Sappho Is Burning

PAGE DUBOIS

SAPPHO IS BURNING

THE UNIVERSITY OF CHICAGO PRESS
CHICAGO AND LONDON

Page duBois is professor of classics and comparative literature at the University of California, San Diego. She is the author of four previous books, including *Sowing the Body: Psychoanalysis and Ancient Representations of Women* (University of Chicago Press, 1988).

The University of Chicago Press, Chicago 60637
The University of Chicago Press, Ltd., London
© 1995 by The University of Chicago
All rights reserved. Published 1995
Printed in the United States of America

05 04 03 01 00 99 98 97 96   1 2 3 4 5
ISBN: 0-226-16755-0 (cloth)

Library of Congress Cataloging-in-Publication Data

DuBois, Page.
    Sappho is burning / Page duBois.
        p.   cm.
    Includes bibliographical references and index.
        1. Sappho—Criticism and interpretation—History.
    2. Greek poetry—Women authors—History and criticism—
    Theory, etc.   3. Lost literature—Greece—History and
    criticism—Theory, etc.   4. Civilization, Modern—Greek
    influences.   5. Women and literature—Greece—History.
    6. Sex in literature.   I. Title.
    PA4409.D8   1995
    884'.01—dc20   95-8407
                                                             CIP

○∞The paper used in this publication meets the minimum requirements of the American National Standard for Information Sciences—Permanence of Paper for Printed Library Materials, ANSI Z39.48-1984.

For Antonia Meltzoff

CONTENTS

PREFACE AND
ACKNOWLEDGMENTS

In adolescence I loved the haiku-like translations of Sappho's fragments composed by Mary Barnard, their austere beauty, a few black lines on the white page. I promised myself to learn the language in which they were first written. I read Sappho in Greek as an undergraduate at Stanford University, with the late T. B. L. Webster, who shared his love of ancient fragments, ceramic and literary, with his students. In years since, I have found that reading the few fragments of Sappho has become more difficult with each encounter. This book is about those difficulties, about the ways that Sappho the poet cannot be assimilated into familiar narratives. She is not part of the patriarchal tradition of Western literature, not part of a project of self-mastery and discipline, not only a poet, perhaps not a "lesbian," not quite a European, not exactly a Greek. She stands for me as a sign of why we still need history, why we should not be satisfied with a one-dimensional, atemporal, global postmodern culture, why the study of history, of distant times and distant places, can provide us the experience of difference, a productive memory of latent fragments of human being, now remote but recoverable through our inquiry into what we have lost.

The chapters of this book are bound together not by a common argument but rather by a desire to register the difficulties of reading Sappho's work. I have used the translations of many Sappho translators, including Mary Barnard, quite deliberately, to indicate how many Sapphos there are, how difficult she is, how impossible it is to know even those few fragments we have, bits and pieces provisionally reconstructed, pored over by centuries of scholars, translated by translators who make texts for *their* readers.[1] It has seemed to me that some of Sappho's readers have easily read her as a humanist, a poet accessible, transparent to the techniques of philology, that others have read her easily as the first lesbian, as a sister, an ancestor in a long chain of like beings. I have wanted here to register Sappho's difference from us, the difficulties of seeing all that we project from our own situations onto the past, and of establishing some dialectical relationship with the past. Richard Wolin remarks, apropos of Walter Benjamin: "It becomes the mission of the present generation to redeem the thwarted hopes, aspirations, and struggles of our ancestors, the disconsolate traces of which are inscribed in our cultural heritage. The ruthless expansion of rationalization renders this vital heritage more opaque and alien to us with each passing day."[2]

These essays on Sappho take different tacks, trying to locate her through triangulation, through various critical orthodoxies and genealogies and narratives of our own. The poems are there, and we approach them at our own risk in trying to read them, trying not to obliterate their otherness while still allowing for the possibility of communication. The poems are really all we have; Sappho is only a name, the name the tradition assigns as the putative origin of a set of fragmentary texts. I have wanted to respect the impossibility of knowing more, and wanted not to produce another romance about this woman who lived long ago.

Several of these essays were written for particular occasions and bear the marks of those occasions. I have revised them but have let the framing of their questions remain, since it seemed to me that the debates of these years, about postmodernism and ancient philosophy, about the history of sexuality, about the body, debates

---

1. All translations are my own unless otherwise noted. Sappho's fragments are usually cited according to their numbering in *Poetarum Lesbiorum fragmenta*, edited by Edgar Lobel and Denys Page (Oxford, 1955), referred to as L.-P. "LSJ" refers to the standard English lexicon of Greek, *A Greek-English Lexicon*, compiled by H. G. Liddell and Robert Scott, revised by H. S. Jones (Oxford, 1968). An asterisk indicates a gap in an ancient manuscript.

2. Richard Wolin, *Walter Benjamin: An Aesthetic of Redemption* (New York, 1982), 235.

that generated conferences and symposia and speeches, are appropriate as frames for thinking about Sappho now. I would like to
thank in particular Jack Peradotto, editor of *Arethusa*, who published my first essay on Sappho, Deirdre von Dornan and Charles
Segal, who invited me to deliver a Loeb lecture at Harvard, David
Tandy at the University of Tennessee, Chuck Platter, Allen Miller,
and David Larmour, for asking me to their conference on Foucault's
History of Sexuality at Texas Tech, Steven Shankman at the University of Oregon for the conference on Plato and Postmodernism,
David Konstan for the series on Feminist Theory and the Classics
at Brown. I am much indebted to the work of other scholars on
Sappho, particularly to Denys Page, to Eva-Maria Voigt, to
Thomas McEvilley, to Anne Pippin Burnett, to David Campbell,
whose labor and scholarship are essential to anyone working on
her poetry.

I owe a great debt to the members of my writing group—Susan
Kirkpatrick, Lisa Lowe, and Winnie Woodhull. They have talked
me through every word of this book. William Fitzgerald's friendship, loyalty, and intellectual example have meant more than I
could ever say. Kristin Ross showed me, with her book on Rim-
baud, *The Emergence of Social Space*, a way back to reading poetry.
Dr. Marianne MacDonald, with her great energy and erudition,
inspires emulation; I owe her a great deal and wish I could recip-
rocate her boundless kindness and generosity. Carolyn Dewald
read much of this book in manuscript, and shared her editorial
wisdom and great knowledge of archaic Greece. I thank Perry
Anderson, who read a draft of an essay on Sappho and offered
penetrating criticism. My friend Melvyn Freilicher has sustained
me through some strange times, and I thank him. And I am grateful
to Fred Jameson, Peter Rose, Rick Berg, Kathryn Shevelow, Ed Lee,
Don Wayne, Susan Smith and Sheldon Nodelman, to the students
in my Sappho seminar, especially Molly Rhodes, and to many of
the members of the hybrid and polyglot Department of Literature
at the University of California at San Diego, especially Judith
Halberstam, who said Sappho is burning.

ONE
Fragmentary Introduction

ἦλθες, ἔγω δέ σ' ἐμαιόμαν,
ὂν δ' ἔψυξας ἔμαν φρένα καιομέναν πόθῳ.

You came, and I was longing for you; you cooled my heart
which was burning with desire.
— Sappho, fragment 48

Are we now living in a world without history? Is the landscape
flattened, filled with objects that interpellate us from within
the codes of the present, objects without density or past? Is subjectivity a fantasy, personal "histories" simply fictional narratives constructed within the template of alienated identity, versions of the
ego that capture only a part of experience? Are we simply processes, discontinuous assemblages of the various appellations of
gender, class, race, and ethnicity? I both like and hate this story.
The fluidity and heterogeneity and Deleuzian flux of the model
are appealing; in some ways it seems to be a response to feminist
critiques of the rigid, bounded, discrete metaphysical subject of
post-Platonic Western culture. It acknowledges *internal* difference,
the fragmentary, disjointed, multiple determinants of quotidian experience, the ways in which we are all spoken by the flow of culture, by familial codes, by work, popular culture, advertising, all
those things that make up what we used to call ideology. The
model of an eternal postmodern present, chaotic and fluctuating,
does permit a sense of boundarylessness, an exhilarating new way
of conceiving of community that imagines an endless process, multiplicity of ties, and mergings with others.

Feminism has to a certain extent produced this theory of identity
and sometimes seems untroubled by it, consciously or not following
the Lacanian dictum that we are all always already "split" and the

1

Althusserian notion that we are constantly "interpellated," called, "hailed," by differing imperatives. There are certainly pleasures involved with this sense of ahistoricity, freedoms to consume, to reinvent oneself daily, hourly. The erasure of history reduces anxiety; we need no longer consider the past, or even the difficulties of the future. We can enjoy the pleasures of discarding the weight of the past, its failures and claims on us, both in the sense of the historical past, revolutions and resistances, and in terms of our private histories, our parents, the Oedipal dramas of subjectivity and its creation. But there are, of course, problems with this model. If we are always only in the present, what is that present, a nanosecond infinitely divisible into an ever smaller unit of time, so that time itself becomes an absurd concept? How could there be even a fictional sense of selfhood, of duration, if there is no access to history? How could anyone ever act, be an agent, have principles and some possibly desirable sense of continuity with the past? Is the erasure of histories, personal and public, just an obedient response to a commodified world, one where we are what we buy, what we wear, what we eat, rather than subjects in some significant relationship to the past, private and public? Do we need some sense of a narrative into which we fit ourselves, a critical relationship to the past, of our own biological lives and of other human lives? And then, if one acknowledges temporality at all, then why not History, why not a master narrative, say one by Marx, one that returns us to the recorded past of human existence, and why not the psychoanalytic narrative of personal development?

Perhaps we must after all hold both these models of existence simultaneously, postmodernist and master narrativists at once, conscious of dwelling both in the postmodern present and also in relation to some pasts—multiple pasts, multiple defining narratives, of private as well as shared experience, of class, of ethnic definition, even of nationality. At least provisionally, we can move between these two ways of understanding being, as both a diffuse flow of contradictory, cacophonous appeals and directives, and as an evolutionary, teleological story. And, if we do have some relationship to history, or History, some sense that time passes and there are meaningful statements to make about this feature of experience, then I want to think here about classical antiquity, and not just as the source of quotation for postmodern architecture but as an unstable object in our construction of a relationship to the past.

How do we construct that narrative? I do not believe it can be through reference to the greatest that was thought or written, to the noble origins of Western civilization. In fact, especially in the United States of America, any narrative of origins must include reference to Asia, Africa, the Pacific Islands, all of the Americas. But it is in part because of the human labor expended on understanding the Greco-Roman past that it has significance for all of us who live in some place in its aftermath. Our relationship to Greek antiquity has been embellished, encrusted, inscribed, and reinscribed for centuries, and it is this relationship that is the most fascinating object to me in studying the Greeks. How can we represent that relationship? In this book I consider the ancient Greek poet Sappho, her anomalous place in the histories we tell ourselves, her unassimilable, eccentric position at the beginnings of some of those stories. She calls attention to the varieties of pasts we have still insufficiently come to know, and to the losses we sustain when we abandon history.

Sappho was born in the seventh century before the common era (B.C.E.) on the island of Lesbos. I should say at the start that when I use the proper name "Sappho" I mean only the voice in the fragments attributed to her, only the assembly of poems assigned to her name. She is not a person, not even a character in a drama or a fiction, but a set of texts gathered in her name. Knowing as little as we do of her life and of the circumstances of performance of her poetry, we cannot even make a sensible distinction between "Sappho the poet" and "Sappho the speaking voice in her poetry." We know her work only in fragments. Although other authors in antiquity report the existence of volumes of Sappho's works, we have only ruins, lines cited in these later authors' work, lines painstakingly reconstructed from ancient papyri exhumed from Egyptian sands. Many have attempted to construct biographies on these magnificent ruins, to invent reassuring narratives of teaching, motherhood, heterosexuality. But such narratives are based on little evidence, on projections based on her poetry, on the accounts of poets and writers who wrote hundreds of years after Sap-

pho's death.[1] Joan DeJean has recently traced with great precision
the vicissitudes of narratives about Sappho from the sixteenth century of the common era (C.E.) to Marguerite Yourcenar's *Feux* in
1937. Her painstaking recreation of the transmission of Sappho's
texts, and of the interested fictions generated about her life, provides a crucial background to any possible reading of Sappho's
works in the present.[2]

Sappho wrote in the seventh century B.C.E., after the great age
of Minoan culture, after the immigration of Greek-speakers into
the Mediterranean basin, after the period of Mycenaean domination over Crete and much of mainland Greece, after the fall of
Mycenae and the dark age which followed it, after the time of
Homer. Hers was an age of earliest literacy, of an Aegean recently
transformed from a devastated region in which the residents had
lost the capacity to write, had lost all the economic rationalization
and hierarchical structure of a warrior and palace culture. As the
Greek world began to recover from the terrible effects of a myste-
rious catastrophe of the twelfth century B.C.E., cities emerged from
the ruins of the past, in the regions of the Aegean world to which
its refugees had fled. Homer the great poet, the first poet of the
Western tradition whose work has come down to us, is now be-
lieved to have written or sung his epic poems in the eighth century
B.C.E.; he was probably a privileged singer, one who served
princes, who sang in great houses not unlike those of the Homeric
heroes. The world of Sappho, at least a century later, was a very
different one, one that valued urbanity as much as militarism. In
her day the cities of the eastern Aegean had become centers of
culture and of luxury; just such a city, Mytilene, close to Asia Mi-

1. For an excellent survey of the issues involved in Sappho biographies, see
Holt N. Parker, "Sappho Schoolmistress," *TAPA* 123 (1993): 309–51. He concludes:
"Analogous to Alcaeus' circle, Sappho's society was a group of women tied by family,
class, politics, and erotic love" (346). See also Mary Lefkowitz, "Critical Stereotypes
and the Poetry of Sappho," *Heroines and Hysterics* (New York, 1981), 59–68.

2. Joan DeJean, *Fictions of Sappho, 1546–1937* (Chicago and London, 1989). See also
Anne Pippin Burnett, *Three Archaic Poets: Archilochus, Alcaeus, Sappho* (Cambridge, Mass.,
1983), for readings of Sappho's poems and for helpful discussion in footnotes of philological debate about the Greek text, much of which is in dispute. I have in general
accepted the readings of the cited textual scholars, and direct the reader elsewhere for
detailed examination of the evidence on disputed readings.

nor, to the wealth and cultivation of the Lydians, harbored not only a surplus that allowed for the development of urban life; it also permitted the often rivalrous aristocracy to which Sappho belonged a life of leisure and high culture. In some fragments Sappho exhibits envy or competitive impulses toward others, perhaps women poets themselves; it has been argued that her lines express sentiments equivalent to those of her male contemporaries, aristocratic competitors in war and civil strife.[3]

For though Sappho belonged to the long-dominant aristocracy, the security of her class was being challenged by emergent social forces and by internal disputes among the aristocratic Lesbian families. The ruling family of Lesbos, the Penthilidai, who traced their origin back to the Homeric hero Agamemnon, had been deposed in the years before Sappho was born, and the poems of Sappho's contemporary Alkaios attest to the turmoil these poets survived. The noble families of Lesbos struggled among themselves for domination of the city of Mytilene and were forced as well to contend with "tyrants." These monarchs, or autocrats, who arose in many cities during this period, often betrayed their aristocratic fellows by allying themselves with lower classes and assuming power. Their legal reforms were instrumental in weakening the aristocracy's hegemony and in paving the way for democratic agitation and control. Pittakos was chosen as leader, *aisymnētēs*, that is, "elected tyrant," by the people of Mytilene, in opposition to aristocratic exiles who included the poet Alkaios (Aristotle, *Politics* 1285 a 30 ff.). Sappho was somehow caught up in these struggles, since we read on the Parian marble of her exile in Sicily for some period during the years 604 to 594.[4]

Sappho writes in full consciousness of her status as an aristocrat, and the occasional moments of satire and humor in her poetry exhibit a strong sense of social hierarchy. She mocks a country girl

3. On Mytilene, see Oswyn Murray, *Early Greece* (Stanford, Calif., 1983), 148ff.

4. For the details of the historical context of Sappho's writing, see Anthony J. Podlecki, *The Early Greek Poets and Their Times* (Vancouver, 1984), 62–88. On the Parian marble, see *Translated Documents of Greece and Rome*, ed. Robert K. Sherk, vol. 1, *Archaic Times to the End of the Peloponnesian War*, ed. and trans. Charles W. Fornara, 2d ed. (Cambridge, 1983), 1–3 (omitting mention of Sappho), and F. Jacoby, *Die Fragmente der griechischen Historiker* (Berlin and Leiden, 1923–).

as *agroiōtis,* "rustic," ignorant about elegancies of dress, in fragment 57. Another woman is described dismissively, almost contemptuously, as uneducated in fragment 55:

> But when you die you will lie there, and afterwards there will never be any recollection of you or any longing [*pothos*] for you since you have no share in the roses of Pieria; unseen in the house of Hades also, flown from our midst, you will go to and fro among the shadowy corpses.[5]

Sappho appears in her verses aware of her privileged status as a cultivated aristocrat whose poetic context has been formed by male poets' epic celebration of war and warrior culture.[6]

Along with such figures as Arkhilokhos, Sappho is part of a great turn in the poetic tradition and in the very history of the development of subjectivity. Homer and Hesiod, her predecessors in the epic age, speak of themselves less as individual men than as conduits of divine inspiration, as transmitters of truth and lies, of stories and genealogies, of histories that the gods and muses know, which they convey to the mouths of the poets. Sappho and the poets who are her near contemporaries are among the first to inhabit fully the first person singular, to use the word "I" to anchor their poetic speech, to hollow out for their listeners and readers the cultural space for individual subjectivity. For us the existence of a self with interiority, with a silent, private consciousness, harboring secrets of fantasy, imagination, sexuality, may seem perfectly inevitable. But this, like other assumptions of twentieth-century culture, is a construction, the result of a centuries-long process, of many transformations, accretions, and losses. We see in the work of Sappho the very beginnings of this process, the construction of selfhood, of the fiction of subjectivity at its origins. The community of Homeric heroes, of men feasting around a campfire, dividing up the spoils of battle—spoils which included the women of the conquered people—conceived of identity as collective; the hero's selfhood was diffusely connected with his

_____

5. David A. Campbell, trans. and ed., *Greek Lyric I: Sappho and Alcaeus* (Cambridge, Mass., 1982), 98–99.

6. On the elevated status of women aristocrats, see Murray, *Early Greece,* 44, and Jean-Pierre Vernant, "Le mariage," in *Mythe et société en Grèce ancienne* (Paris, 1974).

tribe, with the name of his father, with the legacy of heroic actions his name would carry in the memory of the future. It is only in the age of the burgeoning city, of a newly emerging possibility of democracy, of popular agitation against traditional aristocratic rule, that noble birth and blood begin to become less important than individual citizens' separate status and identities, identities that will become putatively equal and interchangeable in the radical democracy of fifth-century Athens.

Sappho is a crucial figure in this process of separating out individuality from the communal mass of preurban society. Her poetic representations of desire and subjectivity, of an "I" that sings and wills, that suffers jealousy and longing, begin to open up a space for private, interior life, a life that will not be fully realized for centuries to come, and that may in our present be superseded by newly diffuse forms of electronic, cyberspatial identity. Her poetic project seems to include the establishing of an individual form of identity, a figuring of human energy that now seems commonplace to us, but that was once an astonishing social and intellectual phenomenon in a world in which the heroic family had long been the only matrix within which significant life could be lived and represented in verse.

The power of Sappho's poetry consists not only in her representation of a new stage in the thinking of existence, of the place of the individual and her desire, not only in her evocation of pleasure, luxury, and meditation on loss; it is also a superb example of turning preexisting poetic materials to a new use, to a poetic project different from that for which they were first composed, one that Sappho is sure will bring her immortality in the memory of her readers. Helen, an ambiguous object of exchange in Homer's hands, becomes an agent of desire in Sappho's. Sappho refigures Homer's poetic formulation of flight and pursuit. Warriors pursue each other in elegant patterns of variation throughout the Homeric corpus. Man ambushes man, chases him through the ranks of warriors and chariots, around trees, around the city wall of Troy, engages in the endless pursuit and flight of single combat. Sappho takes a crucial motif of the battlefield, this situation which epitomizes enmity, the establishing of hierarchy that is martial domination, and uses it to speak of love. The poem called fragment 1

(L.-P.) plays with the roles of pursuer and pursued so crucial on the battlefield; this is the translation of John J. Winkler:

> Intricate, undying Aphrodite, snare-weaver, child of Zeus, I
>   pray thee,
> do not tame my spirit, great lady, with pain and sorrow. But
>   come to me
> now if ever before you heard my voice from afar and leaving
>   your father's
> house, yoked golden chariot and came. Beautiful sparrows
>   swiftly brought you
> to the murky ground with a quick flutter of wings from the
>   sky's height
> through clean air. They were quick in coming. You, blessed
>   goddess,
> a smile on your divine face, asked what did I suffer, this time
>   again,
> and why did I call, this time again, and what did I in my
>   frenzied heart
> most want to happen. Whom am I to persuade, this time
>   again . . .
> to lead to your affection? Who, O Sappho, does you wrong?
>   For one who flees will
> soon pursue, one who rejects gifts will soon be making
>   offers, and one who
> does not love will soon be loving, even against her will.
>   Come to me even now
> release me from these mean anxieties, and do what my heart
>   wants done,
> you yourself be my ally.[7]

Here the voice in the poem invokes Aphrodite, begs her to descend to earth, to the narrator's side, as she has come in the past,

7. John J. Winkler, "Double Consciousness in Sappho's Lyrics," in *The Constraints of Desire: The Anthropology of Sex and Gender in Ancient Greece* (New York and London, 1990), 167–68. See pages 166–76 for a full and fascinating reading of this poem. See also David A. Campbell, *The Golden Lyre: The Themes of the Greek Lyric Poets* (London, 1983), 10–13, who includes the observation that Sappho used no "b" sounds in this poem. Claude Calame sees quasi-juridical language in this poem, a sign of the institutional nature of Sappho's bond with the members of her "circle." See Claude Calame, *Les choeurs de jeunes filles en Grèce archaïque*, 2 vols. (Rome, 1977), 368–69.

begs her to transform the girl who now flees into one who pursues, the one who receives gifts into one who offers them. In Greek, the identification of the gender of the beloved, the one now pursued, is delayed until the very last word of the penultimate stanza, *etheloisa*. The reversibility of these roles, the tricks of fortune in love that make one the lover, the other the beloved, are playfully yet hauntingly represented here. The voice of Sappho supplicates the female god to intervene in a scene of pursuit and flight between two women; Sappho reinscribes her probable source, Homer's *Iliad*, making hers a poem of homoerotic courtship. This is not to say that Sappho is gentle and feminine and desires to subvert the violence and enmity of the masculine war machine. Some contemporary readers have interpreted Sapphic love as different in kind from that of her fellow lyric poets, arguing for a sort of *écriture féminine*, an erotics of reciprocity in her work. In my view, she, like other archaic lyric poets, seems at least in this poem to have seen love as a battlefield, the terrain of erotic struggle one of victory and loss, of pain as well as pleasure. Her vision of eros shares with theirs a desire for domination; the beloved, "even against her will," *kouk etheloisa*, will become the lover. This scenario of pursuit and flight, of subject and control, seems to me to give the lie to an essentialized, ahistorical version of passive or even reciprocal feminine sexuality; Sappho participates more in the aristocratic drive for domination, in the agonistic arena of Greek social relations, than in some projected vision of nonviolent eros. The other woman will be forced by Aphrodite to love and pursue Sappho, even though she is unwilling, and Aphrodite will be her "ally," "fellow-fighter," *summakhos*, a word that connotes battle. Sappho cannot readily be assimilated into some versions of feminist utopianism.

Reading Sappho's poetry requires, as well as a historical sense, an appreciation of her aesthetic practices, often either focused on exclusively by formalists or minimized by sexologists. An implicit narrative of loss and a concomitant yearning drives Sappho's poetry, but unlike Homeric poetics, which recall a historically distant and irrecoverable age of heroism, Sappho's often conjure up past pleasure, addressing an imagined lover who remains absent, who comes to life only through words. Although there are many poems so fragmentary that we cannot deduce their themes, and others that seem to celebrate weddings, in the most complete extant poems the voice of the narrator again and again describes a distant, unattainable object of desire. This pattern is characteristic not only of the invocation of the distant Aphrodite in fragment 1, but also of the Anaktoria poem (fr. 31), recalling Anaktoria "not present," and the poem for Atthis (fr. 96), mourning the girl now far away in Lydia. In many poems we find a relationship between desire and withholding, or presence and absence, which seems to have moved Sappho to write, to create in the elusive, allusive word the absent one, the desired one. In fragments 105 a and c, discussed here in the chapter called "The Aesthetics of the Fragment," fragments which some scholars believe not to be Sappho's work, two disparate fragments which describe an apple left high on a tree and a flower trampled underfoot, floral metaphors often used of maidens, Sappho's lines enact the drama of desire and withholding, presence and absence: "As the sweet-apple reddens on the bough-top, on the top of the topmost branch" (Campbell). The apple here is unattainable, high on its branch; the simile conjures up the apple even as it records its distance, its *hauteur*. Like the gatherers, the reader recognizes the beauty of the fruit but can never reach it. This fragment exemplifies Sapphic poetics, and allows us to thematize the act of reading itself as a recording of the experience of absence, the process of seeing and not seeing simultaneously. We can know the apple only through the poem, but the poem cannot be the apple, can only realize for us its unattainability. The reader assumes the position of the thwarted gatherers, of the assumed suitors, of the poet; the act of reading is an attempt to constitute the missing fruit, the missing maiden, to bring them to life in words that must always betray the materiality of the real. Sappho's fragmentary lines can be read in contrast to the conventional themes in later Greek poetry, especially in later Greek tragedy, describing women as objects of exchange, as fields to be plowed, tablets to be inscribed.[8] In Sappho's fragments, women are rather the yearned for, the unattainable objects of desire.

Although we know almost nothing about the performance of Sappho's poems, about the immediate environment of her production of them, it seems clear from the language she uses that she

8. See Page duBois, *Sowing the Body: Psychoanalysis and Ancient Representations of Women* (Chicago, 1988).

writes often as a woman "narrator," in a feminine voice, often desiring other women. For twentieth-century readers of her verse,
this dimension of her work offers a continuity with contemporary
lesbian practices, although it is difficult to reconcile certain of Sappho's lyrics with a view based on the present, often exclusively
female objects of lesbian desire. A fragment the context of which
is lost expresses sentiments that may be more typical of the pederastic poetry of Sappho's contemporaries:

> Mother dear, I
> can't finish my
> weaving
> > You may
> blame Aphrodite
>
> soft as she is
>
> she has almost
> killed me with
> love [*pothōi*] for that boy
> > (fr. 102)[9]

"That boy," so translated by Mary Barnard, in Greek *paidos*, may
just as well be a child, boy or girl, or a slave, as the dictionary has
it "man or maid."[10] Here is a place where our desire to know Sappho's desire is thwarted, because the ancient word does not specify
gender or social condition or even age, and thus does not definitively establish what is now called "sexual preference" in the case
of this poet.

Nonetheless, such poetry, expressive of the female poet's desire,
can transform our view of classical antiquity as an exclusively male-
dominated society, one in which women had no voice, no desire,
or only the parodic lust of Aristophanes' female characters. In
other fragments, Sappho's voice presents a powerful challenge to
what has often been seen as a monolithically phallic economy, an
untroubled history of symmetrical heterosexuality, of masculine
domination and female submission triumphant through all of

9. Mary Barnard, trans., *Sappho: A New Translation* (Berkeley, Calif., 1958), no. 12.
10. H. G. Liddell and Robert Scott, comps., *A Greek-English Lexicon*, rev. H. S. Jones
(Oxford, 1948); hereafter cited as LSJ.

Western culture. Sappho celebrates not household labor and fertility, not the role of the good wife, but rather desire and yearning, the amorous pleasures women share on soft beds; in poem 94 the narrator remembers:

> All the garlands woven
> Around your delicate neck,
> Fashioned from a hundred flowers.
> All the fragrance of myrrh
> Fit for a queen and rare
> Worn on your fresh young skin beside me,
> While on the softest beds
> From the quiet hands of maids
> No Ionian was so fêted.
>
>   (fr. 94)

Sappho sings of her love and desire for women and she sings wedding songs; she thus disrupts both the narratives of untroubled heterosexuality and of an essentialized lesbian continuum from antiquity.

The desire Sappho expresses for women has parallels in the choral songs written by the Spartan poet Alkman to be sung by female choirs. The third fragment of Alkman, part of a *partheneion*, or "maiden song," contains these lines:

> . . . and with limb-loosening desire [*pothōi*] and she looks (at me?) more meltingly than sleep or death, and not in vain is she sweet . . .[11]

Even though such lines seem to point to a shared atmosphere of female eros within archaic culture, Sappho's expression of homoerotic desire has led to immense difficulties in the transmission and appreciation of her work.[12] Although ancient Greek poets and critics seem to have had no problems with Sappho's clearly articu-

---

11. David A. Campbell, trans., *Greek Lyric II: Anacreon, Anacreontea, Choral Lyric from Olympus to Alcman* (Cambridge, Mass., and London, 1988), 378–79.

12. On these songs, see especially Claude Calame, *Les choeurs*. On the Sapphic circle, see Calame, *Les choeurs*, vol. 1, *Morphologie, fonction religieuse et sociale*, 367–72. See also Bruno Gentili, "The Ways of Love in Thiasos and Symposium," in *Poetry and Its Public in Ancient Greece: From Homer to the Fifth Century*, trans. A. Thomas Cole (Baltimore and London, 1988), 72–104.

lated desire for women, both scandalized Christians of subsequent generations and scholars in the early modern and modern eras have spent much ink on the question of Sapphic desire.[13] Some have claimed that Sappho "ventriloquates" male desire, that she speaks for men in singing of the love for women. Some have argued that she participates in a genre peculiar to archaic poetry, in which adolescent girls desired each other in preparation for lives of heterosexuality and reproduction. Others have imagined that Sappho was some sort of schoolmistress, a poet who trained girls in the arts of the muses, sent them away, and yearned for them forever after. Editors and translators have tried to erase, correct, ignore the clear textual traces of lesbian desire in Sappho's poetry. Recently, however, political struggles for gay and lesbian rights and work in the history of sexuality have enabled a different reading of Greek culture, allowing us to escape, condemn, and even to historicize the anachronistic homophobia of much of the Judaeo-Christian tradition in its attitudes toward classical antiquity.

Michel Foucault and others have argued, for example, that the social role of "homosexual" is really a construction of recent centuries, that the cultural demand that individuals choose a sexual identity and name themselves according to their object of desire is a product of a particular and recent moment in human history.[14] The sexual practices of the ancient Greeks have interested historians of sexuality, particularly because of what seems to be a unique institution in Western culture, the open and often celebrated practice of pederasty, eros between young men and boys, in the classical city. It has been argued recently that sexual identity was constructed in classical culture not on the basis of the gender of one's sexual partner but rather on one's position in sexual acts, as active or passive, dominating or receiving, penetrating or penetrated.[15] Sexual practices were thought of in terms of power—power over

13. See, for example, Ulrich von Wilamowitz-Moellendorf, *Sappho und Simonides* (Berlin, 1913).

14. See K. J. Dover, *Greek Homosexuality* (Cambirdge, Mass., 1978); Michel Foucault, *The Use of Pleasure*, vol. 2 of The History of Sexuality, trans. Robert Hurley (New York, 1986).

15. David M. Halperin, *One Hundred Years of Homosexuality and Other Essays on Greek Love* (New York, 1990). This argument has generated intense criticism from such scholars as Amy Richlin in articles noted in later chapters on Foucault.

others, control over oneself. The male Greek citizen was the subject of domination and desire; women, slaves, and boys were his objects. Such an argument sheds light on our difference from the ancient Greeks and supports the view that sexual identity, like other features of human society, varies historically, that identities are constructed differently in different social and economic circumstances. With such an interpretation of the changing forms that identity takes in human history, we can no longer rely on common sense, on our historically bound ideas about human "nature," to explain away cultural differences in the domain of sexuality.

There is little said of women's desire for women in the classical age; Plato in the dialogue called the *Symposium* (189d–191e) has his character Aristophanes speak of prehistoric creatures composed of male/male, male/female, and female/female halves, to account for what we now call lesbian desire. But we are forced to conclude from the paucity of evidence concerning women's sexuality either that there was no lesbian practice in antiquity after Sappho (highly unlikely), or that it was so improper a subject that it could not be alluded to (also unlikely given that Aristophanes, for example, speaks with great relish of a variety of sexual behaviors), or that it was taken for granted and considered insignificant, like many other aspects of women's lives. The latter explanation seems to me most likely. If what were thought of as sexual practices characteristically involved penetration by a hierarchically superior being, the continuum of lesbian practices, even penetration with dildoes, may not have seemed like "sexual" acts in the eyes of the Greeks. In what we might see as a range of sexual behaviors, performed from adolescence to old age, with most women marrying and having children, with various modes of sexual expression, woman-woman sex, not leading to reproduction, may have seemed irrelevant to the men of the classical city, engaged as they were in such weighty matters as politics, the maintenance of honor, and the seduction of boys. Women, on the other hand, may have taken pleasure with each other, as they did in Sappho's day, without a poet by to record their desire.

Can we conclude that the desire for women was part of a rich and varied sexual existence for women of Sappho's class, that they, like male aristocrats, could conduct an erotic life that included as objects of desire both males and females? This seems to me the most likely conclusion, although it disrupts both the narrative of lesbian essentialism and that of the unquestionable heterosexuality of the great Lesbian poet. Does the form that the erotic takes in Sappho's poetry, her emphasis on her desire for women, contradict the thesis that the gender of one's sexual partner was irrelevant to the ancient Greeks? The sixth-century lyric poet Anakreon writes of a girl from Lesbos who rejects his advances:

> Once again golden-haired Love strikes me with his purple ball and summons me to play with the girl in the fancy sandals; but she—she comes from Lesbos with its proud cities—finds fault with my hair because it is white, and gapes after another—girl![16]

Questions about such women's sexuality are subjects for studies that do not make the existence of women a footnote to the history of men. Perhaps we can best read the portrait of eroticism in Sappho's verse as typically that of an aristocrat of the archaic period, and Sappho's desire as polymorphous, constructed with an view toward domination rather than exclusively toward women. In any case, although Sappho's lesbian desire has proven intolerable to generations of male classical scholars, it never affected her high reputation as a poet in antiquity.[17] She was called the tenth Muse; Cicero records the presence of a statue of Sappho in the marketplace of Syracuse in Sicily: "What owner, public or private, should possess this work of Silanion, so perfect, so elegant, so highly finished, rather than the elegant and learned Verres?" (Cicero, *Verr.* 2.4.125–27). We must conclude that Sappho's expressions of love for women were completely acceptable to her readers in ancient Greece, since they excite no comment, neither praise nor blame.

Sappho has been claimed by philologists and by lesbians, cate-

---

16. Campbell, *Greek Lyric*, fr. 358, 2:56–57. Gentili argues that the girl, a typical "Lesbian" in the Greek sense (she like other women from the island of Lesbos performs fellatio), in fact gapes not after another girl but after the hair (pubic) of "another guest" at a symposium (Gentili, *Poetry and Its Public*, 96).

17. On Sappho's contemporary reputation, see Gentili, "Holy Sappho," *Poetry and Its Public*, 216–22.

gories only intermittently overlapping, and their claims mark out a
crucial and contested territory for interpretation of the poet and
her place in history. In the hands of the philologists, disapproval
of Sappho's poetic techniques abounds. Denys Page, one of her
recent editors (1955—recent in terms of classical scholarship, that
is) frequently chides her, as I will show in the chapters that follow. Gordon Kirkwood comments on her "conventional" depiction
of nature.[18] R. L. Fowler, in a book published in 1987, remarks
concerning the possible influence of two Homeric passages on
poem 1:

> Neither passage is a model for Sappho. Indeed, the indica-
> tions Sappho gives to her audience are so weak and indeci-
> sive that the poem must be termed a failure. Yet it is not; the
> details of her description have full meaning within their own
> context.[19]

Must the poem be termed a failure? Or not? Fowler elsewhere reveals some characteristic philological prejudices that affect evaluation of Sappho as a poet—belief in common sense and in the
ahistorical absolute "natural" as an explanatory category. For example, in a paragraph on page 62, the argument quickly describes
"ring-composition" as "entirely natural," "unavoidable," "naturally"
ending by repeating the opening statement, "obvious and psycho-
logically natural," like examples in any "normal conversation."[20]

A more theoretically self-conscious and sophisticated direction
is being pursued by the classicist Marilyn Skinner in a series of
essays on the Sapphic tradition. She argues for the recovery of a
lost female poetic tradition in ancient Greece and for Sappho's
poetics as a basis for organizing female experience:

18. Gordon M. Kirkwood, *Early Greek Monody: The History of a Poetic Type* (Ithaca,
N.Y., and London, 1974), 127.

19. R. L. Fowler, *The Nature of Early Greek Lyric: Three Preliminary Studies* (Toronto,
1987), 39. Fowler is disputing the views of Jesper Svenbro in "Sappho and Diomedes,"
Museum Philologum Londiniense 1 (1975): 37–49.

20. Fowler also finds fault with the work of Hermann Frankel and Bruno Snell,
arguing that they depend on an imagined passage from mythical to rational thinking,
derived ultimately from the writings of Henri Lévy-Bruhl, which he dismisses. On the
dismissal or trivialization of Sappho's works, see Josephine Balmer, trans., *Sappho: Poems
and Fragments* (Newcastle upon Tyne, 1992), 7–8.

Through imaginative identification with the first-person speaker, a girl would have absorbed survival tricks for living within a patriarchal culture: formulas for resisting misogynistic assumptions and so protecting self-esteem, for expressing active female desire, for bonding deeply with other women, and for accepting the underlying ambiguities and absences of full closure inherent in both human discourse and human life.[21]

Skinner's work, by teasing out the little evidence we have and by relying on contemporary work on women's writing, seeks to establish "the missing half of the Greco-Roman gender dialectic."[22]

Such a historically and philologically informed reading of the Sapphic tradition in antiquity has certain affinities with the contemporary views of Judy Grahn, who sees Sappho as a first lesbian, a sister in the past, an ancestor for lesbians in the present.[23] Hers is an essentialist view, based on the evidence of Sappho's sexuality, and can be read in relation to the important debate about nature and culture, or genes and construction, concerning primarily male homosexuality and recently (re)generated in the works of John Boswell and Michel Foucault.[24] In *The Highest Apple: Sappho and the Lesbian Poetic Tradition*, Grahn recounts a powerful and enabling narrative about an early history for human culture, a time when society was "based primarily on womanly powers." Sappho stands at

---

21. Marilyn Skinner, "Woman and Language in Archaic Greece," in *Feminist Theory and the Classics*, ed. Nancy Sorkin Rabinowitz and Amy Richlin (New York and London, 1993), 135. See also Marilyn Skinner, "Sapphic Nossis," *Arethusa* 22 (1989): 5–18, and "Nossis *Thelyglossos*: The Private Text and the Public Book," in *Women's History and Ancient History*, ed. Sarah B. Pomeroy (Chapel Hill, N.C., 1991), 20–47.

22. Skinner, "Woman and Language," 138.

23. Judy Grahn, *The Highest Apple: Sappho and the Lesbian Poetic Tradition* (San Francisco, 1985). See also Judy Grahn, *The Work of a Common Woman: The Collected Poetry of Judy Grahn, 1964–1977* (Trumansburg, N.Y., 1978). On Grahn, see among others, Margot Gayle Backus, "Judy Grahn and the Lesbian Invocational Elegy: Testimonial and Prophetic Responses to Social Death in 'A Woman Is Talking to Death,'" *Signs* 18:4 (1993): 815–37, and Sue-Ellen Case, "Judy Grahn's Gynopoetics: The Queen of Swords," *Studies in the Literary Imagination* 21:2 (1988): 47–67. On lesbians' interest in the Lesbian Sappho, see Susan Gubar, "Sapphistries," *Signs* 10 (1984): 43–62.

24. On this debate, see Eve Kosofsky Sedgwick, *Epistemology of the Closet* (Berkeley and Los Angeles, 1990).

the end of this period of human history, stands for a tradition that is suppressed and yet endures:

> I take the apple that Sappho said reddened on the topmost branch . . . to mean "female powers." I take it to mean the centrality of women to themselves, to each other, and to their society. That apple remained, intact, safe from colonization and suppression, on the topmost branch, and in the fragmented history of a Lesbian poet and her underground descendants.[25]

Both the classicists and the gay and lesbian theorists and historians have much to contribute to our readings of Sappho, although I would distinguish between those that assume fixed subject positions, or a humanistically informed ahistorical consciousness, and those that allow for historical difference even in such matters as sexual identity.[26] My own readings of Sappho must be set alongside these, and represent not a quarrel with them, but another story.

In raising such issues as the open celebration of women's desire for women, Sappho's poems afford an occasion for the contemplation of the problem of the historical in contemporary culture. I don't want to read antiquity through a Lacanian lens, imagining that human nature throughout all time and in all places is adequately described by psychoanalytic theory.[27] But one useful way, among others, to take up the problem of living in the present and in relation to the past might be through describing our relationship to past and present, a peculiar, historically specific relationship, in terms adumbrated by Jacques Lacan. Because Lacan's version of temporality is complicated and heterogeneous, because it allows us to understand subjectivity as a process, the ego as a fictional construct, our sense of our past as troubled, reft by unconscious elements, constructed provisionally from the point of view of present realities, our gender identities as unstable and provisional too, it may be a useful example, as a loosely read allegory, of how to think about a past of greater duration, a master narrative of histori-

---

25. Grahn, "Highest Apple," 10–11.
26. On this question, see Sedgwick, *Epistemology*, esp. 1–63.
27. See duBois, *Sowing the Body*, 7–17.

cal process. I want to stress here that I see this use of Lacanian theory as essentially illegitimate within the terms Lacan himself conceives, and that the analogy I draw between the historical and the psychological cannot be pressed too hard. Nonetheless, Lacan's work is potentially illuminating for a model of the provisional, self-conscious, unnervingly temporary relationship one constructs between oneself and any form of narrative, any history, personal or collective.[28]

Lacan argues that in the domain of the symbolic, after the child's acquisition of language, the site of prelinguistic, pre-Oedipal "imaginary" existence is recalled as a "body-in-pieces," a fragmented and disparate collection of body parts. And, furthermore, the "I" of the child is produced in the mirror stage as a fiction. Lacan says:

> We have only to understand the mirror stage as an *identification*, in the full sense that analysis gives to the term: namely, the transformation that takes place in the subject when he assumes an image. . . .
>
> This jubilant assumption of his specular image by the child at the *infans* stage, still sunk in his motor incapacity and nursling dependence, would seem to exhibit in an exemplary situation the symbolic matrix in which the *I* is precipitated in a primordial form. . . .
>
> This form would have to be called the Ideal-I. . . . This form situates the agency of the ego, before its social determination, in a fictional direction, which will always remain irreducible for the individual alone.[29]

The "I" is specular, permanent, and nonetheless alienated, as in a mirror; it produces, in a temporal dialectic, another set of images of what precedes it. If the child celebrates, jubilates, as Lacan puts it, in the alienated recognition of a whole body in the fictional surface of the mirror, she or he also from the point of view of

28. See also Peter Dews, *Logics of Disintegration: Post-Structuralist Thought and the Claims of Critical Theory* (London, 1987).

29. Jacques Lacan, "The mirror stage as formative of the function of the I as revealed in psychoanalytic experience," in *Ecrits: A Selection*, trans. Alan Sheridan (New York and London, 1977), 2.

the fictional integrity recalls or constructs a previous state of disintegration.

> The *mirror stage* is a drama whose internal thrust is precipitated from insufficiency to anticipation—and which manufactures for the subject, caught up in the lure of spatial identification, the succession of phantasies that extends from a fragmented body-image to a form of its totality that I shall call orthopaedic.[30]

The subject, even after it enters into the social network of the symbolic, of collective language, alternates between a fictional "I" and an invented memory, a phantasy, of a time before the capture of this "I," a time when the body was fragmented, the agent and object of earliest aggressivity.[31]

The dialectic between two states, the specular ego and the body in pieces, might serve as a model for the relation between the postmodern ahistoricity of a self in process, and a historicist sense of duration. Such a view would first of all recognize the broken, fragmented quality of the past. And it would also recognize the necessarily fictional yet necessary fiction of the assumption of an "I," a shifter producing the text that is history, an "I" that can assume agency, that creates a relationship to a past and a possible future.

Such a model of historicism might be especially productive for reflecting on the postmodern thinker's relationship to classical Greek antiquity. Our historiographical desire, our need to constitute antiquity as a whole and the "Greeks" in particular as coherent objects, even though all we have of them is heterogeneous fragments, smacks of the need to produce for our own jubilation some mirror image, some wholeness that resembles what we wish were our own. We need to be conscious of an ongoing tension between our desire to register fragmentation and our desire to invent integrity.

For example, what do we do with the fragments, literal fragments, of ancient literary texts? Who are the scholars, supposed agents of integrity and coherence, who desire to mend that past, to make it whole? When considering these texts, Sappho's espe-

---

30. Ibid., 4–5.
31. See Jacques Lacan, "Aggressivity in psychoanalysis," in *Ecrits,* 8–29.

cially, I find useful Lacan's way of thinking about the alternation between the fictional whole, the "I," and the fragmentary past, as a process, as a dialectic. When we read a fragmentary text like Sappho's, we may be conscious of the possibility of dismemberment, of the fragility of wholeness, of corporeal and psychic integrity, even as our identity as readers is fashioned against the background of such dismemberment. Historiography is a process, a recognition of the fictionality, the scriptural status of the story we tell assembled from the fragments of the past, objects, bits of stuff embedded in other narratives or standing alone, receiving their status as fragments only from our point of view within a narrative. We use these fragments as we seek coherence.

The classical Greeks themselves, inventing history, inventing a relationship of difference rather than repetition with the past, took the fragments of oral history, of memories and legends, and made their own stories. In the invention of democracy, they constructed a narrative of a break, a radical difference between past and present. E. R. Dodds wrote of the discomfort produced in the sixth and fifth centuries B.C.E. by the democratizers' sense that they had violated their obligation to their fathers.[32] They had betrayed the demand for repetition of traditional culture characteristic of aristocratic, analphabetic culture, a sense that society survives by reenacting the significant gestures of the past, by replacing one leader with his son, by respecting the spaces and rituals and objects inherited from the past. The democracy broke the link with the past in changing legal practices, in electing magistrates. Even though every culture alters the practices of the past, some, especially those based on oral traditions, believe that they are literally and perfectly imitating what has gone before. The recognition and even celebration of rupture with cultural inheritance created, in Dodds' view, anxiety and a sense of parricidal betrayal in the classical Greeks that accompanied the first attempts at history, at making sense of the past by seeing it as temporally other, different in a new way. Although the Greeks from the time of Homer had spoken of their difference from the time of the heroes, of a rupture between themselves and the generation of the Trojan War, the writing of history as opposed to epic poetry meant a new kind of

32. E. R. Dodds, *The Greeks and the Irrational* (Berkeley, Calif., 1951).

break, an attempt to bring the account of time from the moment of the Trojan War up to the writer's present, and to assemble the fragments of the past in such a way as to show difference, to account for the institutions of Herodotos' present, for example, by showing how things had changed. Although Herodotos seems concerned to show the continuity between the past and the present, doing lateral, horizontal, geographical labor, writing about the relations between the Greeks and their neighbors, seemingly less interested in history per se, vertical, chronological history, except as it illuminates the differences and similarities between the Greeks and the Scythians, Persians, Egyptians, it may be that he stresses continuity because he is in fact aware of how much things have changed, how radical a break there is between his own time and that of the generations before his.

Might we see the classical Greeks' concerns with past and present, with fragmentation and writing as similar to the Platonic processes of separation and assembly, of *diaeresis* and *synagogē*? An imagined origin, fragmentation, separation, division, then reassembly? And is there a resemblance here to the Lacanian dialectic between the symbolic and the imaginary? Can one hold both in tension, knowledge of separation and separateness, knowledge of provisional, tentative unity?

Another model of historicism, one quite different from that loosely derivable from Lacan, is one that depends on the work of Walter Benjamin. I would like to use both of these models, not to choose between them but to let them illuminate one another. Benjamin's idea of history is firmly rooted in the present, in a reality that calls to the past, that looks backward for moments in the past that speak to the present and to the future. He uses the image of the *angelus novus*, the angel flying backwards, propelled furiously into the future by the past.

> Where we perceive a chain of events, he sees one single catastrophe which keeps piling wreckage upon wreckage and hurls it in front of his feet. The angel would like to stay, awaken the dead, and make whole what has been smashed. But a storm is blowing from Paradise. . . .[33]

33. Walter Benjamin, "Theses on the Philosophy of History," in *Illuminations: Essays and Reflections*, ed. Hannah Arendt, trans. Harry Zohn (New York, 1969), 257–58.

Benjamin stresses the interested nature of our inquiry into the past, our residence in the present, our obligation to the remains of the dead. "Only that historian will have the gift of fanning the spark of hope in the past who is firmly convinced that even the dead will not be safe from the enemy if he wins. And this enemy has not ceased to be victorious."[34] Richard Wolin has written eloquently about Benjamin's relationship to the remnants, the fragments that are history:[35]

> In face of the boundless and irrepressible triumph of the forces of rationalization in the modern era and the concomitant destruction of all traces of premodern, traditional life, Benjamin's great fear was that along with all remnants of tradition the all-important index of redemption which the past provides would also fall victim to the oblivion of forgetting—resulting in the most hollow and defective civilization imaginable, a civilization without origins, without memory.[36]

Benjamin insists on the necessity of a relationship to the past, one rooted in interest, in the commitment of the historian to remember the past and to change the present for the future. Only the recollection of the past can save the present from becoming an impoverished, ruthlessly rationalized desert, a landscape without memory, without hope.

We can hold these two visions of the past together, the one model based on Lacan, in which the historian provisionally imagines a coherent story while recognizing that it is a fiction, and the other based on Benjamin, in which a relationship with shards of the past is established like a bolt of lightning, in which we suddenly see something new, in which we recognize the losses we

---

34. Ibid., 255.

35. "Benjamin's Kabbalistically influenced conception of the philosophy of history helps to account for his preoccupation with fragmentary works of art as opposed to totality-oriented, classical art—works such as *Trauerspiel*, Baudelaire's *Fleurs du mal*, and Kafka's parables. For only such 'profane' works of art undercut the illusory Enlightenment vision of cumulative historical progress and its concomitant myth of the infinite perfectability of man" (Richard Wolin, *Walter Benjamin: An Aesthetic of Redemption* [New York, 1982], 59). See also Gary Smith, ed., *On Walter Benjamin: Critical Essays and Recollections* (Cambridge, Mass., 1988), and Gary Smith, ed., *Benjamin: Philosophy, History, Aesthetics* (Chicago, 1989).

36. Wolin, *Walter Benjamin*, 264.

have sustained in living in the present, the need for a commitment to changing the present, to redeeming possibilities of human being in the future. Both of these versions of the historical can, I believe, open up into a reading of the Greco-Roman tradition, and in particular of the ancient Greek poet Sappho.

The classical tradition, long privileged as the source of all that is unique about our past, is just one of many traditions informing postmodern, multiethnic reality.[37] We can no longer sustain the fantasy that we are all pure descendants of a homogeneous, ethnically pure and high-minded ancient Greece, its democracy, its philosophy, long celebrated as the paradise lost of Western civilization. There are many strains that make up contemporary culture, indigenous peoples, centuries and generations of immigration from throughout the world.

And even within the Greco-Roman tradition, there are voices that survive in opposition within a seemingly univocal culture. Sappho, one of the handful of women whose poetry has come down to us from antiquity, sings not of democracy and philosophy, not even of work and war, not of the instrumentalizing of the eroticized body, but of the individual and her subjective body, of "the most beautiful," of erotic desire and yearning. Sappho writes of Aphrodite the goddess of sexuality, of soft beds, roses, groves sacred to the goddess, of jealousy, desire, and the absence of one's beloved. Setting themselves against the warrior culture of the epic poet Homer, against the values of labor and reproduction emerging in the nascent city-states of the Greek world, Sappho's fragmentary, broken lines celebrate pleasure and women's bodies, and her work has the potential to disrupt many of the most treasured conceptions about the Western tradition.

Can we construct a narrative about the past by using the fragments of the past, the fragments of the Sapphic corpus, one that allows for a consciousness of the past's inaccessibility, of the fictional quality of our narrative, as a reading of Lacan might suggest? Can we, like Benjamin, read the past with a sense of urgency and of the reclaiming of the lost shards of the past, a remembrance that honors the dead? Can we justify the study of classical antiquity in

---

37. See Jacques Derrida, "'Nous autres Grecs,'" in *Nos Grecs et leurs modernes: Les stratégies contemporaines d'appropriation de l'antiquité*, ed. Barbara Cassin (Paris, 1992), 251–76.

our present day, one in which we are caught up gazing at a future without history? We encounter in the culture of the ancient Greeks not only a culture named as the origin of our own. We also must come to terms with its otherness, with constructions of identity, sexuality, and society that differ radically from our own and reveal the arbitrary nature of arrangements we take for granted in our society of compulsory heterosexuality, of egoism and consumerism.

The figure of Sappho, the verse of Sappho, disrupt various paradigms of Western civilization. Hers is a troubling place at its purported origins. She is a woman but also an aristocrat, a Greek, but one turned toward Asia, a poet who writes as a philosopher before philosophy, a writer who speaks of sexuality that can be identified neither with Michel Foucault's account of Greek sexuality nor with many versions of contemporary lesbian sexuality. She is named as the tenth muse, yet the nine books of her poetry survive only in fragments. She disorients, troubles, undoes many conventional notions of the history of poetry, the history of philosophy, the history of sexuality. We need to read her again. And we need to see that Sappho can stand as a supplement to our reigning ideas about classical culture and to the discipline of classics, which has often depended upon devaluation of the very principles Sappho's fragments, as fragments, embody. We must rethink the rhetorical structure of Platonic dialogues, the themes animating Homeric figures, classical historiography, and even the Westernness of the West in relation to another kind of writing, one we inherit in the fragmentary form of Sappho's verse. Hers is a spare yet voluptuous language, a poetics that refuses the call to subordinate erotics to metaphysics. Sappho represents the feminine that philosophy silences, while contemporary scholarship often simply reproduces the political semiotics of classical Greek discourse in this respect. Such a judgment is just as true of scholarship that follows in the path of Michel Foucault as it is of classical philology. These modern scholars read the classical tradition as it asks to be read, abjecting the kind of thinking, writing, and Asiatic Greekness represented by Sappho. Sappho has become the other of later metaphysical philosophy, history, discourses of mastery and physical discipline, precisely because she offered aesthetic, philosophical, and ideological alternatives to the Eurocentric notions that

Western humanism has so long revered. In fact, the ancient world moved between these antitheses, and acknowledging them can enrich and enable a living encounter with ancient culture within postmodernity.

Sappho stands as an alternative to a certain classical tradition, a tradition not confined to antiquity. One can read these traditions against each other, Sappho against the austerity of the ancient philosophers, against Foucault who reads their austerity as the origin of the desiring subject, against Lacan and his patriarchal triangle, against the traditions of classical scholarship that occult Sappho's existence, her practice, her voluptuosity, her gaze toward the East, her emphasis on pleasure and on human being. The reigning notion of the classics, as transmitted to us by conservatives, depends upon devaluing these elements of the classical tradition, even though they persist as an undercurrent, a countercurrent, a secret pleasure that belies the austerity celebrated by contemporary critics.

Sappho's legacy lies in fragments, and we can use her fragmentary corpus as a supplement to destabilize a reading of Greek antiquity as sober, classical, balanced, austere, masculine, the origins of the West. Sappho's fragments stand as a supplement in the sense that they unbalance the classical, pedimental, Attic Greek, and insist upon a lyrical, sensual, emotionally laden textuality, disrupting and interrupting a mainstream of the representation of Greek thought and culture as a disciplined wholeness. That wholeness was itself only a fragment of a larger whole, a fluid and fragmentary collectivity.

We should be reading texts like Sappho's in postmodernity, texts that recall alternative traditions, that undermine master narratives and myths of austerity and mastery and fixed boundaries. Postmodernism appears to be tearing down the classification system that identifies a position within modern North American and European culture with a body that is always and only either male or female, white or black, rich or poor, good or bad. The new postmodern body observes the aesthetics of the fragment, is not as ahistorical as its critics claim, because it offers a compensatorily discontinuous and affective record of change, not as hostile to masculine Eurocentricity as it boasts and as its critics fear, because the two are in fact mutually defining. Reading fragmentarily, reading

historically distant cultures with a recognition of their fragmentary, partial, latent messages about human culture, should be part
of the project of postmodernism.

This is my attempt at a reading, just one reading. I have seen
Sappho as a text of broken texts, my reading as an effort, from
various heterogeneous perspectives informed by current critical
questions, to think about her. Sappho's poems, fragments, confront the reader with an almost hallucinatory luminosity at times,
perhaps because they are fragments, but also because they are signs
of the breaking apart of the Homeric poetic world, like bits of
brocade torn from a whole fabric. Her poetry epitomizes the *blanc*,
the blank, the whiteness of the page marked only by scattered,
shattered words. Her poetry can produce anxiety because it exemplifies lack, and Sappho herself sometimes becomes a fetish
object, made whole, perfect, sealed on the page by translators who
are made uncomfortable by the holes in her writing.[38]
    The transmission of Sappho's texts reveals the heterogeneous,
layered, uneven processes of history. We find her work sometimes
preserved whole, or cited in the fragmentary works of other ancient authors, or on shreds of ancient papyri. One poem, fragment 2, *deuru m'ek Krētas*, "Hither to me from Crete, to this holy
temple, where is your pleasant grove of apple-trees, and altars fragrant with smoke of frankincense . . ."—a call to the goddess Aphrodite—was discovered on a potsherd, a broken, fragmentary
piece of ancient ceramic.[39] It seems to have been written by someone in the third century B.C.E., written without line breaks in the
stanza, but with spaces after the stanzas. Denys Page remarks: "The
writer was either very careless or very ignorant, or both."[40] We owe
this poem of Sappho to an unknown writer who used a piece of
pottery broken off from a whole, a vase, painted or not, used by
women perhaps to carry water, or by drinkers at a symposium. The
writer used the fragment to record some of Sappho's lines, a broken

    38. On fetishism, see Emily Apter and William Pietz, eds., *Fetishism as Cultural Dis-
course* (Ithaca, N.Y., 1993).
    39. M. Norsa, *Ann. R. Scuola di Pisa*, ser. 2 (1937) 6:8ff.
    40. Denys Page, *Sappho and Alcaeus: An Introduction to the Study of Ancient Lesbian Poetry*
(Oxford, 1955), 35.

remnant of a poem once whole, discovered as precious rubble inscribed more than two millennia ago. There is no original text, no
"right," perfect, whole object; we have only a broken bit of ceramic, mediated by centuries. Other poems are found woven into
the works of other writers, in a complex fabric composed not to
express individual "authorship," but organized according to other
criteria. Athenaeus, a third-century C.E. writer from Naucratis, in
Egypt, gives us fragment 101 in the course of his *Deipnosophistai*,
"The Learned Banquet," a description of a banquet lasting for days,
a record of the guests' conversation with authorial commentary, a
huge compendium of dissertations and citations on a multitude of
themes. Fragment 101 is embedded in an extended discussion of
symposiac hand washing and "towels," in a peculiar and dazzling
display of erudition:

> A linen towel [*ōmolinon*] is mentioned by Cratinus in *Archi-
> lochi*: "Her hair swathed heavily in coarse towels, full of all
> unworthiness." And Sappho, when in the fifth book of her
> *Lyric Poems* she addresses Aphrodite, "These towels of radiant
> purple Mnasis hath sent to thee from Phocaea, gifts worthy
> to veil thy cheeks," means that the towels are an ornamental
> head-covering, as Hecataeus, or whoever wrote the account
> of travels entitled *Asia*, makes clear: "The women have towels
> on their heads."[41]

Fragment 101, abounding in textual difficulties, is removed from
its context in the text of Athenaeus by textual editors, numbered,
and placed into the series of fragments, then to be emended or
amended, that make up the corpus of Sappho. How is it possible
adequately to take account of the aleatory, contingent, layered,
disturbing incoherence and fragmentariness of the preservation of
these poems? A crucial question for the presentation of the Sapphic text has always been how to represent the absences, the
holes, the gaps in the poetic object; how does a publisher, without
sanitizing, rectifying, fetishizing, print these fragments, show the
tears, frangible edges, erasures, abrasions? Sappho herself persists
elusively always as an absent source for the texts these various es-

---

41. Athenaeus, *The Deipnosophists*, trans. Charles Burton Gulick (London and New
York, 1930), ix. 410e.

says consider, as an origin we can never know. Her texts, as we receive them, insist on the impossibility of recapturing the lost body.

My reading of Sappho seeks to argue for historicist study that comes to terms with a historical perspective, a belief that history matters. And it seeks to establish some Benjaminian, Lacanian, hermeneutic connection between these historically distant objects and our actually existing situation. If my readings often suggest that Sappho has been left out of crucial historical narratives, or if acknowledged left unread, my own experience of reading her poetry includes, in addition to the recognition of her place in archaic society, in addition to the recognition of neglect of her texts in many histories, a sense of a complex immediacy in her work. I would characterize my experience of reading Sappho's fragments as marked by what the Greeks called *pothos*.[42] This word is often translated as "yearning," or "longing," or "regret." As Socrates says in the *Cratylus*:

> The word *pothos* [yearning] signifies that it pertains not to that which is present, but to that which is elsewhere [*allothi pou*] or absent, and therefore the same feeling which is called *himeros* when its object is present, is called *pothos* when it is absent.[43]

Sappho's poems often evoke *pothos*, a yearning for someone absent, for a lost time, a lost pleasure, and her poems re-create, in a longing mode, that time, that person, those pleasures, but always at a distance, framed by the poet's voice in the present of the poem, recalling, recollecting. For me, this relationship connects not only with the pleasures of reading her poems, but also with my experience of Sappho as the absent one, the poet we can never know, and of my encounter with all the Greeks, with this period of history now long gone, accessible only through fragmentary texts, as objects of yearning or longing that will never be satisfied. My desire is not to return to a world now lost, one in many ways more terrible than our own, marked by cruelty, torture, slavery, and misogyny, as well as by democracy, but rather a desire to *know* that world in all its

---

42. See Anne Carson, *Eros the Bittersweet: An Essay* (Princeton, 1986).
43. H. N. Fowler, trans., *Plato*, vol. 4 (Cambridge, Mass., and London, 1926), 420a.

complexity and ambition. It is the experience of loss and regret, of looking back, that both Benjamin and Lacan address—the look back at another form of social and economic organization, one different from the commodified alienated relations we know, or the yearning characteristic of "the imaginary," nostalgia for the mirror phase, a time of fusion and wholeness—that *pothos* evokes for me. The study of Sappho implicates me not only in reading her poems; it is also exemplary of a certain relationship to the past, of an always insatiable historical longing to know other times, other places.

TWO

The Aesthetics of
the Fragment

We have tended to see the ancient world as a set of objects—
vases, seal rings, poems. If our gaze is extended, we discuss
such matters as these objects' makers, the conditions of their production or the field of objects among which a single object has
meaning. Even the social history of art has assumed a transparency
in the relationship between ourselves and the past, a positivist perspective on antiquity's accessibility to our gaze. What is the desire
of the scholar confronted by fragments of papyrus, of stone, shards
of vases, bits of ancient culture that have always stood for lack?
How can classicists think again about our will to make the broken
material evidence of the past whole? Must our relationship to archaic civilization be one of mastery and narrativization? I want to
look at several instances, material and literary, of fragments from
archaic Greek culture, and think about how to refigure them in
new histories. What are we to make of these broken things, these
fragments, bits of the past assembled for our gaze through random
events of destruction and discovery? And who are "we"? The work
of such people as Martin Bernal, Homi Bhabha, and Gayatri Spivak
has called attention to the coercive, Eurocentric, colonialist, often
racist presumptions of much of the scholarly tradition to which

Ideas presented in this chapter were first expressed in my contribution to *De Gustibus:
Essays for Alain Renoir*, ed. John Miles Foley, The Albert Bates Lord Studies in Oral Tradition (New York and London, 1992).

classicists belong.[1] How can we think about class, ethnicity, and race, as well as gender, in formulations about our relationship to the ancient world? How can we think about being more than passive readers of these objects, interpreting them and taking into account our intentions, our labors? Is it enough to remind students and readers of our texts that women existed in antiquity, that we know certain facts about them? Is it enough merely to enlarge the scope of positivist history, to increase the body of knowledge about women of the past? Or even to see how women are constructed in ancient society, to understand the mechanisms of the production of sexual difference in ancient artistic and literary practices? There is more at stake than supplying the deficiencies of past science, and we need to understand that our labors figure in the disciplinary and intellectual debates of the present.

If, in our scholarly work, we call attention to the existence of women and a sex/gender system in antiquity, we may also be arguing, in an allegorical fashion, for our own place, for recognition in contemporary academic disciplines. But I wonder if we cannot go further, to think about what kinds of historical and contemporary desire are being stimulated or satisfied by our gaze at the archaic past. Are we gripped by nostalgia, hungering for a world that seems forever and happily closed, fixed in frozen motion like the figures on Keats' Grecian urn? Or do we want to find an origin, the first moments of Western misogyny, in the hope that uncovering the prejudices against women, coexistent with all Western literary, artistic and philosophical practices, will allow us to move beyond such prejudice in the future? What is the desire of the feminist scholar of antiquity? I think we should be contesting the project of such neoconservatives as William Bennett and Allan Bloom, who desire to see in antiquity a paradise lost, a distinctly European, pure and homogeneous origin for Western civilization.[2] Their nostalgia for a certain version of the ancient past betrays a nostalgia for Plato's academy, for an exclusive, masculine conversation that

1. Martin Bernal, *Black Athena: The Afroasiatic Roots of Classical Civilization*, vol. 1, *The Fabrication of Ancient Greece, 1785–1985* (New Brunswick, N.J., 1987); Gayatri Spivak, *In Other Worlds* (London, 1987); Homi K. Bhabha, *Locations of Culture* (London and New York, 1994).

2. Allan Bloom, *The Closing of the American Mind* (New York, 1987); William J. Bennett, ed., *The Book of Virtues: A Treasury of Great Moral Stories* (New York, 1993).

avoids the heterogeneity and general messiness of contemporary culture.

In the effort to think theoretically about our scholarly practices and our place in the intellectual debates of the postmodern age, I find psychoanalytic theory to be invaluable. I have argued against the ahistorical importation of psychoanalytic categories into our understanding of ancient culture. It seems to me unhelpful, and even dangerously essentializing and conservative, to argue that gendering is the same in all cultures and in all historical periods. When we understand the function of the Oedipus complex in twentieth-century America, when we understand the role of the imaginary, and "suturing," in late capitalist cinema, we have not deciphered, I believe, Aeschylus' *Oresteia*, or the numerous representations of the Gorgon in archaic pedimental sculpture.[3] The work of Sigmund Freud and of Jacques Lacan, however, does seem to me useful for the project described earlier, the theorization of *our own* relationship to antiquity. If we can think about why we look at ancient works of art, what kinds of desire—desire, that is, as a longing for what we cannot have—what kinds of desire are being satisfied by our attention to these artifacts from the past, if we can clarify our perspective on the past, we may see differently the importance of our work, the fact that our writing is not simply a recording of the truth about the past but labor itself, the product of a dialectic between the material culture of antiquity and ourselves.

Marx argued that the Greeks constituted the childhood of mankind, that the past represents for us a lost whole, some former integrity now destroyed. Is that what motivates one of the primary impulses of classical scholarship, the desire to find what is missing, to deny the broken, fragmentary quality of our inheritance from the past? The efforts of many literary and art historical scholars are bent on this effort, not necessarily assuming a metaphysical origin, a perfection that once characterized the past, but nonetheless behaving as if the most important project of modern contemporary scholarship is restoration, recovery, reintegration of what is in fact irrecoverably lost. Yet if we limit ourselves to a simple recording of the truth of antiquity, the restoring of absent characters to the

3. On gender in cinema studies, see, e.g., Kaja Silverman, *Male Subjectivity at the Margins* (New York and London, 1992).

drama, we miss an opportunity to examine further why such a restoration matters. In 1980 Peter Fuller attempted to account for the enduring fascination of the Venus de Milo, depending for his argument on the materialism of Sebastiano Timpanaro and on Melanie Klein's work on part-objects. His essay, called "The Venus and 'Internal Objects,'" interests me because he wanted, as I do, to theorize the position of the viewer of the object of art, wanted to describe the ways in which we connect to the broken remnants of the ancient world.[4] Fuller seems to believe, however, in the *transparency* of the statue and to want to make a claim for our unmediated access to it. "The sculpture's immediate relation to the body is not significantly changed by socio-economic transformations, and this relation forms the *sine qua non* of the statue's survival as something other than a historical document." He further argues for "the apparent aesthetic superiority of the present mutilated version over its original." Fuller claims that its present state allows us to experience an "externalisation" of the Kleinian "internal objects," to believe that the "Mother" has survived our infantile aggressive attacks.[5] Furthermore, the mutilated state of the statue encourages us to complete it internally; those who find the statue in its fragmentary state disturbing may identify with its mutilation, seeing themselves as fragmented, or experience the desire to mutilate the other further.

My difficulties with Fuller's argument stem from his claims for an invariable stratum of biological givens in human experience, which he believes provides the basis for a degree of constancy in all human beings' responses to works of art.[6] Part of the project of feminist theory, however, has been to undermine such assumptions, which tend to regard the masculine body, experience, and response as normative and therefore the touchstone of the human.[7]

---

4. Peter Fuller, "The Venus and 'Internal Objects,'" in *Art and Psychoanalysis* (London, 1980), 71–129. He points out that Freud was unimpressed with the statue; even more intriguing is the story "that the statue had been found intact and had subsequently been deliberately mutilated" (88).

5. Ibid., 104, 120, 121.

6. Fuller says, e.g., "One reason why this statue remains transparent to us . . ." (ibid., 103–4), when I would argue that it is precisely not transparent.

7. See Elizabeth Grosz, *Volatile Bodies: Toward a Corporeal Feminism* (Bloomington, Ind., 1994).

Furthermore, since Foucault, many historians are likely to recognize cultural differences in historically distant periods, to see the organization of social relations, even especially the experience of the body, as produced by specific formations of power and knowledge. I am more inclined to see difference than similarity in archaic culture, and, as a sort of historical anthropologist, to look for differences in history first of all by trying to see what kinds of desire we project on artifacts from the past. Our contemporary hunger for wholeness, for restoration of a phantasied but lost bodily integrity, or our fear of fragmentation, of the powerlessness of the not-yet-whole, can affect our relation to our cultural past as well as our own psychic history.

My argument is for a recognition of our own relationship to the fragmented artifacts of the archaic past, be they the few lines of poetry left to us by Sappho, or broken ostraka, painted potsherds, solitary columns marking the sites of great, lost temples. Rather than focusing on the restoration of lost wholes, or even on the tragic impossibility of the reconstitution, rather than looking exclusively at the real, the past to which we must always have a fleeting and receding relationship, perhaps we should look also at our own desires, our investments in these lost objects, these shattered fragments of the past.

What is our connection to them? What kind of consequences would follow from recognizing our own position as gazers, as viewers of the fragments of the ancient world? It could be said that recognition of the fragmentariness of the remains of the ancient world would counter the ideological use of antiquity by those who dream of a paradise lost, an unending Platonic symposium, a white male conversation never interrupted by difference, by work, slaves, or women. Their interested description of a monolithic, whole, elite and aristocratic Greece is countered by our recognition of our interests, also at stake in the representation of antiquity. Does looking at the fragments of the ancient world confirm our sense of postmodernist fragmentation, of the inevitably split and dispersed character of social existence? Does it comfort us to know that the ancient world now lies in ruins, that a culture so often exploitative and misogynist has crumbled? Do we feel the pleasures of survivors, who have outlived that world, lived to dominate it through our analyses? Does the contemplation of ruins remind us of our own mortality, but also comfort us with the recognition of survival of some ruins?

What would work that recognized all these questions look like? It might reflect on the fact that art historians of antiquity must work in an imaginary museum, a theater of the mind that juxtaposes objects now far removed from one another and from their places of origin. The materiality of the Parthenon, for example, is embodied in several nation-states, in a complex history of neglect, imperial ambition, and economic disparity. The Elgin Marbles will probably not be restored to the Greeks, who are fast becoming the proletariat of the new Europe. The scholar who works on the Parthenon frieze must encounter striking historical realities in restoring in her imagination a whole, unbroken, unfragmented Parthenon. Perhaps we should not treat such features as incidental, as needing bracketing so that real work can take place. Perhaps the labor of the art historian, traveling from Athens to Paris to London, should be part of the story of these objects for us. Perhaps we could make more of the ways in which ancient art means for us now, how we arrive at it, what historical and social and heterogeneous factors mark our relationship to it, and, what is of greater significance to me here, to the fragments to ancient poetry.

Embedded in fragments in the critical assessments of later, still ancient commentators and literary theorists, unearthed in shreds of papyrus from the sands of Egypt, scribbled on potsherds, the earliest lyric poems of our tradition survive as shattered remnants of a great flowering of culture after centuries of illiteracy and silence that succeeded the collapse of Mycenaean civilization. Literary critics have for the most part read those archaic Greek poems that are most whole, most like the textual objects familiar to us from the world of print, poems with beginnings, middles, and ends, poems that at the worst have *cruces*, a few *lacunae*, perhaps a missing line, syllable, phoneme. These poems with recognizable shape, few ellipses, barely mutilated, are the poems printed in translations, in anthologies. Critics have been grateful that the vagaries of transmission have permitted access to a few whole poems, that, for example, the Arkhilokhos fragment found in Cologne survived centuries of neglect, that Longinus happened to have used

Sappho's fragment 31 as an illustration of sublimity in selection and combination (*On the Sublime* 10. 1–2), even though Longinus' treatise is itself irretrievably partial and damaged. These poems allow us to develop models of the structure of whole poems, of poetic development and narrative patterning.

But what of the poem-fragments from which we cannot construct a whole, lines repeated to illustrate a point, lines retrieved accidentally from a papyrus so damaged that there is no hope of more? Are we simply bound to wait, in expectation that more fragments will be discovered, to confirm or deny the conjectures of textual critics? Can we do more than to place the irretrievably fragmentary remains of these poets in the limbo of the unreadable, as uncanny, damaged and partial ruins of antiquity?

These poems seem to lack the charm ancient ruined sites once held for lovers of antiquity, the romantic appeal of the constructed ruin in the eighteenth-century garden. Perhaps they call up in us some of the same dread as the armless, noseless statuary of antiquity. Just as the sight of ruined, mutilated bodies that were first crafted to recall the beauties and perfection of the human form causes a primitive shudder, as well as the fascination described by Peter Fuller, so too the ellipses in the published archaic fragments, recalling stopped mouths, messages gone astray, the utter failure of communication across a distance of centuries, provoke discomfort. Beyond the psychological obstacles, these poems present problems of reading for the critic. Their incompleteness causes unease. We have learned to read whole poems, and to see some kind of narrative in whole poems. But how can one speak of poetic development when only one line, one metaphor remains? There is no accessible narrative in some of these fragments; or narrative is of necessity truncated. There is inevitably a sense of something missing, of something yet to be supplied. The critic waits for completion, a completion which may never occur, or she recognizes the sensation of working in the dark, of vulnerability to that text which might appear, which might contradict her reading, or subsume it in a fuller, more adequate reading of a fuller, more adequate poem.

One of the impulses of philology has been to attack the problem of the fragment directly. Classical scholarship and biblical scholarship have always been in part efforts of restoration. Philologists have tried to make whole what was broken—to imagine and guess at the missing parts, to repair what was transmitted inaccurately, to change, excise, add, to return to the original and perfect text that we can never know. Their work has been immensely valuable, in reading, deciphering, presenting to us in legible form much that would be inaccessible without the intervention of centuries of erudition. Their efforts at restoration must continue, as labor over textual mysteries, as supplementation of our ignorance. But until the day of glorious resurrection, when all the bodies of ancient poems are miraculously restored in their integrity, what are we to do with the fragments of such a poet as Sappho? Are we to leave them aside until they are miraculously restored? Are we to continue to long for wholeness, to imagine, for example, what the whole poem that surrounds a two-line fragment must be?

Recent literary theory, in celebrating the fragmentary, offers the possibility of another kind of reading, renders it more pleasurable, allows as well for the reading of the fragment, the line, the image, within a study of the culture of the whole, a study based less on literary forms than on cultural practices. And perhaps because of the rediscovery of Nietzsche, that eccentric philologist, work on contemporary culture has recognized the aesthetic particularity of the fragment. The very search for integrity and indivisibility, in all things, has been called into question, not only by the heirs of Nietzsche, but by his feminist descendants, witting or not, who see the emphasis on wholeness and integrity, on the full body, as a strategy of scholarship that has traditionally excluded the female, identified as different, heterogeneous, incomplete in herself, a disturbance in the scholarly body.[8] Aristotle describes the female as a "deformed" (*pepērōmenon*) male (*Generation of Animals* 737a), because the menses lack the crucial ingredient, the principle of soul. The project of scientific textual studies has been to supply the text's "lack," to reduce the fragmented, partial quality of embodied, material texts. But the wholeness associated with the male, dependent upon constructing the female as lack, is always an illusion; our recognition of this illusory integrity leads us to challenge

8. See Peter J. Burgard, ed., *Nietzsche and the Feminine* (Charlottesville, N.C., and London, 1994).

the historically authorized inferior status of that lack associated with the female. We can accept the fragmentary for what it is, appreciate the few words of Sappho that we have inherited, rather than setting them, for example, against the fuller, more adequate corpus of Pindar, and naming him the greater poet.

We have come to recognize that our access to the past is always fragmented, our construction of our past interested, particular, and historically determined. We are dependent on accidents of transmission—fire, war, loss. Our access to so recent a phenomenon as the early years of television is partial, arbitrary, subject to the peculiarities of archival storage and technological limitation. Our knowledge of daily life in ancient Rome is also limited, perhaps no more fragmentary than our knowledge concerning female literacy in eighteenth-century England, or the history of the !Kung. What remains to us of the past, what we know of the present, of the consciousness of others, for example, is fragmentary. One way of responding to this recognition is to pursue a dream of wholeness, transparency, perfect access to what we desire to know. Another is to accept the partiality of our experience, to seek, even as we yearn for more, more facts, more words and artifacts, more lines of Sappho, more poems of Sappho, to read what we have.

Rather than discarding the truly fragmentary as illegible, hopelessly damaged, frustratingly elusive, I want here to attempt a reading that accepts some very broken lines of Sappho's poetry, as they stand.[9] I will give a formal analysis of two fragments, then consider several contexts, the epic, other lyrics, the social relations of gender, that illuminate these lines. From reading at the level of the phoneme, I will move to the relations of intertextuality that situate these fragments, to the aesthetics of distance and unattainability that characterizes Sappho's verse.

9. Some of the most interesting work on Sappho in recent years focuses on her corpus as a whole, on the social and sexual world depicted there. See John J. Winkler, "Gardens of Nymphs: Public and Private in Sappho's Lyrics," in *Reflections of Women in Antiquity*, ed. Helene P. Foley (New York, 1981), 63–89, and Eva Stehle Stigers, "Sappho's Private World," in ibid., 45–61; J. Hallett, "Sappho and Her Social Context," *Signs* 4 (1979): 447–64; see also the response of Eva Stigers to Hallett, "Romantic Sensuality, Poetic Sense," *Signs* 4 (1979): 464–71; Bruno Gentili, "La veneranda Saffo," *Quaderni urbinati di cultura classica* 2 (1966): 37–62, and Bruno Gentili, "Nel tiaso saffico," in *Le donne in Grecia*, ed. Giampiera Arrigoni (Rome and Bari, 1985).

oion to glukumalon ereuthetai akrōi ep'usdōi
akron ep'akrotatōi lelanthonto de malodropēes
ou man eklelathont', all'ouk edunant' epikesthai
(105a L.-P.)

Like the sweet apple turning red on the branch-top, on the
top of the topmost branch, and the gatherers did not notice
it, rather, they did notice, but could not reach up to take it.

oian tan uakinthon en ōresi poimenes andres
possi katasteiboisi, khamai de to porphuron anthos . . .
(105c L.-P.)

Like the hyacinth in the hills which the shepherd people step
on, trampling into the ground the flower in its purple.

These two fragments were not preserved together. The first
comes from Syrianus' commentary on Hermogenes' *Peri Ideōn;* the
first line is mentioned by the scholiast on Theokritos 11.39, and
Himerios (*Or.* 116) discusses the poem, saying that Sappho compared the groom to Akhilleus, the bride to an apple.[10] The second
fragment is recorded in Demetrios' *Peri hermeneias* without attribution. The similarity to the first fragment suggests that both are part
of *epithalamia*, wedding songs. One context, we will see, is the epic.

In my reading of these two fragments of Sappho, 105a and
105c, I will consider the formal aspects of the lines of verse, as well
as the literary and social contexts in which they can be read. The
meter of these two fragments is dactylic hexameter. This is appropriate for the epithalamion, or wedding song, and it also recalls the
epic, sung and recorded in the same meter. As in the epic, there is
correption, the shortening of a long vowel when followed by another vowel, between *ereuthetai* and *akrōi*, between *akrōi* and *ep'* in
the first line of the first fragment, and the first omicron of *malodropēes* is scanned as short because followed by a mute and a liquid.
The second fragment also contains epic features: *en* rather than *enn,*
the doubling of the sigma in *possi, de te* in the last line. These ele-

10. David A. Campbell, *Greek Lyric Poetry: A Selection of Early Greek Lyric, Elegiac and
Iambic Poetry* (Basingstoke and London, 1967), 282. On this fragment, see Anne Carson,
Eros the Bittersweet (Princeton, N.J., 1986), 26–29.

ments reinforce the epic resonance of the fragments; the epic is one possible whole to which these fragments might belong.

Fragment 105a begins with *oion*, "like," the word introducing a comparison. It thus calls attention to the fragmentary status of the fragment, the thing being compared forever absent, available only to the imagination. If the comparison is general, Homer characteristically uses *hoios te*, as in *hoios te Ares*, "some such one as Ares." This *oion* is a specific comparison, different from those Homeric similes that begin adverbially with *hōs*, to introduce not a thing or a person, but an action, a situation. This word introduced a metaphor, if we take Aristotle's definition of metaphor:

> Metaphor is the application of a strange [*allotriou*] term either transferred from the genus and applied to the species or from the species and applied to the genus, or from one species to another or else by analogy. (*Poetics* 1457b)

The simile is an extended metaphor, as Demetrios says (*Peri hermeneias* 232). The bride, if this is indeed an epithalamion, or the girl, if this is a poem of praise like the poem for Atthis, Sappho's fragment 96, is compared in her *being*, not in action, to the thing that follows the word "like," *oion*. She is like fruit; the compound word *glukumalon*, "sweet-apple," doubles the sense of both of its separate components. The apple is a sweet-apple, more than a simple fruit. The syllable *-on* echoes the identical syllable in *oion*; this sound resounds throughout the three lines of the fragment.

The word *ereuthetai*, "reddens," the verb, is at the center of the first line of the fragment and anchors it, its color spreading forward and backward in the line. Thus the *oion* introduces not just the existence of the sweet-apple, but also an action—yet an action inseparable from its being. As the sweet-apple reddens and thus ripens, so the girl blushes and ripens. As the apple lives and grows, it reddens, turning from the immature fruit; the girl matures inevitably as well. Did the Greek audience associate this girl, blushing with modesty and shame as is proper to a maiden, or browning in the sun, with Artemis' virginity, coltish and wild?

The phrase *akrōi ep'usdōi*, "on the branch-top," with its epic correption, introduces distance. The sweet-apple reddens on high. The Aeolic word *usdos*, like *odzos*, "branch," can mean an offshoot or scion, human offspring. It continues the metaphorical equation of fruit and girl. *Akron* can mean not only highest, topmost in a spatial and physical sense, but can also have an evaluative sense, meaning highest, most excellent. The words *akrōi ep'usdōi*/*akron ep'akrotatōi* ("on the branch top, on the top of the topmost branch") suggest a qualitative as well as a spatial situation. This sweet-apple is the best, the highest of the high, the most distant from the common ground. The most physically distant, the highest, is also best. And *akron* suggests completeness, the fullness of time: the sweet-apple reddens on the perfected branch. The omegas of *akrōi* and *osdōi* complete the line with an internal rhyme.

The word *akrōi* is repeated, with variation, in the polyptoton of the following line, where the connotations of excellence and perfection are further stressed. *Akron*, at the beginning of the line, echoes the *-on* ending of *oion* at the beginning of the fragment, while also referring, by means of lexical and grammatical repetition, to the end of the preceding line. *Akron ep'akrotatōi* "on the top of the topmost branch," in its structure resembles the phrase *akrōi ep'usdōi*; the repetition thus insists on absolute distance, and on the sweet-apple's place at the acme. The lyric voice, the observer, the reader are all far below, gazing up at the perfection of the ripening fruit. This line, unlike the first, with the central placement of *ereuthetai*, breaks into two phrases. The first, with its repetition of root, sound, ending, binds the line to the one before; the second phrase establishes a further development of the narrative, by bringing other observers into the universe of the poem. *Lelathonto* "they did not notice" has the same number of syllables as *akrotatōi*, as well as a similar final syllable; the word also contains the syllable *-on*, which figured in *oion, glukumalon, akron*. It is thus bound at the level of sound to what precedes. Chiasmus is created with the word *malodropēes*, "gatherers." Just as *akron* repeats *akrōi* from the first line, it repeats the syllable *mal-* from *glukumalon*. The effect is to suggest the inevitability of the picking of fruit, since the very name of these persons, the noun that establishes their existence, includes both the name of the fruit and the name of their labor. As it ripens, fruit must fall into the hands of gatherers. The word *lelathonto*, however, suspends the necessity of this narrative. Although fruit grows only to be picked, this fruit, thus far, has escaped the notice of the pluckers.

The verb *ereuthetai* is in the present tense; the sweet-apple continues to redden, to ripen. The verb *lelathonto*, a perfect, suggests that, up to this moment, the gatherers have forgotten this single perfected fruit. The contrast between the two tenses opens the narrative to a present possibility; they have forgotten, or overlooked, or passed over until now. And here the fragment turns, the voice of the poet correcting or supplementing itself. *Ou man* changes direction, the *-an* of *man* echoing the beginnings of the two previous lines, but contradicting what has gone before. *Lelathonto* is repeated with variation in the third line; *ek-lelathonto* is "they did (not)indeed forget (the sweet-apple) entirely." This move strengthens the reader's or listener's sense of the apple's perfection; if it were truly so fine, how could the gatherers have neglected it? In fact they did see and desire it, but it was out of reach, too far, too good for them. This line, like the preceding one, breaks into two limbs; although the lines differ metrically, both have caesura, with *lelathonto* directly following the break in the fragment's second line, *ekelathont'* directly preceding the caesura in the third line. The negative *ou* of the first colon of the third line is followed by the negative *ouk* in the second part. The present and perfect tenses are capped by the imperfect of *edunant'*, "they could (not)," again hinting at an imminent break with the past. The *ep-*, prefix of *epikesthai*, "reach it," repeats the *ep-* near the end of the first line, and closes the fragment with a reiteration of the distance and inaccessibility of the perfected fruit. The common gatherers know of this fruit after all, know of it so far out of reach, but could never, until this moment of Sappho's song, bring it down.

The coupling of fragment 105c with 105a may be an arbitrary one. The second fragment is given, without the author's name, by Demetrios. It resembles the first in meter, and may therefore come from an epithalamion, a wedding song. It is also structurally similar to the lines analyzed above, presenting a likeness, a comparison. The question of interpretation is brought to the fore by the fragmentary status of these five lines of poetry. My choice to read these two fragments together, as a sequence, as a disjunctive narrative, requires a certain recognition of the arbitrariness of interpretation. The context of the lines is the Sapphic corpus, early lyric poetry in general, the background of Homeric epic, the archaeological evidence for social and cultural life in the archaic age.

The frame chosen already determines one interpretation. As I choose to read these fragments together, I construct my object, two different moments in a connected or related lyric situation.

The second simile begins like the first, with *oian*, "like," the feminine form of the word introducing a comparison. The sound *-an/ -on* is present here as well, in the definite article *tan*, in the ending of *uakinthon*, "hyacinth." Interestingly, although here the hyacinth is feminine, in the *Iliad* (14.348) it is masculine. Homer twice describes Athena's transformation of Odysseus and the arrangement of his hair "that hung down like hyacinth petals" (*kad de karētos/ oulas hēke komas, huakinthinōi anthei homoias*) (6.231 = 23.158). In a fragmentary pederastic poem, Anakreon (346) describes Aphrodite tethering her horses in a field of hyacinths. Horses often connote the exciting of desire, the will to tame an unbroken filly (Anakreon 84), or the indomitable will itself, as in Plato's representation of the charioteer in the *Phaedrus* (246a). The combination of horses and hyacinths conveys a mood of masculine eros and of the desirability of the male. The feminizing of this hyacinth may be a completely accidental arbitrary feature of a gendered language, but it allows once again for a metaphor of the bride, appropriate to an epithalamion, or to praise of a young girl.

As Anakreon's hyacinths are trampled by Aphrodite's horses, so this hyacinth is affected by an alien presence. The flower is in the mountains, like the sweet fruit of the first fragment distant from human haunts. The phrase *en ōresi*, "in the mountains," occupies the central place in its line, but is followed directly by *poimenes andres*, *Poimenes* alone means herdsmen or shepherds, so the word *andres*, "men," serves to stress the masculine identity of these human beings who appear in the natural setting.[11] The line, like those of the first fragment, contains variations on the syllable *-an*; here *poimenes andres* connects the end of the line with its beginning, while the *-es* endings on the two final words provide a kind of rhyme.

The second line of the fragment establishes an almost tragic mood in response to the destruction of the flower. The sweet-apple of the first fragment was, until the poet spoke, out of reach. The hyacinth has fallen. The word *possi*, "feet," repeats the *p* of *poimenes*; it also suggests *posis*, sometimes written *possis*, "husband," in the

11. See also Alkman 56.4.

dative singular *posei*. The accusative *uakinthon* is now seen for what it is, the object of the verb *katasteiboisi*, "tread." The flower which stood alone at the fragment's beginning is drawn into a narrative, trodden down by the feet of herding men, with a hint for later readers of a husband's presence. If this is a simile about the loss of virginity, it has neither the celebratory nor the bawdy effect of some epithalamia. Read as the cap to the first simile, the unattainable sweet-apple, this scene of unheeding destruction turns the mood of distance and yearning to one of loss and regret.

The second line breaks into two elements. The abruptness of *khamai*, "on the ground," introduces a harshness into the scene, accentuating the unaspirated *k* of *katasteiboisi*. The word *khamai* is set off emphatically by the words *de te* that follow; they provide a sort of epic breathing space to underline the implicit humiliation and loss of the flower. The last two words of this fragment bring the hyacinth back in memory; it is like a Vergilian poppy cut down in the field. The words *porphuron anthos*, "purple flower," repeat the phoneme *-on/-an*, with the rhyme that forms them into an indissociable couplet. The *anthos*, "flower," last word of the fragment, recalls the first element of the comparison, *uakinthon*, and generalizes its specificity. The phrase directly echoes the last two words of the first line, *poimenes andres*. The words of each begin with *p* and *a*, and they are metrically identical. The metrical and phonic repetition contrasts the destructive herdsmen with the purple flower. Homer, who apparently did not know the *porphura*, the *murex* from which purple dye was obtained, seems to use the word *porphuron* to denote a dark gleam, without the specification of color. He speaks of "purple" blood. Sappho, or whoever the author of this fragment is, has the antiquity, the double extension of the word, to work with; the word connotes both the color of the hyacinth flower and its association with the dark-gleaming sea, cloud, blood. The destruction of the mountain flower at the feet of the herdsmen is accomplished even as the integrity of the hyacinth is reinvoked.

The simile of the apple recalls features of the Homeric epics. Although the action of the *Iliad* is confined to the bare and often bloody plain before Troy, the constant use of similes opens the poem to a normative world beyond the battlefield, one in which artisans labor, trees grow, shepherds herd their flocks. Throughout the Sapphic corpus lines like these, saturated with Homeric refer-

ence, embody an awareness of the epic context, its militarism, its
atmosphere of masculine combat and struggle. The epic similes are
often fragments of the natural or artisanal world set down in the
conflictual arena of the battlefield; the referent of the Homeric
simile is a world of material objects and practices outside the world
of war. In a similar way the Sappho fragments insert the Homeric
simile into the celebratory world of the marriage song, bringing
into the listener's or reader's consciousness both the heroic context
and the natural or pastoral world juxtaposed with it. Indeed if, as
Himerios says, the groom in the poem from which these lines remain was compared to the epic hero Achilles, then the epic world
is part of the frame of these lines, as much a context for this fragment as the lost words of the whole epithalamion.

Sappho often uses and simultaneously refuses the material of
the Homeric universe.[12] The first fragment, 105a, seems to evoke
in particular two moments in the *Iliad;* the first occurs in the description by Odysseus of a snake omen:

[The snake] made toward the plane tree.
Thereupon were innocent children, the young of the
     sparrow,
cowering underneath the leaves at the uttermost branch tip
     [*ozōi ep'akrotatōi*] . . .

                                              (2.310–12)

The snake devours all the birds, even though they are hidden at
the farthest tip of the branch; the intertextual resonance with
Sappho's lines casts darkness over the fruit at the topmost branch
of the tree in Sappho's lines. The second passage is less directly
evoked by Sappho, yet for me it appeared by association in my
mind as I read her lines, and we must assume such familiarity with
the Homeric text in an ancient audience. The Homeric lines describe the wounding of Menelaos by Pandaros:

straightway from the cut there gushed a cloud of dark
     blood.

---

12. See Leah Rissman, *Love as War: Homeric Allusion in the Poetry of Sappho* (Konigstein/
Ts., 1983), and J. D. Marry, "Sappho and the Heroic Ideal," *Arethusa* 12 (1979): 271–
92.

As when some Maionian woman or Karian with purple
colours ivory, to make it a cheek piece for horses;
. . .
so Menelaos, your shapely thighs were stained with the
   colour
of blood, and your legs also and the ankles beneath them.
                                          (4.140–44)

Here too the Homeric allusion in Sappho's lines projects menace
for the young girl/apple/hyacinth. As John J. Winkler points out in
his analysis of this fragment:

> The verb *ereuthō,* "grow red," and its cognates are used of
> blood or other red liquid appearing on the surface of an ob-
> ject which is painted or stained or when the skin suffuses
> with blood.[13]

Although Homer does not use the verb *ereuthō* in the passage describing the staining of the ivory, and the staining of Menelaos'
body, the semantic network sustains an association between the
ripening fruit and the wounded body of the hero. The context of
the lines surrounding the two Homeric passages I have cited gives
the resonating images a vastly different meaning from that suggested by Sappho's fragment. In Homer the image of the branch
prefigures slaughter in battle; the natural world is made to echo the
heroic. In the *Iliad,* the simile often has an ironic effect; the simile
of the ivory worked by the artisan has an uncanny quality of distancing the listener, enabling her to attempt to forget the flowing
of blood. Because the object in the simile and the thing compared
are nonetheless always both present, always both absent, the process of comparison is destabilizing, and an uncanny sensation is
produced, of horror and admiration simultaneously.

   Let us examine further the menace, the darkness that the epic
context allusively casts over Sappho's apple/girl. In the *Iliad,* apart
from the women of Troy, prizes of war, and those goddesses who
themselves engage in the battle, women have little place. The Iliadic universe is a profoundly masculine one, where male force

   13. John J. Winkler, *The Constraints of Desire: The Anthropology of Sex and Gender in Ancient Greece* (New York and London, 1990), 183.

dominates, where female influence consists in such acts as Thetis' provision of arms for her doomed son, where Hera's only moment of power over Zeus derives from the deception of the girdle. In this context, the similes are an alternate world of relief from war. The simile of the ripening fruit thus evokes the whole series of images of the Homeric similes, many of which depict a natural universe, another scene contrasted to the arena of dust, sweat, and blood of the struggling armies. What is particularly fascinating about Sappho's simile is its implied recognition of the alternative posed by the parallel universe of the Homeric similes. Further, if we are to read these two fragments together in some kind of narrative sequence, we may perceive that Sappho responds to the Homeric epic by representing violence as integral to the natural, pastoral, demilitarized zone as well as to the world of battle.

Even if the two fragments are not read as a disjunctive narrative, the probable context of the epithalamion suggests that the ripening fruit forgotten or unattainable by the gatherers will finally be gathered in the marriage ceremony, that it is all the sweeter for having been out of reach, reddening and ripening undisturbed. Only the most determined and worthy of suitors, he who gathers most carefully and best, who appreciates perfection of ripeness, will receive this beauty reserved for him.

Yet the imminence of the husband's possession has an incipiently threatening quality. In the simile, the mention of the *malo-dropēes*, "gatherers," is slightly ominous, indicating the inevitability of the fruit's acquisition. And, as the Homeric allusions suggest, the metaphor of the ripe fruit, used throughout lyric poetry, has its dark side as well. The fruit ripens for the picker, who consumes and thus destroys it. A famed poem (or fragment) of Ibykos transfers the menace of the plucker of fruit to a generalized atmosphere of doom: here the voice of the male poet registers the violence always potential in eros:

> In spring time the Kydonian quinces (*malides*) watered by running streams, there where the maiden nymphs have their secret garden, and grapes that grow round in shade of the tendriled vine, ripen.
>
> Now in this season for me there is no rest from love. Out

of the hard bright sky, a Thracian north wind blowing with
searing rages and hurt—dark, pitiless, sent by Aphrodite—
Love [erōs] rocks and tosses my heart. (286)

This poem, preserved by Athenaios, sets the erotic figure of ripening fruit against the violent wind of Eros. Here the women's
world, the Nymphs' garden, the natural processes of maturation are
menaced by a natural aggression. The poem recalls another fragment of Sappho:

Love [erōs] shook my heart
Like a wind in the mountains battering the oaks.

(47)

Love, the male god, is a violent wind for Sappho and for the later
Ibykos. The ripe fruit can be shaken from the trees and wasted on
the ground. In Ibykos' poem the lyric speaker is rocked and shaken
by Eros; Sappho's "I" is shaken too, and she then uses a simile, introduced like the Homeric similes with ōs, to compare herself to
the battered oaks of the mountain. The tender and delicate apples,
quinces, on their tree-tops, are vulnerable to the winds of Eros.

Apples are like cheeks, like maidens' breasts. The Doric form
malo-, in place of the Attic mēlo-, allows the word to echo the adjective malthakos, meaning, when used positively, "soft, gentle, mild,"
and malassō, which means "soften" (and perhaps a hint of maleros,
"fierce, devouring," used of fire in the Iliad). The softness of the
apple/breasts stresses their vulnerability to the winds of Eros, the
violence of masculine desire. As B. H. Fowler points out apropos
of the scene of Persephone's flower gathering in the Homeric
Hymn to Demeter: "gardens and the plucking of blossoms occur
in other passages of Greek literature which describe girls who are
about to lose their virginity." She remarks that "apples and roses
are both tokens of love, a part of courtship."[14] The emphasis on

---

14. B. H. Fowler, "The Archaic Aesthetic," *American Journal of Philology* 105 (1985):
142, 141. See also Anne Pippin Burnett, *Three Archaic Poets: Archilocus, Alcaeus, Sappho*
(Cambridge, Mass., 1983), 266ff.; and Helen Foley, ed., *The Homeric Hymn to Demeter:
Translation, Commentary, and Interpretive Essays* (Princeton, N.J., 1994), which includes
Marylin Arthur, "Politics and Pomegranates: An Interpretation of the Homeric Hymn
to Demeter," first published in *Arethusa* 10:1 (1977): 7–47.

imminent marriage and the loss of innocence seems more appropriate to the simile of the lone ripening fruit in the Sappho fragment, while the transfer from the gifts of courtship to the object
of desire, the bride herself as fruit, evokes the possibilities of destruction, with the fruit's consumption, and waste, if it languishes
and falls unnoticed from the tree. (Archilochus uses the word *pe-
peira*, "ripe," to describe the girl in the Cologne fragment.)

In Aeschylus' *Suppliants* the anxious father of the Danaids,
threatened with violence and rape by their Egyptian suitors, uses
similar language to suggest the delicacy and vulnerability of his
distraught daughters:

> I beg
> You not to bring me shame, you who have
> That bloom which draws men's eyes: there is no simple
> Guard for fruit most delicate, that beasts
> And men, both winged and footed, ravage . . .[15]

Danaos' almost obsessive preoccupation with his daughters' sweetness and fragility, his fear of contact with their suitors, make clear
the perceived dangers of the transition from *parthenos* to *gunē*, from
maiden to wife, in the Greeks' version of female life. As Giulia Sissa
shows in a recent book, silence, the closure of the upper and lower
"mouths" of the girl's body, is a crucial attribute of virginity:

> Le vocabulaire hippocratique montre une première cristalli-
> sation très forte: une homonymie parfaite qui dédouble le
> corps de la femme en un haut et un bas symétriques. A la
> bouche (*stoma*) de la nourriture et de la parole, qui s'ouvre sur
> le visage, repond en bas une autre bouche, le *stoma* uterin.[16]

---

15. Aeschylus, *The Suppliant Maidens*, trans. S. G. Benardete, in *The Complete Greek
Tragedies*, ed. David Grene and Richmond Lattimore (Chicago, 1967), ll. 994-1000. On
this play, see Froma Zeitlin, "The Politics of Eros in the Danaid Trilogy of Aeschylus,"
in *Innovations of Antiquity*, ed. Ralph Hexter and Daniel Selden (New York, 1992),
203–52.

16. "The Hippocratic vocabulary demonstrates one very strong primary crystalli-
zation: a perfect homonymy that doubles the woman's body into symmetrical upper
and lower halves. To the mouth (*stoma*) which eats and speaks, which opens in the face,
corresponds below another mouth, the uterine *stoma*." Giulia Sissa, *Le corps virginal: La
virginité féminine en Grèce ancienne* (Paris, 1987), 76.

The maiden is not only physically *intacta;* she is also silent. The apples on the tree, the Kydonian quinces of Ibykos' poem, the Danaids threatening to hang themselves in silent testimony to the Egyptians' violence, all these are signs of appropriate silence for a Greek maiden. In Sappho's poem, the blushing ripening fruit is patient, waiting, silent.

An implicit narrative of desire is visible here, in fragment 105a, as it is in other poems of the Sapphic corpus. The voice of the poet describes a distant, unattainable object of desire. The same pattern is characteristic of such poems as the invocation of the distant Aphrodite (fr. 1 L.-P.), the Anaktoria poem (fr. 16), recalling Anaktoria *ou pareoisas,* "not present," the poem for Atthis (fr. 96), remembering a girl now far away in Lydia. Thomas McEvilley, in his reading of fragment 2, identifies this poem as paradigmatic for all of Sappho's works. The poem summons Aphrodite to a Cretan grove, described in detail, with its apple grove (*alsos malōn*), fragrant altars, stream, roses, meadow.

> Come to me from Krete to this holy
> temple, to the apple grove,
> the altars smoking with frankincense,
>
> cold water ripples through apple
> branches, the whole place shadowed
> in roses, from the murmuring leaves
> deep sleep descends,
>
> where horses graze, the meadow blooms
> spring flowers, the winds
> breathe softly . . .
> *
>
> Here, Kypris, after gathering . . . ,
> pour into golden cups
> nectar lavishly
> mingled with joys.[17]

17. Diane Rayor, trans., *Sappho's Lyre: Archaic Lyric and Women Poets of Ancient Greece* (Berkeley and Los Angeles, 1991), fr. 2, 53.

The poem was found recorded on a potsherd; McEvilley claims, against some others, that the poem is nearly complete as we have it, "internally adequate as it stands."[18] For him, its fragmentary quality is almost an illusion; he is concerned to read a narrative, to see poetic development in the text.

Although I do not share his concern to restore, make whole again this potsherd, McEvilley's analysis of fragment 2 establishes a valuable set of terms for Sappho's poetics. He argues that "the poem itself becomes a visual pun, with Sappho at the end."[19] The poem has for McEvilley a "spiritual" function, depicting not an actual but a symbolic scene. The poem *is* the grove, the grove is poetry. Most important is McEvilley's noting of the dynamic of presence and absence in this poem:

> The grove is a general image of a relationship of desire and withholding, of emptiness and fullness, of art and life, that is acted out in various specific forms in the other poems.[20]

The relationship of desire and withholding, of presence and absence seems to move Sappho to write, to create in the elusive, illusive fragmentary net of words the absent one, the desired one. In fragment 105a, the poet's gaze in the simile enacts the drama of desire and withholding, presence and absence. The fragmentary status of these lines enables us further to thematize reading as desire. The reader assumes the position of the thwarted gatherers, of the assumed suitors, of the poet; the act of reading is an attempt to constitute the missing fruit, the missing maiden, to bring them to life in words that must always betray the materiality of the real.

The paradigmatic narrative of Sappho described by McEvilley, the "relationship of desire and withholding, of emptiness and fullness" is, if we read these two fragments together in a disjunctive sequence, represented characteristically, in ways that have affinities with other poems of Sappho that we know. The distance, absence, of the sweet-apple are bound up with desire for the unattainable fruit. And the hyacinth, once fallen from an imagined height,

18. Thomas McEvilley, "Sappho, Fragment Two," *Phoenix* 26 (1972): 323–33.
19. Ibid., 333.
20. Ibid.

is destroyed. The fragments suggest an aesthetic of distance, of the beauty of the unreachable object of desire, suggest the superiority of the unattainable. Like the voice of the poet in other poems, yearning for a girl, for Aphrodite's presence to help her win the girl, watching her beloved seated next to a man, remembering the girl Atthis loves, the voice in these fragments values the absent object of desire, regrets the fall of the sweet flower in the present, to the ground, to the realm of men, of daily work. The sweetness of the desired object is lost when it enters the realm of marriage, adulthood, consumption.

Perhaps the same aesthetic valorizes for us the fragmentary corpus of Sappho, mined as it is with lacunae, loss, incompletion, imperfection. The art of reading is problematized in the encounter with these fragments, as the reader is made to confront her desire, her desires for wholeness, for more, for coherence, for linear, narrative familiarity. The effect of reading these tiny remnants of ancient lyric is the realization that all texts are fragments, parts of some elusive whole, whether it is the absent corpus of all ancient lyric, the "social text," the biographical details of the poet's life. We can always only read the part, the ruin, the shard of a lost vase, what is left to us, whether the poet be the long-dead Lesbian of the seventh century B.C. or the poet next door. Reading the explicitly fragmentary lines of these poems reveals the premises of our interpretive practices based on the desire for a whole always out of reach, denying the fragmentary nature of all cultural artifacts.

Another fragment of Sappho reads: "But I claim there will be some who remember us when we are gone."[21] Do we want simply to remember the everyday life of multitudes of women now dead, whom we can never know? Do we want to restore to them a narrative of which they have been deprived? Perhaps the dream of a restored wholeness, perfection, completion is caught up in the patriarchal, metaphysical tradition of absolute union with God the Father. Perhaps if we accept the necessity of fragmentation, the ways in which our access to any past is limited, our access to any narrative determined in part by our own desires, we can contemplate a new relationship between ourselves and the archaic past,

21. Richmond Lattimore, ed. and trans., *Greek Lyrics*, 2d ed. (Chicago, 1960), 41.

one that focuses not only on its irretrievability, but also on what pleasures it offers, what identifications or estrangements it allows, how it can be used in contemporary debates about community, subjectivity, the place of art, what kinds of empowerment or utopianism or imagination of the future it enables.

THREE
Sappho's Body-in-Pieces

One of Walter Benjamin's theses on the philosophy of history expresses scorn for a certain view of historicism. He wrote: "Historicism gives the 'eternal' image of the past; historical materialism supplies a unique experience with the past. The historical materialist leaves it to others to be drained by the whore called 'Once upon a time' in historicism's bordello. He remains in control of his powers, man enough to blast open the continuum of history."[1] Benjamin here argues, in scandalously sexist terms, against a kind of historicism called by Fredric Jameson "existential historicism," that aesthetic contemplation of an immutable past called "once upon a time," "the experience . . . by which *historicity* as such is manifested, by means of the contact between the historian's mind in the present and a given synchronic cultural complex from the past."[2] I argue here for a historical materialist historicism, one that is not content merely to contemplate the past from the point of view of an autonomous subject in the present, who comes into contact with the collective past, but that rather engages with the past in order to generate some vision of a utopian future. And if Benja-

An earlier version of this chapter was composed for the Princeton University Lecture Series on Gender.

1. Walter Benjamin, "Theses on the Philosophy of History," in *Illuminations: Essays and Reflections*, ed. Hannah Arendt, trans. Harry Zohn (New York, 1969), 262.

2. Fredric Jameson, "Marxism and Historicism," in *Syntax of History*, vol. 2 of *The Ideologies of Theory: Essays, 1971–1986* (Minneapolis, 1988), 157.

min, in his vision of the aestheticizing, contemplative version of historicism, uses the image of the whore in historicism's bordello, feminism needs not only to reject such degrading imagery but also to consider a dialectical materialist theory of history, to use Marxism, to see difference, to put into question contemporary assumptions about such concepts as gender, sex, sexual difference and to struggle for change.

We may need a counter to what I see as feminism's continuing and sometimes exclusive emphasis on the present, a circumstance in which even an "existential" historicism might have much to offer. If we focus on the nineteenth and twentieth centuries, see only contemporary women writers, reflect only on what is to be done in the next few months, the next few years, we limit ourselves radically in speculation, in strategies and tactics, in the invention of new realities. It seems important to reinsert the possibility of utopian thinking into feminist work, and to argue that historicism, a certain variety of historicism, can expand the vocabulary of possibilities for all work on gender. This chapter is not only an argument for feminists to adopt a theory of history but also perhaps a regression to a pre-postmodernist vision of history and progress. I realize that such a line is out of fashion, that postmodernity has erased history, rendering all of our experience flat and one-dimensional, that the concepts of past and future, of linear time, evoke unfortunate associations with master narratives, with the humanist trajectory of patriarchy. But to refuse any model of historical difference and change limits us inevitably to a purely aleatory experience of time, without the possibility of political and intellectual change and practice, and will restrict us to a passive observation of the machine of the world as it displays itself and us. I argue for a Marxist-feminist historicism, one that includes not only a narrative about the past but a vision of equality and emancipation in the future not only for women but for everyone.

Historicism will allow us to claim other histories for our political and intellectual work, allow us to see other peoples, other ideas of gendering, power, and sexual difference that help us see beyond the horizons of our own culture's essentializing notions of gender and difference. The ancient Greeks are, for me, a particularly suggestive example for historicist work, in part because we often name them as our origin, in part because they are in fact radically differ-

ent from us. And fragmentation can stand as a figure for a difference in approach from the traditional classicist drive for wholeness
and integrity, origins and continuity rather than recognition of
difference.

Before reading Sappho's poem 31, let me recall some ways in
which fragments figure in ancient culture, and undo from the first
any possible confidence concerning the integrity and stability of
this distant place and time. Ancient Dionysiac ritual included reference to a *sparagmos*, the ritual dismemberment and devouring of
animals in Bacchic celebration. Sophocles' heroine Antigone is
haunted by the figure of her brother's broken and unburied body.
The Athenians buried the broken bodies of the *korai*, the cult sta-
tues of Athena, after the Persian invasion at the beginning of the
fifth century; they used broken pieces of statuary and masonry to
refashion the wall that protected the city. The various Greek tribes
saw themselves and their settlements as fragmentary, disseminated
bits, broken off into individual cities from original unitary founding ancestors' families, saw their colonies as similarly dispersed
fragments of an original whole.

What is the political meaning for Athenians both of tribal dispersion after the death of their founder Ion, and of the dissemination of citizens in colonization? What are the discourses in historical texts on dialects, what are the political attempts to establish
leagues, to reconstitute wholeness? The Athenians, in their imaginary integrity and homogeneity, descended from a single ancestor,
or sprouted from the earth, lived surrounded by refugees, slaves
and foreigners, the metics, broken away from their places of origin.
The Athenians in particular seem to have seen their existence as a
community as haunted by a dialectic between integrity and dissemination. How did they think about democracy—the dispersed,
heterogeneous votes, scattered bits of broken shells, ostraka,
pebbles broken from rocks, shards once part of whole bodies of
vases—transformed through the vote into a single unified voice of
the majority, of the polis as a new whole?

And what is writing itself, the inscription on the ostraka that led
to ostracism? Writing is the scattered letters, lots, seeds, like the
dragon's teeth of Thebes, the gift of Kadmos, like the fragmented
bodies of Actaeon and Pentheus, sons of his house, like the stones
of the wall of Thebes, moved by the singing of Amphion and

Zethus, like the severed, singing head of Orpheus, dismembered
by maenads. Can we consider the imaginary opposition between
Thebes and Athens in terms of this slippage, this oscillation between fragmentation and integrity, Thebes as the site of dispersion
and dismemberment, Athens the city of remembering, recollection, democracy which is the unification of the once dispersed and
scattered?[3]

The period of the earliest democracy and of the Persian Wars,
the latter part of the sixth century B.C.E. and the early part of the
fifth, exhibit the Greeks' own fascination with fragments. An *ostrakon* is an oyster shell. The term came to be applied to broken bits
of pottery. The ceramic vases of the Greeks, when broken, pro-
vided myriad shards. Vases came to bear the names of potter and
painter, of donor, of the recipient of the gift, epigraphs naming the
figures in paintings; they bore writing on them, random letters at
first, when the painter wanted to demonstrate his ability to write,
then parts of words, names, whole words, whole names, even sen-
tences. Was it these inscribed words, painted and fired into the
surfaces of the rounded vases and then split off from their former
sites, that led the Athenians to see these broken pieces of vases as
proper surfaces for the names of those who were becoming too
prominent, who threatened to unbalance the democracy and who
thus had to be exiled? The word *ostrakon* has an interesting history,
moving as it does from the split leaves of the oyster, the two sides
of the bivalve, to an extended meaning, the broken-up bits of the
vases, which might have vaguely recalled oyster shells. The mound
of Testaccio in Rome, a hill of waste, of shell and broken pieces of
pottery, still looms as a considerable elevation in the modern city.
Archaeologists excavating in the modern city of Athens discovered
a cache of 190 ostraka, all bearing the name of Themistokles written in just a few hands. They conjecture that Themistokles' political opponents were plotting to have him ostracized, and planned
to distribute these potsherds either to the illiterate or to supporters
who would be organized to vote against their enemy.

---

3. On Thebes and Athens, see Froma Zeitlin, "Thebes: Theater of Self and Society
in Athenian Drama," in *Nothing To Do with Dionysos? Athenian Drama in Its Social Context,* ed.
John J. Winkler and Froma I. Zeitlin (Princeton, N.J., 1990), 130–67.

In a significant parallel to the Athenian practice of using pottery fragments for the most important type of voting, the casting out of a prominent man from among the citizens, the citizens of Syracuse in Sicily, a Corinthian foundation, engaged in a political ritual called *petalismos*, after the *petala*, or olive leaves, used in voting. Homer, in a famous passage, likens the generations of human beings to leaves on a tree:

> As is the generation of leaves, so is that of humanity
> The wind scatters the leaves on the ground, but the live
>   timber
> burgeons with leaves again in the season of spring
>   returning.
> So one generation of men will grow while another dies.[4]

Olive leaves were a convenient and available source of writing material in the Mediterranean, but it is nonetheless significant that this act of scapegoating and expelling a member of the ancient community of Syracuse would use the medium of leaves, the once living and then fallen parts of the olive tree.[5] These practices of expulsion take up fragmentary elements of ordinary life, use them to mark someone and to expel him, in order to reconstitute the integrity of the city. The fragments are the instruments of the construction of a new whole, one renewed and strengthened by the breaking off of one of its parts, one of the citizen members of the polity.

Voting in the assembly of Athens took place by a show of hands and does not exhibit the characteristics of the casting of names into a pool for ostracism. However, voting by juries in legal trials was done by secret ballot, and thus has affinities with ostracism; it

---

4. *The Iliad of Homer*, trans. Richmond Lattimore (Chicago, 1951), 6.146–50.

5. On ostracism, see also Jean-Pierre Vernant, "Ambiguity and Reversal: On the Enigmatic Structure of *Oedipus Rex*," trans. Page duBois, *New Literary History* 9 : 3 (1978): 475–501. "It [ostracism] was all organised so as to make it possible for the popular feeling that the Greeks called *phthonos* (a mixture of envy and religious distrust of anyone who rose too high or was too successful) to manifest itself in the most spontaneous and unanimous fashion (there had to be at least 6,000 voters) regardless of any rule of law or rational justification. The only things held against the ostracised man were the very superior qualities which had raised him above the common herd, and his exaggerated good luck which might call down the wrath of the gods upon the town" (488).

is remarkable that these two kinds of activity fall into the same field because of the Greeks' physical practices of voting with objects. Questions concerning individuals (*ep'andri*) were decided with secret ballot (*psēphisma*, from *psēphos*, voting-stone, voting-pebble), even in the assembly, and the decisions of juries on individuals similarly used pebbles dropped into an urn, a black stone for conviction or a white one for acquittal. These deliberations, pointed at an individual member of the community, required a secret ballot, one conducted by means of these fragments, *ostraka*, potsherds, and pebbles, when what was at stake was the punishment or removal of one element of the polity. It is as if all these practices were understood as efforts at cleansing and repair, the reestablishing of balance after a moment of fragmentation and harm brought on the group by the efforts of a single person on his own behalf. The selfish acts of conspirators, criminals, and potential tyrants split the community; the fragments used to name such actors, or to condemn them, served to renegotiate the bonds of community and to create a new whole, one no longer split and fragmented by the actions of the culprit. So both the ostracism and the jury system of Athens might be said to exhibit similarities to the process of historiography, the recognition of fragmentation, the use of fragments to negotiate some change, and the provisional, temporary, establishing of coherence.

The metaphorics of the discourses and practices of the Athenians, in some sense our ancestors, in some sense descendants of Greeks of the archaic age, like Sappho, themselves exhibit a sense of fragmentation, dismemberment. The Greek words that derive from *speirō*, "sow," interestingly combine the metaphorics of dissemination with those of fragmentation and dismemberment. It is as if the ear of grain, the source of seeds, is seen as a whole from which parts are stripped, in a move that transfers that act of separation from the *sparagmos*, which is in fact derived from *spaō*, "draw, tear, rend," rather than from the verb for sowing. In a typically unscientific but interesting ancient etymology, there is a confusion between these two verbs and their derivatives which makes both of them partake of the connotations of the other, sowing becoming rending, rending becoming sowing, the Sown Men, the Spartoi of Thebes, the ancestors of the dismembered members of the

house of Thebes, Dionysos, Aktaion, and Pentheus.[6] All these ety-
mological nets and metaphors, although applied to the city of
Thebes, are known from Athenian tragedy, from Athenian accounts of the history of that state.

The semantic complex associated with sowing and rending connects the practices of agriculture, which functioned to unite the
community, with myths and rituals of dismemberment. In the *Bacchae*, for example, a messenger describes the ripping apart, the *sparagmos* of the ruler of Thebes, Pentheus:

> Ignoring his cries of pity,
> she seized his left arm at the wrist; then, planting
> her foot upon his chest, she pulled, wrenching away
>   [*apesparaxen*]
> the arm at the shoulder. . . .
> Ino, meanwhile, on the other wide, was scratching off
> his flesh. Then Autonoe and the whole horde
> of Bacchae swarmed upon him. Shouts everywhere,
> he screaming with what little breath was left,
> they shrieking in triumph. One tore off an arm,
> another a foot still warm in its shoe. His ribs
> were clawed clean of flesh [*sparagmois*] and every hand
> was smeared with blood as they played ball [*diesphairizde*]
>   with scraps
> of Pentheus' body.
>   The pitiful remains lie scattered,
> one piece among the sharp rocks, others
> lying lost among the leaves in the depths
> of the forest. His mother, picking up his head,
> impaled it on her wand. She seems to think it is
> some mountain lion's head which she carries in triumph.[7]

The passage has some of the baroque strangeness of the scene of
Creousa's melting flesh in the *Medea*; Euripides links by a half-pun

---

6. Cf. *sparganon*, in plural "swaddling clothes," "and so, in Trag., remembrances of
one's childhood, tokens by which a person's extraction is discovered" (LSJ.). Presumably
Oedipus' scarred ankles would be such tokens, Oedipus also of the house of Thebes.

7. Euripides, *The Bacchae*, trans. William Arrowsmith, *The Complete Greek Tragedies*, ed.
David Grene and Richmond Lattimore (Chicago, 1959), ll. 1124–42.

the dismemberment and playing ball. The sundered shoulder recalls the body of Pelops, partially consumed at the feast of Atreus
and Thyestes, although his shoulder was replaced by one of ivory,
and he lived on. While this Bacchic scene is hardly agricultural, it
does associate the choruses, the dancing groups of bacchants, with
the chorus of the theater, performing before that assembly of the
city of Athens that unifies them in the act of watching and seeing.
Although this tragedy was supposedly written in Macedonia during Euripides' exile there, it was performed in Athens.

Other relevant scenes of tearing apart, ripping apart, include
the image of the city at the time of the Peloponnesian War, when
parties struggled against one another and when people turned
against each other in fear of Sparta. The ancient historian Thucydides writes about the rebuilding of the walls of the city of Athens
after the Persians sacked and burned the city's akropolis. They built
broken pieces of the old wall into the new, constructing a fabric
consisting partly of stones, the "bones of the mother," and partly
of fragments of earlier man-made structures. Although these elements of the visual culture of Athens may seem distant, these classical Athenian texts to have little to do with the archaic Lesbian
Sappho, they demonstrate a cultural preoccupation with the fragmentary that goes beyond the fact that the Greeks of the archaic
and classical ages were widely dispersed across a great geographical territory. They saw themselves as scattered parts of a former
whole, and the tribes, then dispersions of peoples, then colonization as dialectically related phenomena.

This essay considers the figure of fragmentation of the body in
relation to the world of the ancient Greeks and to our own naturalized notions about the body. I am concerned with postmodernity's focus on contemporary culture and with the concomitant
loss of a perspective on past and future that might enable other
visions of bodies, sexualities, genders. Our lack of relationship to
the past, our refusal of its fragmentedness, may depend on a psychological resistance to the fragmented body, a resistance that
Jacques Lacan's work can perhaps help us to understand. Our fear
of coming to terms with the fragmented historical past leads us to
re-member its dismemberment, often to falsify that past. Such mis-
recognitions have implications not only for how we read the past
and its fragments but also for how we read the world and women's

place in it. Sappho's poems, their form and the ways in which we receive them, can exemplify an alternative aesthetic. Seeing the possibilities of this alternative—recognizing and accepting our own fragmentation and the inevitably fragmented past—has implications for how we treat bodies of poetry, bodies in poetry, and bodies in the world.

In a recent book called *Rethinking Art History*, Donald Preziosi characterizes his discipline in terms that cast light on classics as a field. He argues that "the discipline . . . serves to project or to validate a certain kind of viewing Subject: ideally, passive consumers, and, in more contemporary contexts, educated and discerning cryptographers—but receivers of messages all the same." He points out further that the discipline actually "shares with other humanistic disciplines . . . a highly complex and self-perpetuating analytic theater of power and knowledge, a discourse always written in the third person singular."[8] I am especially concerned here with the ways in which the field of classics projects and validates a similar Subject, "the classicist," who is at once consumer, cryptographer, and receiver of messages, but who has rarely acknowledged rhetorically his own power and presence in the act of interpretation of the fragments of antiquity, assuming rather a transparency, an unmediated access to the remnants of the past.

My question here is: How do classicists come to terms with ancient culture? What sort of subject does ancient culture produce, in the person of the classicist? And how can contemporary theory, especially psychoanalysis, help us think the relationship we have to antiquity?

Classicists receive antiquity in pieces, as fragments. There are various attempts to come to terms with the material of the past, both to break it up further, into more manageable entities, and to recover an imagined lost unity. Paradoxically, both those attempts to reunite lost parts and to break down the past can deter readers from the act of interpretation, from considering what the past means for us, what it makes of us. One way of responding to this recognition is to pursue a dream of wholeness, transparency, per-

---

8. Donald Preziosi, *Rethinking Art History: Meditations on a Coy Science* (New Haven, Conn., and London, 1989), 52.

fect access to what we desire to know through such scholarly practices as "conjectures," imagining the word that might have once
been where there is now a gap. Another is to try to manage the
instability of our relationship to the past by reducing it to atoms
accessible to philological science, through the production of a
scholary apparatus and commentary, through the perusal of lexi-
cons, catalogs of all the words, fixing them into alphabetic lists.
Another is to accept the partiality of our experience, to seek, even
as we yearn for more—more fact, more words and artifacts, more
lines of Sappho, more poems of Sappho—to read what we have in
light of who we are now.

Speaking of those ancient writers whose work "counted for
something," in praise of Horace, Nietzsche said:

> This mosaic of words, in which every unit spreads its
> power to the left and to the right over the whole, by its
> sound, by its place in the sentence, and by its meaning, this
> *minimum* in the compass and number of the signs, and the
> *maximum* of energy in the signs which is thereby achieved—
> all this is Roman, and, if you will believe me, noble *par
> excellence*.[9]

Nietzsche's appreciation of Horace does not concern the fragment,
nor is it directed to archaic Greek poetry, nor does his praise of
Horace as noble suit my purpose. But his remarks on the *minimum*
of signs, *maximum* of energy might direct a reading of the fragmentary, one that attempts, not romantically, not lamenting the loss
that surrounds the fragment, not to restore its lacks, but to read the
minimal signs of the fragment with a maximum of energy.

What follows is a reading of a necessarily fragmented poem of
Sappho, one that attempts to recognize the fragmentary state of
my own encounter with the poem.

This is Sappho's poem 31:

> To me he seems like a god
> as he sits facing you and
> hears you near as you speak
> softly and laugh

9. Friedrich Nietzsche, *The Twilight of the Idols: or, How to Philosophise with the Hammer,*
trans. Anthony M. Ludovici (New York, 1964), 113.

in a sweet echo that jolts
the heart in my ribs. For now
as I look at you my voice
is empty and

can say nothing as my tongue
cracks and slender fire is quick
under my skin. My eyes are dead
to light, my ears

pound, and sweat pours over me.
I convulse, greener than grass,
and feel my mind slip as I
   go close to death.[10]

φαίνεταί μοι κῆνος ἴσος
   θέοισιν
ἔμμεν' ὤνηρ, ὄττις ἐνάντιός
   τοι
ἰσδάνει καὶ πλάσιον ἆδυ
   φωνεί-
σας ὐπακούει

καὶ γελαίσας ἰμέροεν, τό μ' ἦ
   μὰν
καρδίαν ἐν στήθεσιν
   ἐπτόαισεν
ὠς γὰρ ἔς σ' ἴδω βρόχε᾽ ὤς με
   φώναι-
σ' οὐδ' ἒν ἔτ' εἴκει,

ἀλλὰ κὰμ μὲν γλῶσσά ⟨μ'⟩
   ἔαγε, λέπτον
δ' αὔτικα χρῷ πῦρ
   ὐπαδεδρόμηκεν,
ὀππάτεσσι δ' οὐδ' ἒν ὄρημμ',
   ἐπιρρόμ-
βεισι δ' ἄκουαι,

10. Willis Barnstone, trans., *Sappho and the Greek Lyric Poets* (New York, 1988), fr. 31.

κὰδ δέ μ' ἴδρως κακχέεται,
τρόμος δὲ
παῖσαν ἄγρει, χλωροτέρα δὲ
ποίας
ἔμμι, τεθνάκην δ' ὀλίγω
†ιδεύης
φαίνομ' ἔμ' αὔτ[ᾳ.

ἀλλὰ πὰν τόλματον, ἐπεὶ †καὶ
πένητα†[11]

The lines break off here, into fragments. This poem was much ad-
mired in antiquity; Plato seems to echo it in the *Phaedrus* when
Socrates describes the symptoms of love as beauty enters through
the eyes:

> . . . first there come upon him a shuddering and a measuring
> of . . . awe. . . . Next, with the passing of the shudder, a
> strange sweating and fever seizes him.[12]

Catullus translated this poem, retaining the gender markers of the
object of desire and transforming it into a heterosexual text. Longinus, in citing the poem in his work, speaks of the skill with which
Sappho picks out and binds together the most striking and intense
of the symptoms of love.[13]

Sappho's selection of *akra*, of high moments, is a fragmentation
of experience, in that it must perforce break up the flow of lived
time. Poetry performs such a splitting up of experience through
selection. But piled on top of this sense of fragmentation is another, one peculiar to the thematics of this particular poem, in
which the body is represented as falling into fragments, seen as a
series of discrete, unconnected, disjunctive responses. As Longinus
points out in remarks that have been found inadequate in the twentieth century but that suit my purpose admirably:

11. David A. Campbell, *Greek Lyric Poetry: A Selection of Early Greek Lyric, Elegiac and
Iambic Poetry* (Basingstoke and London, 1967), 44.

12. Plato, *Collected Dialogues*, ed. Edith Hamilton and Huntington Cairns (Princeton,
N.J., 1961), 497.

13. See David A. Campbell, *The Golden Lyre: The Themes of the Greek Lyric Poets* (London, 1983), 13–14.

Is it not wonderful [literally, *ou thaumazdeis?* are you not amazed?] how she summons at the same time soul body hearing tongue sight colour, all as though they had wandered off apart from herself?[14]

Longinus says that the poet constructs of all these things a *sunodos,* a meeting, a junction. The poem is a crossroads of emotions, a reassembly of the fragmented, disparate parts of the poetic "I" that have "wandered off apart from herself." These parts are her heart, which is given a separate existence in her breast, her voice, which escapes her, her broken tongue, her skin, over which fire runs, her blinded eyes, her humming ears. This is Eros the limb-loosener, *lusimelēs,* the one that unstrings the assembly of the body and brings the "I" here close to death.

Much has been written about this poem, some of it illustrating my view that classicists perpetuate a certain kind of subject, one rooted in reason, deciphering the cryptic fragments of the past, speculating endlessly about contexts about which evidence can never be regained. This is true of the argument about whether Sappho's bodily disintegration is caused by jealousy or fear, whether the occasion of the poem is a wedding feast, Sappho an observer overcome by envy of the bridegroom, or full of awestruck praise for the magnificence of the newly married. One particularly obfuscating debate concerns the issue of Sappho's homosexuality,[15] as in George Devereux's essay, "The Nature of Sappho's Seizure in Fr. 31 as Evidence of Her Inversion" (1970).[16] A belief in the tragedy of homosexual existence colors Thomas McEvilley's otherwise help-

14. "Longinus," *On the Sublime,* in Aristotle, *The Poetics,* "Longinus," *On the Sublime,* Demetrius, *On Style* (Cambridge, Mass., and London, 1932), 10.3.

15. For a valuable corrective, see André Lardinois, "Lesbian Sappho and Sappho of Lesbos," in *From Sappho to De Sade: Moments in the History of Sexuality,* ed. Jan Bremmer (London and New York, 1989), 15–35.

16. George Devereux, "The Nature of Sappho's Seizure in Fr. 31 as Evidence of Her Inversion," *Classical Quarterly* 20 (1970): 17ff. For a response, see Miroslav Marcovich, "Sappho Fr. 31: Anxiety Attack or Love Declaration," in *Studies in Greek Poetry,* Illinois Classical Studies Suppl. 1 (Atlanta, 1991), 29–46. Other more illuminating studies are Eva Stehle Stigers, "Sappho's Private World," in *Reflections of Women in Antiquity,* ed. Helene P. Foley (New York, 1981), 45–61, and John J. Winkler, "Gardens of Nymphs: Public and Private in Sappho's Lyrics," in ibid., 63–89.

ful reading of the poem in a way that seems postromantic to me; his essay is subtitled "The Face behind the Mask"! He argues that the beginning of the poem suggests a hymeneal occasion, but that then the poem veers into a private voice. As he describes what he terms the "dramatic situation," "Sappho has been asked to write or sing the wedding song, and she has begun nicely; then the sight of the beauty of the bride sends her out of control, calling up her very ambivalent feelings about homosexuality and married happiness." I actually find this rather unpersuasive and irreconcilable with the reading that argues that the fear and disintegration produced by the sight of the beloved are elements of praise, of suggesting the divine beauty of the beloved woman. It is not clear to me that Sappho's desire for girls produced ambivalence about homosexuality at all; we could read her songs of regret and longing as her ontological situation, her aesthetic response to the separation from the beloved that almost all lovers experience.[17]

As Charles Segal points out, this poem is saturated with reference to the world of oral poetry. In a fascinating essay, he writes in detail about the poem's patterns of alliteration and assonance, features that contribute to its incantatory quality, and that link it with the oral tradition.[18] Jesper Svenbro reads it as Sappho's allegory about reading:

> Coming as she did from the oral tradition, she set up the disappearance of the writer in a new way—not by using the third person for herself, but by giving an allegorical description of her own death by writing.[19]

---

17. Thomas McEvilley, "Sappho, Fragment Thirty-One: The Face behind the Mask," *Phoenix* 32 (1978): 14. "She is showing us the extreme disharmony which she must have felt inwardly on such occasions. She seems to be the first poet who has left us a record of what has since become a familiar situation: the poet as a sensitive soul suffering feelings of frustration and alienation from the problems of relating his or her work to conventional social realities. Needless to say, in this case the situation was aggravated by Sappho's homosexuality" (15). McEvilley's tragic homosexual, like the "tragic mulatto" or the tormented Romantic poet, seems a highly ideological figure.

18. Charles Segal, "Eros and Incantation: Sappho and Oral Poetry," *Arethusa* 7 (1974): 139–57.

19. Jesper Svenbro, "Death by Writing: Sappho, the Poem, and the Reader," in *Phrasikleia: An Anthropology of Reading in Ancient Greece*, trans. Janet Lloyd (1988; Ithaca, N.Y., 1993), 152.

Leah Rissman, in *Love as War*, discusses fragment 31 in terms of the "application of Homeric battle simile and terminology to lovers."[20] Her argument supports the view that Sappho's symptoms suggest not jealousy of the man who is her beloved's companion, but rather that the whole poem is in some sense a poem of praise, that the poet is stunned by the woman's beauty, which has the kind of effect on her that the aegis of Athena had on Penelope's suitors in the *Odyssey*. The woman in this scene is divine, the man heroic. Rissman says: "Both Sappho and the poet of the *Iliad* are concerned with contrasting the behavior of winners and losers. Sappho's catalogue of her own reactions to a woman is similar to the Homeric catalogue of the coward's response to the stress of ambush: both lists include pallor and unsteadiness of heart."[21] Fragment 31 is, therefore, a marriage poem in her view, a poem of praise in which the man is presented as godlike, the woman as divine; the poem elevates marriage by investing it with the heroic grandeur of the Homeric situation.[22]

More persuasive than McEvilley's remarks on Sappho's homosexual alienation are his observations on the diction of fragment 31, which support Rissman's commentary about the profoundly Homeric quality of Sapphic reference. He points out that *kardia*, "heart," does not occur elsewhere in our fragments; that *glōssa* is unusual, since Sappho usually refers not to tongue but to voice, that "fire" does not occur elsewhere. "Only in fr. 31 are the unpleasant physical sensations of heat and cold a part of Sappho's poetic world. They are . . . intrusions from the uncontrollable realm of physical circumstance from which Sappho's poetry usually provides escape." Ears do not appear elsewhere, and sweat too is Homeric, and inelegant. McEvilley points out that "in Sappho's general practice, parts of the body are mentioned only as containers of erotic beauty." He argues that all this diction is meant to "make explicit the difference between the real and the poetic worlds."

20. Leah Rissman, *Love as War: Homeric Allusion in the Poetry of Sappho* (Konigstein, 1983), 72.

21. Ibid., 89.

22. Anne Pippin Burnett shares this view, seeing the singer of fr. 31 as fearful, approaching someone who has aroused her desire. *Three Archaic Poets: Archilochus, Alcaeus, Sappho* (Cambridge, Mass., 1983), 219; see 230ff. for a useful bibliography of work on fr. 31.

"Now for once the grim facts of bodily death become overwhelmingly clear and close: she is mortal; her tongue of songs is broken, sweat pours down her body."[23] The poem alludes to the Homeric descriptions of the body, using cruder, more corporeal language than that of other poems in its depiction of the poet's collapse.

In a particularly startling image, for example, Sappho says: *glōssa eage*, variously translated "my tongue broke," "my tongue shivered," "my tongue cracked." Denys Page complains that the hiatus would be irregular, and the meaning "my tongue is broken" unsatisfactory; David Campbell nonetheless points out that Lucretius 3.155 seems to echo this passage in *infringi linguam*, and in the invocation to the catalog of ships in *Iliad* 2, the poet asks for the Muses' help with the words, "I could not tell over the multitude of them nor name them, not if I had ten tongues and ten mouths, not if I had a voice never to be broken [*phonē d'arrēktos*] (*Iliad* 2.488–90).[24] Sappho here alludes to this curious feature of the Homeric body, the frangible tongue, and in her poem the hiatus, the two vowels coming together, could be seen to "break" the tongue, to force an awkward, dysphonious phrase, a stumbling into the gap between the two vowels that produces a simulacrum of the poetic "I"'s distress in the reader.

Nancy Vickers has written brilliantly about the ways in which Renaissance lyric, the poems of Petrarch and his imitators perform a sort of dismemberment of the female body, how in their blazons and ekphrases, their descriptions of the physical appearance of the beloved, their lines anatomize, "cut up" the limbs, the parts of women.[25] Such an observation recalls the feminist critiques of contemporary advertising and pornography, which similarly dismember and commodify the parts of women's bodies. Such dismemberment produces not disorder but the control of anatomization. What is particularly fascinating about Sappho's poem is that here the woman herself sees the disorder in the body in love, sees herself objectified as a body in pieces, disjointed, a broken set of organs, limbs, bodily functions.

23. McEvilley, "Sappho, Fragment Thirty-One," 16, 17, 18.

24. Page, *Sappho and Alcaeus*; Campbell, *Greek Lyric Poetry*, 272.

25. Nancy J. Vickers, "The Body Re-Membered: Petrarchan Lyrics and the Strategies of Description," in *Mimesis: From Mirror to Method, Augustine to Descartes*, ed. J. D. Lyons and S. G. Nichols (Hanover, N.H., 1982), 100–109.

Whether or not the poem depicts envy or praise expressed as fear—both seem simultaneously possible—readers interested in psychoanalysis might see this poem as an ideal text to demonstrate the universal value of psychoanalytic theory. Such work would point to the universality of the human condition and to the capacity of psychoanalysis to describe and illuminate all human desire.[26] Sappho's poem is an important example of a poetics based on recollection, the conscious mind recalling a moment of bodily alienation of a sort that might be thought to exemplify the Lacanian dialectic of imaginary and symbolic. Can we use the work of Lacan to describe the effects on Sappho of the sight of her lover? Lacan speaks, for example, in terms that might seem familiar to the reader of Sappho, of a body in pieces:

> This fragmented body . . . usually manifests itself in dreams when the movement of the analysis encounters a certain level of aggressive disintegration in the individual. It then appears in the form of disjointed limbs, or of those organs presented in exoscopy, growing wings and taking up arms for intestinal persecutions—the very same that the visionary Hieronymus Bosch has fixed, for all time, in painting, in their ascent from the fifteenth century to the imaginary zenith of modern man.[27]

Although Sappho's fragment 31 seems beautifully to exemplify Lacan's description of the Boschian vision, what follows is an argument against the view that Sappho's catalog of broken body parts proves the universal descriptive value of Lacanian psychoanalysis. This poem, I argue, reveals not transcendent human nature, not universal human psychic structures, but rather historical difference, a moment in the constitution of the aristocratic self, perhaps even before the theorization of gender per se. The "I" that speaks and writes, the "I" that is produced in that moment, regards the past, a disordered, fragmented past, from a present in which the poem itself and the fiction of subjectivity represented in it are

26. For a psychoanalytic reading of a classical corpus, see Micaela Janan, *When the Lamp Is Shattered: Desire and Narrative in Catullus* (Carbondale, Ill., 1994).

27. Jacques Lacan, *Ecrits: A Selection*, trans. Alan Sheridan (New York and London, 1977), 4–5.

constituted against the backdrop of fragmentation. The "I" of the poem comes out of that fragmentation, is constructed from it. The *sunodos*, the junction, must be read historically, neither generalized to describe some absolute and general proposition of feminine composition, nor used to prove the universality of our postmodern ideas of split subjectivity.

I would argue instead for a historicist understanding of this poem, recalling Bruno Snell's pages on the Homeric body. He argues that the Homeric authors and audience understood the body as such not to exist, but rather to be an assembly of parts, of functions, of disparate organs loosely allied, commanded independently by gods and men. Snell says:

> Of course the Homeric man had a body exactly like the later Greeks, but he did not know it *qua* body, but merely as the sum total of his limbs. This is another way of saying that the Homeric Greeks did not yet have a body in the modern sense of the word; body, *sōma*, is a later interpretation of what was originally comprehended as *melē*, or *guia*, limbs."[28]

Snell makes a connection between this conception of the human form and its representation in early Greek art:

> Not until the classical art of the fifth century do we find attempts to depict the body as an organic unity whose parts are mutually correlated. In the preceding period the body is a mere construct of independent parts variously put together.[29]

The tribal, collective, prepolitical world of the Homeric heroes represents the body, or rather what will become the body, as similar to its own social organization, a loose confederation, a tenuous grouping of parts.

Although Snell's work has been called into question by some, the arguments of such scholars as Robert Renehan, in his essay on *sōma*, do not seem to me to discredit Snell's point.[30] I appreciate the

28. Bruno Snell, *The Discovery of the Mind: The Greek Origins of European Thought*, trans. T. G. Rosenmeyer (Cambridge, Mass., 1953), 8.

29. Ibid., 6.

30. Robert Renehan, "The Meaning of *Sōma* in Homer," *California Studies in Classical Antiquity* 12 (1981), 269–82.

objections made to the orthodoxy following Snell, who contended that the word *sōma* never refers to a living body. Furthermore, there are problems with seeing lyric poetry in relation to Homeric epic in such a way that we see only a Hegelian, nineteenth-century evolution, an inevitable progression, a Lévy-Bruhlian passage from myth to reason. I share many scholars' objections to these versions of historical inevitability. But I do not have the same difficulty with the notion that there is a difference, a *historical* difference, between Sappho and Homer and that their views of the body may differ. Snell's argument seems to me to be a particularly valuable intervention in the question of the *historicity* of the body.

Set against the background of this understanding of human beings' physical existence, Sappho's disordered, fragmented body takes on a different resonance than if it were to be understood only as figuring in the Lacanian imaginary. The subject, the "I" of archaic lyric, is generated in the earliest urban, that is, literally "political" setting, internal to the voice of a dominant aristocracy. According to Snell, these poems record the beginning of the historical evolution of selfhood, of individuality, the aristocratic origins of what will become the male citizens of the ancient *polis*, the city-state, and Michel Foucault's subject of philosophy in the Platonic tradition. Although I do not suggest that Sappho read Bruno Snell, or that she had a historical sense of distance from the Homeric past, Sappho's poem nonetheless recalls the relatively archaic view of the body represented for her in Homeric poetry. There is no historical consciousness for Sappho equal to Snell's in its formal grasp of a shift in consciousness between Homer's day and her own; rather, Sappho adopts here a traditional, conventional, epic description of the body, familiar to her and her audience from the traditional poetry, to express what appears to be a disintegration of her own body. If the relation of Sappho's description of her own physical distress to the earlier Homeric sense of the body may not be conscious for Sappho, it has definite consequences nonetheless. Sappho's view of eros *lusimelēs*, that love that disunites the only recently constituted body, suggests that eros returns that body to a past state, to an alliance of functions, a loose set of organic capacities; what she represents is a turning back from a tenuously held subjectivity, that new sense of the poet as an "I," back to an archaic sense of identity.

Lacan's work on the relationship between the body in pieces and
the ego, though not directly applicable to Sappho's poetic universe, might, as I argued in the introduction, shed light on the
question of what we make of the fragments, literal fragments, of
ancient poetry. Who are we, these supposed agents of integrity
and coherence, who desire to mend that past? I find especially useful, when considering these texts, Lacan's way of thinking about
the alternation between the fictional whole, the "I," and the fragmentary past, as an ongoing dialectic; we are always conscious of
the possibility of dismemberment, of the fragility of wholeness, of
corporeal and psychic integrity, even as our identity is fashioned
against the background of such dismemberment.

In approaching the Greeks in this way, fragmentation stands as
a figure that both illuminates a contemporary relationship to the
past and that recognizes in the Greeks themselves a certain contestation of figures of integrity and coherence. Such an approach
might be seen to differ from a more traditional classicist drive for
wholeness and integrity, recognition of origin and continuity, or
from the need to fragment, to atomize, to render manageable and
not-yet-interpretable the data we receive from antiquity.

It is crucial to understand that the pleasure Sappho's poem 31
affords us, in our positions as psychoanalytic subjects of the twentieth century, is not the same as that of the audience of Sappho's
day. If Sappho's listeners heard an account of historical archaism,
of dissolution back into undifferentiated collectivity, we may project a psychological state described by Lacan. And we recognize
Sappho's distance from Homer, our distance from both. The richer
reading of this poem would acknowledge all these dimensions, historical and contemporary, and would measure the distance between one pleasure and another. And this poem, in its evocation of
distress, even of anguish, of the exaggerated pains of love, is a pleasure for us to read. The "I" as contemporary reader can appreciate
Sappho's recollection of suffering because the poem has constructed coherence from disorder, reconstituted subjectivity out of
a body in pieces. The pleasure of this reconstitution is what allows
for readerly transference, to refer to a psychoanalytic model. If the
male lover, who sits across from, *enantios*, vis-à-vis Sappho's object
of desire, is caught in a specular, dyadic relationship to her, gazing
at her, the voice of the poet has entered the domain of language,

acknowledges the passage of time and the possibility of a linguistic recovery of her fragmented body. The reader's pleasure comes from an appreciation of the disintegration the poet describes, the undeniable pain of eros, of a disordering desire that shatters the tongue, that brings the "I" to a place near death, but also from the security of that "I" that speaks the poem, the voice that gazes retrospectively at the experience of fragmentation, and from it creates a crossroads, a poem, and a self. And there is further the historical dimension of our reading, a sense of distance from the fragments of Sappho's work, a sense of another distance, internal to the poem, in which the Homeric body serves as a figure for the lover. If, as Shoshana Felman argues, we are both analyst and analysand as we read, if therefore we experience both transference and countertransference, if we see ourselves as authority and as subject to the authority of the text, then such readings might take account of the contradictory drives for integrity and for atomization, for mastery of a disturbing past.[31] The self constituted against a background of disorder can be a self of pleasure and authority that recognizes its construction of itself out of fragmentation, that acknowledges its own fictionality, its own historicity. And we as its readers can recognize our implication in its drama and our own situation in the late twentieth century, gazing at the fragments of the past, trying to work them into a story about ourselves, a story that enables action in the present, for the future. We can use the pleasures of that story, rethinking our relationship to the Greeks, to their privileged position in our history, countering the inherited vision of ancient society inhabited by disembodied, philosophical, male citizens.

I would argue for a historical materialist historicism, one that is not content merely to contemplate the past from the point of view of an autonomous subject in the present, who comes into contact with the collective past, but that rather engages with the past in order to generate some vision of historical difference. The ancient Greeks, and Sappho in particular, provide particularly suggestive

31. "With respect to the text, the literary critic occupies thus at once the place of the psychoanalyst (in the relation of interpretation) and the place of the patient (in the relation of transference)." Shoshana Felman, "To Open the Question," in *Literature and Psychoanalysis: The Question of Reading: Otherwise* (Baltimore and London, 1982), 7.

material for historicist work, in part because we so often name the Greeks as our origin, in part because Sappho is in fact so radically different from us, even in such a "natural" domain as life in the body. And if Benjamin, in his vision of the aestheticizing, contemplative version of historicism, uses the image of the whore in historicism's bordello, feminism needs not only to resist such imagery but also to incorporate a materialist theory of history to see historical difference, to have a richer sense of possibility, to put into question our assumptions about the natural body.

FOUR

Sappho in
the Text of Plato

There is a moment in the *Symposium* in which Socrates speaks of the disruptive, troubling presence of the woman at the scene of philosophy, invoking a creature from mythology. In response to Agathon's speech, he says:

> His speech reminded me so strongly of that master of rhetoric, Gorgias, that I couldn't help thinking of Odysseus, and his fear that Medusa would rise from the lower world among the ghosts, and I was afraid that when Agathon got near the end he would arm his speech against mine with the Gorgon's head of Gorgias' eloquence, and strike me as dumb as stone. (198c)

Of course this is a witty little joke, using the elements of a shared vocabulary among men, teasing Agathon for his effeminacy, and of course I exhibit the heavy-handed literalism of the humorless feminist when I point it out. But I am enough of a Freudian, or even of a new critic, to believe that even jokes can be interpreted. Here the woman who threatens to rise up from the underworld, like the dead mother of Odysseus, endangers speech and the philosophical occasion, the ecstatic contemplation of pederastic love; she threatens to impose silence.

This chapter had its origin in a paper delivered at a conference on Plato and postmodernism at the University of Oregon.

It has become fashionable to argue that Plato is more rhetorical, literary, ironic, self-reflexive than we have always thought, we of the Western metaphysical tradition. Plato does not present, in this view, a systematic philosophy, nor does he argue for specific doctrines. He is engaged in a truly dialogic practice, writing open texts that turn with great rhetorical sophistication upon themselves, that commit conspicuous logical errors, that call attention to their own arbitrariness and to the difficulties inherent in any model of mastery and discipleship. This may well be, although I have not yet been convinced that there is no doctrinal substance presented in the form of these dialogical texts.

But what does it mean to think about Plato in the context of postmodernism? A first question might be: Whose postmodernism? In contrast to Hal Foster's distinction between a postmodernism of resistance and a postmodernism of reaction, E. Ann Kaplan distinguishes between a commercial or co-opted postmodernism, and a utopian postmodernism.[1] Resistance to what, reaction to what, utopia of what? Susan Bordo has argued that postmodernism can be used to collapse gender categories, to erase alterity and historical difference.[2] Postmodernism can be condemned from the point of view of traditional Marxism, as the loss of the coherent subject, the agent of political action, or from the view of cultural feminism, as the abandonment of a dream of wholeness and fusion. But if postmodernism is the logic of late capitalism,[3] or a reaction to modernism, the regime of infinitely proliferating simulacra, or some utterly new and unknowable beast, it may represent an opportunity as well as something to be deplored. I want to argue for a utopian antisexist, antiracist postmodernism, one that celebrates heterogeneity and difference, the fragmentary and erotic always until now kept at the boundaries of Western culture. What I don't want is a postmodernism that rehabilitates the classical authors, that sees postmodernism in Plato and argues that we should return to him because he is us.

1. Hal Foster, "Postmodernism: A Preface," in *The Anti-Aesthetic: Essays on Postmodern Culture*, ed. Hal Foster (Port Townsend, Wash., 1983), ix–xvi; E. Ann Kaplan, "Introduction," *Postmodernism and Its Discontents* (London and New York, 1988), 4.

2. Susan Bordo, "Feminism, Postmodernism and Gender-Skepticism," unpub. paper.

3. See Fredric Jameson, *Postmodernism, or, The Cultural Logic of Late Capitalism* (Durham, N.C., 1991).

In my exploration of Plato and postmodernism I disregard many of the tenets of the philological and philosophical traditions of reading the dialogues, especially the demand that the reader respect their literary integrity, read only the metaphorics of a single dialogue or the narrative imposed by one of them. Instead, I transgress, taking things from different dialogues, reading as if there is an author, someone whose contradictory statements or supporting statements from different texts can be taken to illuminate one another. Someone assigned all these texts to the name of one man, and that fact is part of the history of the text, part of its condition of being. Some poststructuralist readings, new critical, formalist readings, sever the textual object from the context of its production and reproduction. If there is "nothing outside the text," the text for me is not just one dialogue, not just the Platonic corpus, or even all of the social text of ancient Greek society, but also the persistent exclusion of women from philosophical pleasure and labor.

What would it mean to call Sappho up from the underworld, the subtext, and put her in the text of Plato? Literally to put her there, to set her down in the middle of the dialogues, conversations among men? How would her presence affect those conversations, scenes of exploration and discovery, aporia and domination? How would she unsettle and destabilize and trouble the fabric of the debates Socrates finds himself in? What would it mean temporally to scramble the linear sequence of time, to set Sappho the archaic aristocrat in the middle of the classical age, either Socrates' or Plato's time, to place this noblewoman in the scene, the symposium, of the democratic city? Or to find Sappho in Plato's text? To discover the maker of Lesbian erotic verse in the company of the sober and reflective and contemplative philosopher, the one who seems to abhor the body? To measure Sappho's absence from the text of Plato, her expulsion and exclusion from the scene of philosophy? Is Sappho's exclusion necessary? Are her body and its desires intolerable, its speech too lyrical, too hysterical, too caught up in the battles of love, scenes of marriage, physical longing for the beloved to participate in the sober work of philosophy, even an erotic philosophy like Plato's? The great statesman Pericles, in the fifth century B.C.E., set up sumptuary laws, forbade the women of democratic Athens to mourn so extravagantly at funerals, required decorum of them. But Sappho, although a great technician of poetry, one who knows very well how to polish and aim her words, can be indecorous. What if she were there, in the text of philosophy?

The Sappho we receive in postmodernity, a disparate, fragmentary set of texts, speaks of longing for women, is caught up in the worship of Aphrodite, the fertility of pleasure as opposed to reproduction, corporeal or intellectual. This Sappho has not yet complied with the demand of the classical city that women become instruments of the *polis*, or city-state, that they perform their reproductive duties for the sake of the perpetuation of citizen bodies, nor has she complied with the philosophical demand that material pleasure be subordinated to philosophical engendering. Sappho speaks of a "girl," Cleis, said by tradition to have been her daughter:

> I have a beautiful child [*pais*] who looks like golden flowers,
> my darling Cleis, for whom I would not [take] all Lydia or
> lovely . . .[4]

But Sappho has no boy to fight in the cavalry or infantry or fleet, to be one of those soldiers who defends and perpetuates the city's idea of itself. She does not sing the kind of song of which Plato in the *Republic* approves, songs like those composed by Tyrtaeus, inciting men to battle. Songs she sings arouse desire and evoke longing for the lost beloved. If Plato disapproves of men playing women, of audiences of men weeping in the theater, how much more would he disapprove of desire for the body excited in readers and listeners as they encounter Sappho's words. She is bad not only because she desires women but because she speaks of desire without imagining its transcendence except in the act of writing. Although she can play with new categories for thinking about thinking, imagining abstract entities distilled from what objects in the world have in common, as in poem 16, she most wants to remember, to reconstitute the beloved in her absence.

---

4. David A. Campbell, *Greek Lyric I, Sappho and Alcaeus* (Cambridge, Mass., 1982), *Lyric Poetry*, fr. 132 from Hephaestion, *Handbook on Metres.* Judith Hallett argues that the adjective *agapata*, "darling," suggests that Cleis is indeed Sappho's daughter, in "Beloved Cleis," *Quaderni Urbinati di Cultura Classica* n.s. 10 (1982): 21–31.

The woman poet and the man philosopher share the writerly project of recreating the beloved, of marking through writing the absence of the loved one. Plato cannot forget Socrates; Sappho cannot forget the women she loves. But Plato aspires to a denial of corporeal desire, and seeks to sublimate it into another memory, that sight of the ideas that keeps men hunting for truth and beauty, that prevents them from being trapped in the tomb of the body, while Sappho only wants more of the body, only regrets being denied it through absence and distance. Sappho will not deny daily life, the little pleasures of clothing and flowers, even as she invokes a goddess, as she establishes an atmosphere of reverent or teasing supplication. She exhibits no desire to transcend the body, no desire to escape from flesh. Plato rather follows the path of Oedipus at Colonus, leaving the body for some higher, greater pleasure elsewhere, a meta-physical union with divinity and light beyond the mortal sphere.

Try as I may to read Plato as a rhetorician, as a poet, a dramatist, as a self-conscious, self-subverting ironist, he remains that great man whose work stands like a monument at the threshold of Western philosophy.[5] And part of what is most monolithic and rigorous about Plato's work is its exclusion of women. You can talk about the sedimentations of difference in Plato's texts—differences of languages, echoes of Homer, of legal writers, all kinds of heterogeneous discourses. There are games of power, the imagining of the simulacrum, moments of Lyotardian sophistry, and aporias. Nietzsche complains: "In my opinion Plato bundles all the forms of style pell-mell together, in this respect he is one of the first decadents of style." He calls the Platonic dialogue a "revoltingly self-complacent and childish kind of dialectics," perhaps something finally admirable in a postmodern aesthetics.[6] Plato's texts can be self-reflexive, ironic, contingent, refusing to locate the truth in any single human speaker, in lived experience. But when it comes right down to it, contrary to current opinion, I think Plato

5. See Francis Wolff, "Trios: Deleuze, Derrida, Foucault, historiens du platonisme," in *Nos Grecs et leurs modernes: Les Stratégies contemporaines d'appropriation de l'antiquité,* ed. B. Cassin (Paris, 1992), 232–48, with responses following by Deleuze and Derrida.

6. Friedrich Nietzsche, "Things I Owe to the Ancients," in *The Twilight of the Idols; or, How to Philosophise with the Hammer,* trans. Anthony M. Ludovici (New York, 1964), 113–14.

is a hagiographic, antidemocratic antimaterialist, whose work alternates between aspiration toward truth and a sometimes ironic, sometimes resentful recognition of the obstacles to the achievement of a pure and uncontaminated philosophical life. He doesn't have much in common with someone like Kathy Acker or cyberpunk.

The tradition of reverence for Plato's texts, for the handling of his work, speaks to the traditional sense of his work as a system, as a great body of work from a single author. And in the whole corpus of Plato's writings, we find that there are differences that are intolerable; if some of his energy goes toward subordinating and domesticating women to serve the state, even more goes to creating an ideal language community, the community of the dialogues, in which women have no place. Recuperating Plato as a postmodernist, seeing the postmodern dimensions in his work, discovering a disembodied "feminine" in the dialogues can in the work of some critics just continue to erase women from the field, and to read Plato uncritically, in terms of a postmodern aesthetics, may simply mean recuperating Plato's mastery. Even if we conclude finally that he writes a narrative of failed mastery, he writes a *master* narrative, a master *narrative*, a narrative of mastery.[7]

Sappho, life and works, on the other hand, might be read as an alternative text in postmodernity. If we read her biographies, the attempts to make sense of her life, we realize that there is no there there; Sappho the poet is a multiple, unfixed, constantly transmuting subject. She is a Lesbian supposed lesbian who supposedly died for love of a man. She may be a mother who celebrates her erotic desire for women. She writes *epithalamia*, poems written in honor of marriage, even as she mourns her separation from women she has loved. Her poems have come down to us only in the most fragmentary of forms, quoted in other poets' work, translated by Ca-

---

7. Such views go against the grain of many recent readings of Plato, including those of Jacques Derrida, "La pharmacie de Platon," *La dissémination* (Paris, 1972), 69–197, and Harry Berger, Jr., "*Phaedrus* and the Politics of Inscription," in *Textual Fidelity and Textual Disregard*, ed. B. P. Dauenhauer, American University Studies, ser. 3, Comparative Literature 33 (New York, 1990), 81–103. On the *Phaedrus*, see also G. R. F. Ferrari, *Listening to the Cicadas: A Study of Plato's* Phaedrus (Cambridge, 1987). For other new approaches to Plato, see *Platonic Writings, Platonic Readings*, ed. Charles L. Griswold, Jr. (New York, 1988).

tullus, cited by rhetoricians as exemplary texts, found in shreds of papyrus stuffed in sacred crocodiles at Oxyrhynchus in Egypt. There is no text of Sappho, really, just reports, distant sightings, rumors, a few words reputed to be hers. Even many of the poems assigned to her by scholars have features that make attribution questionable—words from the wrong dialect, even her name spelled variously in different situations. To read Sappho now raises questions about desire, gender, fragmented subjectivity, the fragmented text.

What about Plato in the text of Sappho? I discuss in the chapter called "Helen" the philosophical impulse present in Sappho's work, especially in fragment 16, in which the poet says that men speak variously about what is *kalliston*, "the most beautiful," but which Sappho says is *ottō tis eratai*, "what one loves." Such a claim enters into a philosophical project of definition, to argue that abstractions can stand for the particularities of ephemeral and particular experience, that it is not possible to name all the things considered by all people to be most beautiful, but that whatever any person loves will be seen as most beautiful by her or him, and thus we can generalize to this extent about human value and desire. This seems to me to be clearly on the way to Platonic ideas; What is the good? Although Plato imagines the good as emanating from above, radiating down upon humankind, Sappho seeks a definition, gathering and collecting details, using an inductive or synthetic method of definition rather than imagining divine origin for her good. What would a Sapphic philosophy be? In the literal sense of *philosophia*, love of sophia, of wisdom, what would Sappho's wisdom be? To respect the forces of Aphrodite, to enjoy pleasure at the moment at which it is granted to one, to remember what one has loved, perhaps to assuage the pain of what has been lost by its recollection in poetry.

Within the great generic split named by Plato, Sappho the poetic text is not philosophy; philosophy is a phenomenon of the city, the city in which women are restricted to their own rooms in the house, in which few women were educated and capable of refined intellectual debate. The pre-Socratics are not philosophers in our or Plato's sense—they are physicists; even the sophists are rhetoricians more than philosophers. Perhaps it is not possible to imagine women philosophers in Sappho's age or in Plato's, even though Aspasia was a fine rhetorician, even though Diotima was the fictional Socrates' teacher. The women mentioned as belonging to philosophical schools belong for the most part to a later date, to those post-Platonic schools that defied convention. Sappho writes of flowers and beds and groves, of the goddess Aphrodite, without attempting to see in them emanation from an abstraction. Her relation to them is one of recollection and memory; she records past pleasures and anticipates future pleasures. Sappho is concerned with the *aphrodisia*, the things of Aphrodite, that is, desire and pleasure, sexual longing and gratification. Plato honors Apollo, god of mathematics and harmony, music and philosophy, the god who displaced the earth goddess oracle at Delphi, the image of the *kouros*, that discrete, balanced, rational creature who presides over aristocratic culture.

To this point my remarks have focused on philosophy as the figure, poetry as the ground. What would it mean to reverse this relationship, to let Sappho's fragmentary texts judge the Platonic dialogues? What would it mean to place Plato in the text of Sappho? He would surely be uncomfortable, even disapproving of her talk of earthly pleasures, the satisfaction of longing on soft beds. Although at home in the aristocratic atmosphere of the symposia, Plato might not be so welcome in Sappho's universe. If Sappho's poems were performed at aristocratic symposia of the classical age, one can imagine Plato's appreciation of their delicacy and decorum, without being able to imagine Plato in the presence of the chorus of girls, amidst the worshipers of Aphrodite on the island of Lesbos in the archaic age. However, while women are excluded from the discourse of the Platonic dialogues, men appear in Sappho's poems—she speaks of the man sitting next to the woman she loves, of the bridegroom in epithalamia, of her brother, of mythological heroes. Even if we imagine it her desire to be exclusive of men, and some fragments suggest it was not, she does not ignore their existence in the world.

Sappho's poetry often addresses the vocabulary and social norms of heroic male culture, refusing them, turning them to her own purposes. In fragment 16, for example, her exemplum, imagining Helen as an agent rather than a victim of desire, celebrating her own desire for Anaktoria, begins and ends with that which she rejects, horsemen, infantry, the fleet, all the trappings of war. The critique of male concerns, for battle, conquest, domination, echoes throughout her work; if poetry like Sappho's were to judge a work like the *Republic*, it would find a text that allows public life to overpower and annihilate all that Sappho deems important. Philosophy finally constructs a world of individualism, of private striving toward the Forms, where the kind of erotic connection described by Sappho seems impossible because it must always be reduced to a project of self-improvement and social welfare. To read the Sapphic fragments against the dialogues is to call into question the dialogues' confidence, their integrity, their sublimation and denial of the body, their transcendent and totalizing project.

What is at stake in reading Sappho through postmodernism? Doesn't our encounter with her texts require a resistant postmodernism, one that sees desire differently? Sappho's desire has different objects, different subjects from those constructed in the philosophical text. I think we can see her desire as having a liberating dimension, not merely about male dominating female, male dominating male, or even male and male in a reciprocal but ultimately transcendent regard. Sappho's eros seems to me to be not instrumental, not transcendent. Reading her fragmentary texts continually reminds us of particularity, of the material world, of Anaktoria as an example of the general category of "what one loves." Reading her in postmodernity forces the reader to deal with questions of textual production and transmission, with the fragmentary nature of the text we receive from antiquity, with exclusions of all sorts, with the break between public and private universes. Sappho refuses men's military games, but also the instrumentalization of both women and other men in the philosophical project.

Sappho is mentioned in Plato's *Phaedrus*, a dialogue that urges the control and domination of physical desire, its subordination to the metaphysical quest for a higher truth. Socrates says, to justify his response to Lysias' discourse on love, read to him by Phaedrus: "I'm sure I have heard something better, from the fair Sappho maybe, or the wise Anacreon, or perhaps some prose writer" (235c). He goes on to speak of his own discourse as something welling up inside him, "I suppose it can only be that it has been poured into me, through my ears, as into a vessel, from some external source, though in my stupid fashion I have actually forgotten how, and from whom, I heard it" (235cd). This little joke both recapitulates Socrates' critique of poetry in the *Ion*, that poets know nothing but are simply conduits of divine inspiration, and takes a gentle swipe at Phaedrus himself, who has only Lysias' discourse, nothing of his own to say about love.[8] It also prospectively puts into question Socrates' first discourse on love, alienating it from him as if it were something plagiarized or simply repeated from elsewhere. Although he claims to have heard it from somewhere else, from Sappho or the poet Anacreon, its reasoning owes more to the sophists than either of the poets he mentions. In fact, Socrates attributes it to Phaedrus himself, as if his presence caused Socrates to speak such nonsense.

But then, later, notoriously, in his second discourse on love, Socrates seems to echo a famed poem of Sappho on the effects of love, the poem discussed earlier in this book. She says, in fragment 31 (L.-P.):

> Fortunate as the gods he seems to me, that man who sits opposite you, and listens nearby to your sweet voice
>
> And your lovely laughter; that, I vow, has set my heart within my breast a-flutter. For when I look at you a moment, then I have no longer power to speak,
>
> But my tongue keeps silence, straightway a subtle flame has stolen beneath my flesh, with my eyes I see nothing, my ears are humming.
>
> A cold sweat covers me, and a trembling seizes me all over, I am paler than grass, I seem to be not far short of death . . .
>
> But all must be endured, since . . .

As others have noted too, this passage has many features that find an echo in Plato's description of the lover's reaction to the sight of the beloved in the *Phaedrus*. Plato there says:

> When one who is fresh from the mystery, and saw much of the vision, beholds a godlike face or bodily form that truly expresses beauty, first there come upon him a shuddering

---

8. On this passage, see John Sallis, *Being and Logos: The Way of Platonic Dialogue*, 2d ed. (Atlantic Highlands, N.J., 1986), 119–20.

and a measure of that awe which the vision inspired. . . .
Next, with the passing of the shudder, a strange sweating and
fever seizes him. (251a)

The lover experiences symptoms like those of Sappho as she gazes
at her lover; the sensations of pain in Plato's description are due to
the effect of the sight of the beloved on the soul's wings. They are
nourished and stimulated by the beauty of the loved one:

> Meanwhile she [the soul] throbs with ferment in every part,
> and even as a teething child feels an aching and pain in its
> gums when a tooth has first come through, so does the soul
> of him who is beginning to grow his wings feel a ferment and
> painful irritation. (251c)

But then the particles of beauty relieve the soul from its anguish.
When the lovers are parted, it is pained again, and so moves between joy and anguish, suffering from the regret of loss, tasting "a
pleasure that is sweet beyond compare" (251e) when it beholds
him again. Plato echoes and appropriates the female position, and
then uses the occasion to deny the body and to sublimate erotic
desire into philosophy. Despite the remarkable similarities between descriptions of erotic suffering in Plato's prose and Sappho's
verse, there is no such alteration in Sappho's words, only the pain
of watching her beloved. Why is it important to hold on to this?
Plato uses this occasion of erotic desire at the sight of the lover to
argue for sublimation and for the use of this pleasure and pain to
drive the lover further on his quest toward a higher beauty, one
detached from corporeal sensation and mortal bodies. Sappho's
fragmentary lines preserve the traces of a desire that is eventually
appropriated and manipulated, but that has for us a specificity and
a materiality that challenge the received tradition, the canon privi-
leging idealism and transcendence.

The two renderings of desire differ radically. In Plato's hands the
Sapphic model is appropriated and then disembodied, amputated.
Sappho cannot remain in the philosophical text; even the disembodied Sappho, invoked allusively, like other women is exorcised
from the Platonic dialogue. If the woman can be subordinated,
dominated, and incorporated into the Platonic project of transcendence of corporeality, she may be represented, present, but

silent. This is the ease with the representation of Xanthippe in the
Phaedo, the dialogue describing the conversation that took place
just before Socrates' execution by the Athenian state. As Phaedo
recounts, Xanthippe waits with him at the prison for the hour of
execution:

> When we went inside we found Socrates just released
> from his chains, and Xanthippe—you know her!—sitting by
> him with the little boy on her knee. As soon as Xanthippe
> saw us she broke out into the sort of remark you would ex-
> pect from a woman, Oh, Socrates, this is the last time that
> you and your friends will be able to talk together!
>
> Socrates looked at Crito. Crito, he said, someone had bet-
> ter take her home.
>
> Some of Crito's servants led her away crying hysterically.
> (60ab)

The words Plato uses to describe Xanthippe's actions are *boōsan te
kai koptomenēn*, "crying aloud," and "beating her head and breast in
grief." These are ritual gestures of women in mourning, recorded
on vases and in countless texts, the gestures that Pericles tried to
control and censor in the fifth century. Women are equated with
the figure of exaggerated lamentation. In the extravagances of lamentation, they were thought to violate the command that they be
always decorous. In his funeral oration, as Thucydides reports,
Pericles said to the women present who were now widows: "the
greatest glory of a woman is to be least talked about by men,
whether they are praising you or criticizing you" (2,47). The good
woman is neither seen nor heard.

In the *Phaedo*, after the noisy, demonstrative Xanthippe is taken
away, Socrates immediately begins to reflect on pleasure and pain,
suggesting that the pleasure he feels from the removal of the pain
the fetter caused in his leg follows hard upon Xanthippe's departure; her presence was a pain followed by a pleasure, the last conversation, conducted among men, before his death. Like her departure, death will free him from the prison of the body. And he
explores his thoughts about death without her. Women interrupt
the scene of philosophy with hysterical crying, with mourning,
beating their breasts, inappropriate behaviors of all sorts. Xanthippe scandalously calls attention to the male bond, names the

very economy of exclusion, and must be discredited; her words are seen as partial, irrelevant, and disruptive of the mood of the occasion. Throughout this dialogue, which argues that the body of the philosopher is insignificant, that the *ascēsis* of the philosopher is so to detach his soul from his body in life that death is a trifle, women are not allowed to invade or trouble the philosophical enterprise. Xanthippe is removed. When Apollodorous weeps passionately at the prospect of Socrates' death, bringing others to tears, Socrates says: "Really, my friends, what a way to behave! Why, that was my main reason for sending away the women, to prevent this sort of disturbance, because I am told that one should make one's end in a tranquil frame of mind" (117d). Women disturb the tranquility of the scene, reminding the dying of the body and of loss.

Much is made in this dialogue of Socrates' indifference to his body, but one might also read some of his protestations of indifference as desire to exclude women, caretakers of the body, from the final scenes of his life and from the care of his body after death. Greek burial custom dictated that soon after death, the body of the deceased be bathed and so prepared for burial. As Nicole Loraux points out, Socrates subverts the burial ritual.[9] He insists on bathing himself before death, saying: "I prefer to have a bath before drinking the poison, rather than give the women the trouble of washing me when I am dead" (115a). Socrates hopes to protect himself from women's touch, even after death, and his wishes are followed by his followers to the extent that Crito, rather than allowing Socrates' female relatives to perform these last tasks, closed Socrates' mouth and eyes (118a). Loraux concludes: "le groupe des disciples remplace la parenté, les compagnons de pensée ont pris la place des femmes" (the group of disciples replaces his relatives; his companions in thought have taken the place of the women).[10] The *philosophos* is the man who loves (*philei*) wisdom (*sophia*); he stands in contrast to the *philosōmatos*, who loves the body. Women are the lovers and keepers of the body, associated with the flesh and its claims. They have no place at the crowning moment of the

9. Nicole Loraux, "Donc Socrate est immortel," in *Les expériences de Tirésias: Le féminin et l'homme grec* (Paris, 1989), 182.

10. Ibid. See also Emily Vermeule, *Aspects of Death in Early Greek Art and Poetry* (Berkeley, Calif., 1979).

philosopher's life, when, surrounded by admirers, he exhibits his indifference to the loss of his body.

In the *Republic*, poets who encourage laxity are to be expelled from the ideal city, and we might imagine Sappho to be among them. In his conversation, Socrates and his interlocutor agree that the "mixed Lydian" and other such poetic modes must be done away with, "for they are useless even to women who are to make the best of themselves, let alone to men" (398e). It is also decided that "certain Ionian and Lydian modes," called "lax," should be done away with, since they do not serve men in warfare or other "enforced business" (399a), nor in voluntary works of peacetime, persuading and being persuaded. The verses of Sappho might be directly addressed by these projects, since she wrote laments for the slain lover of Aphrodite, Adonis, as well as poems luxuriating in flowers, imported Lydian finery, and the pleasures of the bed. Although Socrates echoes her in his praise of love, it is only to convert her perspective of pain and unrequited love into the labor of philosophy—she would have no place in his ideal republic.

Let me turn to the place of desire for women in the Sapphic fragments and to how this desire is both figured and occluded by the Greek philosophical text. Plato's Aristophanes, a character in the *Symposium*, in his semicomic account of homoerotic love describes round original beings once whole, now separated from their former halves, male/male, male/female, female/female. In describing their fate after separation, in a move typical of classical culture, he omits to describe female/female desire:

> . . . the idea being that if, in all these clippings and clasp-ings, a man should chance upon a woman, conception would take place and the race would be continued, while if man should conjugate with man, he might at least obtain such satisfaction as would allow him to turn his attention and his energies to the everyday affairs of life. (191c)

Throughout this section, Aristophanes emphasizes the effects of desire on men, saying that men "who are slices of the male" show their masculinity, and "these are the most hopeful of the nation's youth, for theirs is the most virile constitution." His only remark concerning female-female desire is: "The woman who is a slice of the original female is attracted by women rather than by men—in fact she is a Lesbian" (191e). The translation of the Greek word here, *hetairistriai*, compresses a complicated history; women who desire women today are called lesbians as a sign of their descent from Sappho of Lesbos. Liddell, Scott, and Jones, authors of the standard dictionary of classical Greek, give as the definition of *hetairistria* another Greek word, *tribas*, perhaps hoping to discourage further inquiry. Under *tribas* they record the following definition: "a woman who practices unnatural vice with herself or with other women." In fact the Greek word *hetairistriai* suggests companionship. The male *hetairoi* were comrades, men who plotted together in political schemes or who were simply associated with each other politically or socially. Aristophanes in Plato's text does not elaborate on women's erotic life with other women. It is allowed for as a matter of symmetry, but it is the redundant third term; male-female sex leads to reproduction, male-male sex demonstrates virility, female-female sex is not characterized. Lesbian sex like that celebrated in Sappho's poetry in the centuries before is not described, except in this briefest allowance for it, in the classical age, even in the works of Aristophanes, which are very explicit about many other imaginable forms of sexual behavior. As I argued earlier, lesbian behavior may have been taken for granted and considered insignificant, a sign of women's comradeship, or pointless, without issue, leading neither to reproduction nor to philosophical progress, or disruptive, distracting women from the many tasks involved in feeding, clothing, nursing, caring for mortal, decaying bodies. Lesbian sex may also be unmentionable, except in some abstract sense, because it represents a threat to phallic sexuality and is thus erased and belittled by Plato and by subsequent generations of scholars.

There are other senses in which women disrupt the scene of Platonic philosophy and are therefore expelled from it. In the *Menexenus* Socrates respectfully repeats his mistress of rhetoric Aspasia's funeral oration for the Athenians, but he ventriloquates her words; she herself cannot be represented as present. And this is in spite of the fact that one of the generic sources for the Platonic dialogue, which is after all a semitheatrical genre, is the classical comedy and tragedy of the fifth century B.C.E., in which comic and tragic writers did represent female characters, even though on the stage these characters were played by male actors.

In the *Symposium,* Socrates and his friends are engaged in witty but weighty conversation, enjoying themselves in a contest of speeches in praise of love. The participants agree at the beginning of the evening to abstain from heavy drinking, and Eryximachus the physician, who has urged that wine be consumed only for refreshment, arguing that inebriation is detrimental to health, says:

> I also propose that we dispense with the services of the flute girl who has just come in, and let her go and play to herself or to the women inside there, whichever she prefers, while we spend our evening in discussion. (176e)

There follows the great sequence of speeches in praise of love, capped by Socrates' Diotima speech discussed by David Halperin in his provocative essay "Why Is Diotima a Woman?"[11] This speech is ventriloquized in the mouth of Socrates, who claims to report what the woman Diotima told him. But she is not present, only brought to the scene through Socrates' memory of her wisdom and teachings. I have argued elsewhere that Socrates' repetition of her teachings is not the respectful, deferential attitude toward women, possessors of occult knowledge, not a recognition of the crucial role of the female in culture, as Arlene Saxonhouse claims,[12] not a rewriting of eroticism to include reciprocity, as David Halperin argues, but rather an appropriation of the Greeks' notions of female powers of prophecy and reproduction and the transmutation of the

11. David Halperin, "Why Is Diotima a Woman?" in *One Hundred Years of Homosexuality and Other Essays on Greek Love* (New York and London, 1990), 113–51. See also Page duBois, "The Platonic Appropriation of Reproduction," *Sowing the Body: Psychoanalysis and Ancient Representations of Women* (Chicago, 1988), 169–83; Halperin says of the argument in this chapter. "The radical *absence* of women's experience—and thus, of the actual feminine—from the ostensibly feminocentric terms of Plato's erotic doctrine should warn us not to interpret Plato's strategy simplistically as a straightforward attempt to appropriate the feminine or as a symbolic theft of women's procreative authority. For Plato's appropriation of the Other works not only by misrecognizing the Other but by constructing 'the other' as a masked version of the same—or, to borrow the language of Julia Kristeva, it works by constructing a 'pseudo-Other'" (145). This seems to me too ingenious, still to disregard the absence of the female from the Platonic dialogues; sympathetic as I am to Halperin's project, I remain unconvinced, and see appropriation.

12. Arlene Saxonhouse, "Eros and the Female in Greek Political Thought: An Interpretation of Plato's Symposium," *Political Theory* 12 (1984): 5–27; see also Arlene Saxonhouse, "The Philosopher and the Female in the Political Thought of Plato," *Political Theory* 4 (1976): 195–212.

philosopher into sovereign reason, the normative male person. This being is the *man* who stands for all human beings, who becomes the subject of philosophy and all intellectual life, rather than one half of the human race. This installation of masculinity as sovereign, as it performs the erasure of difference, the production of subordination and hierarchy, is the antithesis of a utopian, heterogeneous, fluid, "queer" postmodern.

Pace Halperin and Saxonhouse, recognizing "the feminine" while at the same time forbidding entrance to even the simulacra of the female, that is, women, seems to me to be a gesture toward incorporation, appropriation of difference, a difference that is produced, as Halperin himself points out, in men's ideological representations of women. And women, those with female bodies, remain shut out, even when the philosophers strive to become "women," when they enact gynesis.[13] Postmodernism in its utopian version is not about men becoming women, but about a more fluid, or more fragmentary, heterogeneous existence, one without fixed gender identities, with multiple genders, but recognizing the historically produced differences that make up heterogeneity. Plato stands for something else, for purity after aporia, a denial of the body and the exclusion of female persons from intellectual pleasure and labor.

The new orthodoxy about Plato urges us to read him as a complex and various author, his texts as dramatic accounts with their own tensions, ironies, heteroglossia. But some tendencies within the so-called postmodern work to make all differences equal, of the same order, to erase bodies, now historically and ideologically gendered. And Plato's texts form part of the history of those writings of bodies. The exclusion of women and slaves is the condition of being of the dialogues, shaping and engendering them. If we remain inside the dialogues, and within certain versions of postmodernism, ones that ahistorically celebrate the freely circulating circuit of desire without location in historically materialized bodies, we cannot see the conditions of production of texts, the exclusions that make such lyrical claims possible. Even the work of someone like Sarah Kofman, in *Comment s'en sortir,* can rehabilitate

13. See Alice Jardine, *Gynesis: Configurations of Woman and Modernity* (Ithaca, N.Y., 1985).

Plato by finding the presence of the workings of the goddess
Metis, "cunning intelligence," in Plato's text, and end by divorcing
"feminine" processes from women, even women represented in
Plato's text.[14] If we do an immanent critique, a reading from inside,
we must also see what is not there, by reference to a world we
know exists elsewhere, a world of women and work and slavery
and bodies.

In Xenophon's *Memorabilia*, like much of Plato's work a purported
account of Socrates' life and teachings, we find an encounter with
a woman who *is* represented in the text, who speaks with Socrates.
It is not the case that philosophical dialogue in antiquity must always "naturally" and necessarily exclude women, as many have argued, that it is inconceivable and inappropriate for women to be
present at the philosophers' conversation. For in Xenophon's text,
Socrates, hearing of her beauty, goes to visit the *betaira* Xenodote.
They speak of her techniques for attracting lovers, he arguing that
she chases rich men into her nets. She says: "Nets! What nets have
I got?" He answers: "One, surely, that folds well enough—your
body" (3.11.10). Their exchange is remarkable not only in that it
underlines Plato's representation of Socrates' skeptical attitude toward the body. Here the woman's body is a trap, a net, and Socrates
uses a compound of the word *plekō*, "weave," connoting women's
traditional work, to describe the effects of Xenodote's body. But
while Xenophon's Socrates shares the Platonic Socrates' suspicion
of bodies, emphasizing their attractions, their capacity to distract,
more significant is the fact that Xenophon represents women as
attracting, as capable of speech and humor, as present and engaging in conversation with the philosopher. It is not just aristocratic
decorum that shelters women from the exposure of representation
in Plato's dialogues; they cannot be present while philosophy is
happening.

In the *Symposium*, after repeating Diotima's doctrine, Socrates is
seated amidst applause, "when suddenly there came a knocking at
the outer door, followed by the notes of a flute and the sound of
festive brawling in the street" (212c). The drunken Alcibiades is in
the court demanding to see Agathon, and he enters with a flute
girl. "There he stood in the doorway, with a mass of ribbons and

14. See Sarah Kofman, *Comment s'en sortir* (Paris, 1983), and *Socrate(s)* (Paris, 1989).

an enormous wreath of ivy and violets sprouting on his head" (212d). This is the eruption of real eros, of Dionysiac pleasure and drunkenness and flute-girls, an eruption of the heterosexual plea- sures of the symposium into this philosophical occasion, and the intrusion of sexual difference, not simply ventriloquized by So- crates, but embodied in the silent presence of the flute-girl. The woman is allowed to enter, but after Socrates' speech she must re- main silent, must be read in terms of his eloquence about love. The philosopher represents the woman's wisdom, incorporates and ap- propriates it, and then allows her to return subdued and dominated by philosophical truth. One can see the interruption of the flute- girl and of Alcibiades, drunk, ready for pleasure, hungry to tell his story of thwarted desire for Socrates' body, as Plato's own argument for sobriety and hatred of the body, except as a temporary vehicle for the soul. Alcibiades betrayed his city and his friends; he ap- pears in Dionysiac costume, praises tragedy, accompanies a flute- girl. He is a man contaminated by effeminacy, by a love of the body.

Women are hopelessly tied up with the body in ancient Greek culture. They give birth, they nurse the young, they provide food and clothing, they nurse the sick, tend the dying, and bury the dead. In fact, one could read Socrates' hatred of the body as fear and dread of the ministrations of women; in the world of disem- bodied souls, men would no longer need to depend on women. Er, in his description of the land of the dead in the *Republic*, says he saw the soul of Orpheus "selecting the life of a swan, because from hatred of the tribe of women, owing to his death at their hands, it was unwilling to be conceived and born of a woman" (620a). And in the *Phaedo*, Socrates compares himself to a swan: "I believe that the swans (who sing at their death), belonging as they do to Apollo, have prophetic powers and sing because they know the good things that await them in the unseen world, and they are happier on that day than they have ever been before. Now I con- sider that I am in the same service as the swans, and dedicated to the same god" (85b). Socrates, devotee of Apollo, likens himself to this species unborn of woman; he is committed to the god who stands for the discrete, bounded body, geometric abstraction and philosophical harmony, against Dionysos, worshiped by women, drunks, and crazy people.

The woman on the scene of philosophy cries hysterically, plays the flute, encourages drunkenness, threatens silence. Of course she must be encapsulated within the male philosopher's discourse, cited from a temporal distance, enclosed with his frame, not even allowed the ephemeral textual existence of a character in a dialogue. To my mind, this is a scenario of appropriation, subordination, and exclusion, and if there is something about some versions of postmodernism that pleases me, it is the extravagant and insistent presence of such characters as Kathy Acker and Prince, neither of whom would have been invited to the party, to the philosopher's symposium. Kathy Acker says:

> "Had a dream while waking that was running with animals. Wild horses, leopards, red fox, kangaroos, mountain lions, wild dogs. Running over rolling hills. Was able to keep up with the animals and they accepted her.
> Wildness was writing and writing was wildness."[15]

Mine is not a lament, a call for reading Sappho instead of Plato. But let us not use whatever break the entry into postmodernity means merely to reread and reinscribe the canonical texts of our history. The exclusion of women from philosophy should figure in our readings, and if "the female" is included, through metaphor or appropriation, but left out of the dialogical participation that is the philosophical life, then we need to talk about that. One of the difficulties I have always had with the Habermasian ideal speech situation is that it fails to acknowledge and address the inequalities of power, the silences, of some of those I would assume he intends to include in democratic conversation.[16] One of the mechanisms of exclusion, especially in universities and in academic discourse in general, is the weight of a tradition that overlooks traditional exclusions, that sets those aside as irrelevant to the real work of intellectuals. Postmodernist theory can perpetuate this exclusion by pretending that gender has been definitively erased, that there are no inequities, no differences, that we are all simulacra, all equally

15. Kathy Acker, "Humility," in *The Seven Cardinal Virtues*, ed. Alison Fell (London, 1990), 117.
16. See, for example, Jürgen Habermas, "Life-forms, Morality and the Task of the Philosopher," in *Autonomy & Solidarity: Interviews*, ed. Peter Dews (London, 1986), 202.

absent from discourse, present only as polyvalent, polymorphous signs. That discourse can be just the same old story, a refusal of the material world, of historically gendered bodies, that serves the perpetuation of injustice and exclusion. We cannot pretend that others do not essentialize race and gender, even if we wish to inhabit a deterritorialized utopia free of homophobia, racism, and sexism. I still believe that Plato yearns for a disembodied sojourn among the forms, and that some of us might want to contest his sovereign place in the history of Western civilization. I want to make a scene, to make women, among them Sappho, lesbian Lesbian poet, part of the scene.

FIVE

Helen

> Permit me to repeat that we are concerned not with the poet as
> a private person, not with his psychology or his so-called social
> perspective, but with the poem as a philosophical sundial
> telling the time of history.
>
> Theodor Adorno, "On Lyric Poetry and Society"

We can perhaps imagine Sappho in the Platonic symposium, singing her lyrics and disrupting the philosophical conversation of aristocratic truth-seekers with an erotic longing that converts desire to memory rather than to metaphysical aspiration. I once asked a professor of classical philosophy, famous for his work on Parmenides, how he knew the difference between philosophy and poetry. This is of course an (im)pertinent question in the case of Parmenides in particular, since Parmenides' great philosophical work is in verse. My question was in part a reaction to the methodology of the discipline of classical philosophy, of the scholar who extracts from a text, even one in verse, a logical paradigm, a formula that can be rendered in abstract terms, and that disregards questions of rhetoric, versification, imagery, almost as if they were the veil over the philosophical armature of the ancient thinker. He said that he knew what was philosophy and what was poetry by "the questions posed." That is, I presume, a philosopher asks questions about being, while a poet does not, it being in fact unclear to me what questions he thought poets did address. But it was absolutely clear to him that Parmenides was a philosopher, not a poet. At the time I was not yet thinking in particular about Sappho, yet I have wondered since how he would fit her into his story, his his-

Ideas presented in this chapter were first expressed in an article published in *Arethusa* 11 (1978): 89–99.

tory of philosophy, especially her fragment 16, which does seem to me to address questions that philosophers, ever since the invention of the thing called philosophy, have asked. What effect, then, would it have on the history of philosophy to consider Sappho as part, as of one of the multiple points of origin, at its beginnings? Would she have just the disruptive effect on the narrative of the history of philosophy as she would have at the Platonic symposium? Would she not throw into disarray the confidently posed opposition between poetry and philosophy upon which the contemporary philosopher relies, and which Plato makes as a founding move of his philosophy?

In this chapter, while considering Sappho's fragment 16, I want to consider two disconcerting aspects of her work—her place at the beginnings of the philosophical project itself, and in addition, her capacity to disturb the most traditional versions of narrative. This is fragment 16 (L.-P.), with Denys Page's translation:

o]ἰ μὲν ἰππήων στρότον οἰ δὲ πέσδων
οἰ δὲ νάων φαῖσ᾽ ἐπ[ὶ] γᾶν μέλαι[ν]αν
ἔ]μμεναι κάλλιστον, ἔγω δὲ κῆν᾽ ὄτ-
τω τις ἔραται·

πά]γχυ δ᾽ εὔμαρες σύνετον πόησαι
π]άντι τ[ο]ῦτ᾽, ἀ γὰρ πόλυ περσκέθοισα
κάλλος [ἀνθ]ρώπων Ἐλένα [τὸ]ν ἄνδρα
τὸν [πανάρ]ιστον

καλλ[ίποι]σ᾽ ἔβα ᾽ς Τροΐαν πλέοι [σα
κωὐδ[ὲ πα]ῖδος οὐδὲ φίλων το[κ]ήων
πά[μπαν] ἐμνάσθη, ἀλλὰ παράγαγ᾽ αὖταν
]σαν

]αμπτον γὰρ]
] . . . κούφως π[   ]οησ[.]ν
. .]με ῦν Ἀνακτορί[ας ὀ]νέμναι-
σ᾽ οὐ] παρεοίσας·

τᾶ]ς κε βολλοίμαν ἔρατόν τε βᾶμα
κἀμάρυχμα λάμπρον ἴδην προσώπω
ἢ τὰ Λύδων ἄρματα κἀν ὄπλοισι
πεσδομ]άχεντας.

].μεν οὐ δύνατον γένεσθαι
].ν ἀνθρωπ[. . . π]εδέχην δ᾽ ἄρασθαι

Some say a host of horsemen, others of infantry, and others of ships, is the most beautiful thing on the dark earth: but I say, it is what you love.

Full easy it is to make this understood of one and all: for she that far surpassed all mortals in beauty, Helen, her most noble husband

Deserted, and went sailing to Troy, with never a thought for her daughter and dear parents. The [Cyprian goddess] led her from the path . . .

. . . [Which] now has put me in mind of Anactoria far away;

Her lovely way of walking, and the bright radiance of her changing face, would I rather see than your Lydian chariots and infantry full-armed.[1]

I cite the full poem in Greek in part so that even those who do not read Greek can see how broken and elliptical remains this fragment, read painstakingly and tentatively by textual scholars from an Egyptian papyrus.

All readers of the works of Sappho are greatly indebted to such scholars as Denys Page. Yet his literary evaluations of Sappho often infuriate. Here he appears quite unimpressed. He complains of line 7: "The sequence of thought might have been clearer. . . . It seems inelegant then to begin this parable, the point of which is that Helen found *to kalliston* in her lover, by stating she herself surpassed all mortals in this very quality." Of the whole: "The poem opens with a common device. . . . In a phrase which rings dull in our doubtful ears, she proceeds to illustrate the truth of her preamble by calling Helen of Troy in evidence. . . . And the thought is simple as the style is artless. . . . The transition back to the principal subject was perhaps not very adroitly managed." Of the end,

---

1. Denys Page, *Sappho and Alcaeus: An Introduction to the Study of Ancient Lesbian Poetry* (Oxford, 1955), 52–53. On this poem, see David A. Campbell, *The Golden Lyre: The Themes of the Greek Lyric Poets* (London, 1983), 14–15.

"The idea may seem a little fanciful: but this stanza was either a little fanciful or a little dull."[2]

Page obviously feels compelled to evaluate, and find wanting, this work of Sappho.[3] It seems to me, on the contrary, that the very elements with which he finds fault—the catalog, the example of Helen, the return to the catalog at the poem's end—structure it beautifully, while permitting it to open out to a moment of recollection that invokes the radiant presence of Anaktoria. He sees little but literary mediocrity or actual ineptitude in this fragment; I argue that the poem is extraordinary not only for its superb control and unity but also for its ambitions. It is a historically important work, compelling both within what one might call the prehistory of philosophy and within the history of narrative.

The poem begins with a brief catalog, a listing of horsemen, infantry, ships. The phrase "on the dark earth," *epi gan melainan* of line 2 is ambiguous in its position; it refers back to the catalog and forward to the construction, infinitive in Greek, *emmenai kalliston*, "to be the most beautiful." The dark earth is the basis for this host of warriors and warships, and recalls the diction of the Homeric poems.[4] The voice in the poem sets itself, *egō*, against the background of choices, against the dark earth itself, the Homeric earth peopled by warriors. That voice chooses otherwise, saying that the most beautiful thing is "whatsoever one loves."

The rhetoric of the next stanza is designed to overpower the doubter, to offer a demonstration of the principle the first stanza has set forth. The voice in the poem asserts the ease of proof of its earlier statement, and sets out immediately to offer an example of

---

2. Page, *Sappho and Alcaeus*, 53–57. On this poem, see also G. Wills, "The Sapphic 'Umwertung aller Werte,'" *American Journal of Philology* 88 (1967): 434ff.; G. A. Privitera, "Su una nuova interpretazione di S. fr. 16LP," *QUCC* 4 (1967): 182–87; E. M. Stern, "S. fr. 16 LP," *Mnem.* 23 (1970): 348–61; and G. Koniaris, "On Sappho Fr. 16(LP)," *Hermes* 95 (1967): 260ff.

3. See also Gordon Kirkwood: "The device of Priamel is common, and Sappho's use of it lacks the brilliance and force of such Pindaric examples as the beginning of *Olympian* 1." *Early Greek Monody: The History of a Poetic Type* (Ithaca, N.Y., and London, 1974), 107.

4. See Leah Rissman, *Love as War: Homeric Allusion in the Poetry of Sappho* (Konigstein, 1983). The adjective *melainan* might also be taken to modify ships, *naon;* dark ships are Homeric as well.

the truth of that claim. The poet's strategy here is rhetorically subtle; she qualifies her exemplum by calling Helen the woman who most surpassed mortals with respect to beauty. The word "beauty," *kallos*, echoes the abstract, neuter, neutral term *to kalliston*, "the most beautiful," in the stanza that precedes. At first the listener, or reader, associates Helen herself with the abstract *to kalliston* above. But the heroine from the Trojan epic cycle has another function within the poem. She is not herself "the most beautiful thing." She moves toward that thing, drawn by desire, compelled by something missing from the papyrus, by eros, Aphrodite, perhaps.[5] Helen stands alone at first, set up by *polu perskethoisa*, "far surpassing," the hyperbole of which is answered by "her most noble husband," *ton panariston* of line 8; her name is surrounded by superlatives, masculine and feminine. In line 7, which begins with *kallos*, "beauty," the quality for which she is immortal in humankind's memory, she is surrounded by *anthrōpōn*, "human beings," and *andra*, "man." She surpasses all humankind with respect to beauty. The poet's proof is for the moment deferred, but the force of her example, the superiority of Helen to all, is firmly fixed.[6]

The third stanza begins with *kallipois'*, "deserting"; the line ends with *pleoisa*, "sailing." The first letters of the first participle, *kall-*, echo the *kall-* of *kallos*, "beauty," and link the leaving behind, her act of desertion, with her own beauty. The line expresses motion; we see Helen leaving, going, sailing; the *eba*, "went," an aorist, the punctual past tense in Greek, anchors her action in a single past moment. The participles catch her endlessly moving, taking steps, sailing away on a ship that recalls the third element of the catalog at the poem's beginning. The following line sets her motion against

---

5. See Fredric Will, "Sappho and Poetic Motion," *Classical Journal* 61 (1966): 259–62. On this poem, see also Anne Pippin Burnett, *Three Archaic Poets: Archilochus, Alcaeus, Sappho* (Cambridge, Mass., 1983), 277–90. Burnett sees Sappho's comparisons as ironic, proving the blinding power of love.

6. On Helen, see Norman Austin, *Helen of Troy and Her Shameless Phantom* (Ithaca, N.Y., 1994). Austin discusses fragment 16 in "Sappho's Helen and the Problem of the Text" (51–68), and includes an image of the papyrus fragment, found at Oxyrynchus, which contains the troubling remnants of the poem (53). He concludes that "shame is . . . the context that gives the ode its force, since Sappho has selected as the paradigm to prove her argument the woman whose beauty was her shame. But Eros, Sappho argues, knows no shame" (68).

the static force of all that she left behind, all those who should have been dear to her, who, in terms of the Greek ideals of marriage, motherhood and kinship, ought to have satisfied her. She forgets all; the *mna-* of the negated verb form *emnasthē,* "remembered," perhaps plays on the root *man-, main-,* suggesting madness. (Alcaeus, Sappho's contemporary and fellow Lesbian poet, in his poem about Helen, calls her *ekmaneisa,* "maddened," which Denys Page in an uncharacteristically baroque moment translates "driven mad with passion.")[7] The stanza ends with a clause much of which has been lost; someone, something, has led the heroine astray. Page suggests "something like" *ouk aekoisan, Kupris, eukampton gar,* "(Helen) not unwilling, Aphrodite (the Cyprian goddess) led her astray, for she (Helen) was easy to bend."[8]

There follows a fragmentary passage that is legible again at *me nun,* "me, now;" we have moved from the world of epic and legend back to the *egō,* "I," of line 3, and to the present, the singer's time. The next word is *Anaktorias,* the name of the woman who stands in relation to the second half of the poem as Helen of Troy does to the first half. If the logical center of the poem is the generalizing statement of lines 3 and 4, the moment of presence, the phenomenological center, arrives with the name of Anaktoria. We are made aware of her absence with *ou pareoisas,* "not being present"; the participle allows us to imagine her presence as well. Something or someone led Helen "aside," *par-agag';* Anaktoria is not present, not "beside," *par-eoisas.* The participle resonates as well with those used of Helen, *kallipois',* "leaving," and especially *pleoisa,* "sailing," marking the parallelism between these two women. One is legendary, another someone departed from the poet's everyday life. Yet Sappho's memory creates them both; the act of making poetry becomes, in the case of Anaktoria, the act of re-creating the presence of the absent loved one.

The last stanza of the poem completes the process of memory and finally returns the listener to the wider world. The *eraton,* "lovely," echoes *eratai,* "one loves," of line 4, makes whatever is lovely about Anaktoria, her step, her way of walking, partake of

7. Page, *Sappho and Alcaeus,* 275.
8. Ibid., 54.

the general statement at the poem's beginning. The *bama*, "step," "stride," is linked etymologically with the verb *eba*, "went," of line 9, and stresses the connection of Helen with the poet's desire, with the woman Anaktoria. Sappho would rather see her way of walking, her shining face, than the Lydian chariots, than the armed foot soldiers. These last two substantives return the listener to the "prooimion," to the catalog of things that began the poem, ending with the affirmation of desire for Anaktoria that proves the rule of the generalizing statement at the beginning. The voice in the poem prefers what she loves over all those things that others love; she offers thus a proof of her general claim, and in so doing conjures up, summons up, and at the same time praises the object of her memory and desire.

The poem, like others in the Sapphic corpus, plays with time, moving the listener from the past into a vividly realized present, a present that, the poems stress, is really itself the creation of memory. The poet remembers Helen, a figure from long ago, juxtaposes to her Anaktoria, and then causes us to understand that both are distant, recalled in the act of making poetry, in the listeners' experience of hearing, imagining, and in an era of reading out loud, of voicing the poet's praise.[9]

The poem works on an opposition between love and the threat of war outside. In each of the three parts of the lyric Sappho refers to the world of war, the world of men and heroes—in the catalog of warriors and ships, in the mention of Helen, where the Trojan War is unmentioned but inevitably present behind the text, where the beauty of Helen drove men to war, and in the dismissal at the end of chariots and foot soldiers. The notion of desire shimmers through the tripartite rhetorical structure, through the allusions to war and its weaponry and its causes; Sappho's setting for her choice of Anaktoria provides the context for her refusal of alternatives to what she loves.

Richmond Lattimore, the great translator of Homer, mistranslates this poem in a way that reveals the consequences of its compactness, its far-reaching compression. He translates lines 3 and 4

9. On reading aloud, see Jesper Svenbro, *Phrasikleia: An Anthropology of Reading in Ancient Greece*, trans. Janet Lloyd (1988; Ithaca, N.Y., and London, 1993); "the written word (or the writer) makes use of the reader as he could make use of an instrument (that is to say, as an object)" (3).

thus: "but I say she whom one loves best is the loveliest."[10] In fact, the Greek does not mean this, but rather, "I (say it to be) whatsoever one loves." Lattimore's translation, however, brings out an important feature, shared by things and people, essential to the poem's logic. Some people love masses of armed men, some people love ships, some people love Paris (of Troy), and someone loves Anaktoria. Lattimore makes the poem exclusively a love poem, a poem about Anaktoria.

But I would argue, and this is the way in which I see the poem as a prephilosophical text, that Sappho is writing something more, suggesting that there is such a thing as an abstract notion of erōs. At least as important as Anaktoria, and praise of Anaktoria, is the poet's attempt to universalize her insight, to speak in logical terms of the ways in which men's love of the display of battle, Helen's love, her own love for Anaktoria, belong within some more englobing category. She is defining desire with the vocabulary at hand, and her efforts at definition seem to move beyond simple praise of her beloved, and beyond the traditional "priamel" which lists parallel elements and caps them with one climactic final element.[11]

Sappho sets out rhetorically to answer the question: What is *kalliston epi gan melainan*, "the most beautiful (thing) on the dark earth"? Her answer is an attempt to offer a type of definition, a general statement that covers all individual cases—*kalliston*, most beautiful, the most beautiful thing, is "whatever someone loves." The catalog that precedes the general statement is not intended to be exhaustive; it is a triad that includes kinds of men and ships, that by listing varieties stands for all variety. Helen is a particular case, and her action offers proof of the poetic voice's general statement; her beauty and fame are enlisted to give weight to the general definition. Anaktoria is another particular, for Sappho the most beautiful thing on earth, in the poem another element in its proof. The partial listing at the end of the poem closes the "ring,"

10. Richmond Lattimore, *Greek Lyrics* (Chicago, 1960), 40.
11. On the priamel, see Burnett, *Three Archaic Poets*, 281–84, and her notes 7 and 9. She cites the inscription on the Leto temple at Delos, which exhibits a definitional impulse similar to but different from, more abstract than Sappho's: "The most beautiful is the most just; the most sacred is health; the sweetest is possession of what one loves" (283 n. 13).

signaling the conclusion of the lyric and also reminding us paradoxically that while Anaktoria exists briefly for us, recalled to presence through poetry, she is only one case of "the most beautiful," among other cases, since others love Lydian chariots and infantrymen in their panoply.

Bruno Snell says of Sappho's fragment 16, "That one man should contrast his own ideas with those of others is the theme of [this] poem by Sappho." Yet elsewhere I think he comes closer to what is at stake in this particular poem, which is not simply a poem of praise, about personal taste, but rather a move toward a new kind of thinking, toward the cultural production of subjectivity and individualism and reason, *logos*. He says of Archilochus and Sappho: "Both of them are evidently concerned to grasp a piece of genuine reality: to find Being instead of Appearance." [12] Although she might have done so, Sappho is not saying that Anaktoria is equal to *to kalliston*, "the most beautiful." Much of the intensity of the poem derives from the force of her personal preference, her ability to make Anaktoria walk before us; but Anaktoria's presence is tensely, barely contained within a logical and rhetorical structure that gives her memory wider meaning.

Arguments such as Snell's have fallen out of favor in recent years, since they seem to rely on an evolutionary model of human development, one that goes back at least as far as Hegel, that sees human progress from myth to reason, from poetic writings to philosophical logics, that posits an unending rise in human consciousness, with some often unnamed *telos* akin to the realization of absolute spirit. Since Nietzsche, the catastrophes of twentieth-century history including Hiroshima and the Holocaust and the rebirth of torture, since Lévi-Strauss and decolonization, it has become more difficult innocently to see the triumph of reason in the West and to describe a steady trajectory of human progress, with Europe at the vanguard of inevitable enlightenment. Nonetheless, it seems to me unnecessary and even reckless, a throwing out of the baby with the bath water, to conclude that no historicizing narrative is any longer possible. Such an account of Western culture as Michel Foucault's, although it refuses any moral, unless the

12. Bruno Snell, *The Discovery of the Mind: The Greek Origins of European Thought*, trans. T. G. Rosenmeyer (Cambridge, Mass., 1953), 47, 50.

negative one of ever-increasing surveillance of human beings, does allow for the possibility of change over time, and for a tendential description of Western history. Although there are difficulties in positing a single historical narrative for all world history, I continue to believe that it is important to distinguish between one epoch and another, and that to fail to do so leads scholars to posit some unchanging human nature that is much more radically ethnocentric than not.[13] And I see Sappho as a crucial figure in a historical narrative, a particular, local one, that of ancient Greece and thereafter of Hellenizing Western civilization, one that, like Snell's, sees the historical production of the self, of individuality, of the subject, rather than the eternal and unchanging figure of the "human being," whose attributes, desires, and practices we can assume to know through analogy with our own.

The Helen of Sappho's fragment 16 is a figure from the epic cycle, a character of legend; yet she is made to signify something new here, to stand as an example of a general proposition about "the beautiful." Sappho anticipates philosophical argument through the rhetoric of this poem, deploying general statement and examples to prove her point. She moves toward abstraction by employing the presumed substitutability of things, people, and ships, and arrives at a version of definition of the beautiful through the accumulation of detail, through example and personal testimony.

The logical problem differs from that which the Homeric poet sets himself; Sappho's use of example fits into a more hypotactic structure, in which the distinct moments of this poem are set logically and rhetorically in relations of logical subordination. Homer's Phoinix tells the story of Meleager, a hero who withdraws from battle, as an example to persuade the Achilles of the *Iliad* to return to the battle before Troy. He tells of the many supplicants who come to beg Meleager to join the warring Aetolians again and to defend them from their enemies, tells of Meleager's final entry into battle after he had waited so long that his people denied him gifts. Phoinix concludes his exemplum, addressing himself still to Achilles:

13. On the global history problem, see Robert Young, *White Mythologies: Writing History and the West* (London and New York, 1990). See also Partha Chatterjee, *The Nation and its Fragments: Colonial and Postcolonial Histories* (Princeton, N.J., 1993).

yet he [Meleager] drove back the day of evil from them
Listen then; do not have such a thought in your mind; let not
the spirit within you turn you that way, dear friend. It would
   be worse
to defend the ships after they are burning.[14]

Phoinix uses his example to convince Achilles of the folly of his
actions; he is not concerned to describe, to define the nature of
anger or of withdrawal. The story works rhetorically to establish a
pattern, to set Achilles' action in a social and narrative context, to
delineate parallel situations to that of Achilles and to offer parallel
solutions to the problem that faces the hero and his people. And it
offers a rhetorical paradigm for the events of the Trojan cycle as a
whole, for the patterns of withdrawal, supplication, and return,
along with the hero's eventual death, not represented in the *Iliad*
but prefigured in the fate of Meleager.[15] Homer uses this kind of
example rarely; he enlarges the scene of battle more frequently
through simile, sets next to action on the battlefield a scene from
the pastoral world outside the poem's narrative space. Sappho is
moving toward another version of thinking about identity, as different from Homeric notions as her hypotactic style is different
from his parataxis. Along with her representation of personal desire, of an "I" embodied in the poem, goes a new logic of abstract
definition; her several particulars, including the example of Helen
of Troy, are logically subordinated to a whole, as she works
through addition and variation toward that whole.

   The various elements in the poem, the opposition between love
and war, between men and women, between past and present,
serve the definition, create a web of particulars that works to establish that heading subsuming them all. Sappho here seems to be
concerned to say something new with the vocabulary, the terms of
reference of her tradition, and to move toward a type of abstraction that comes into existence more fully in works that might be
called "philosophical," in the context of the classical *polis* after Socrates. Aristotle, for example, in the *Nicomachean Ethics*, attempts to

---

   14. *The Iliad of Homer*, trans. Richmond Lattimore (Chicago, 1951), 9.599–602.
   15. See Gregory Nagy, "Mythological Exemplum in Homer," In *Innovations of Antiquity*, ed. Ralph Hexter and Daniel Selden (New York and London, 1992), 311–31.

define *t'agathon kai to ariston*, the "good and the best," the end at which human actions aim:

> To judge from men's lives, the more or less reasoned conceptions of the good or happiness [*to agathon kai tēn eudaimonian*] that seem to prevail among them are the following. On the one hand the generality of men and the most vulgar identify the good with pleasure, and accordingly are content with the life of enjoyment [*ton bion . . . ton apolaustikon*]. . . .
>
> Men of refinement, on the other hand, and men of action think that the good is honour [*timēn*]. But . . . it is clear . . . that in the opinion at all events of men of action, virtue [*hē aretē*] is a greater good than honour . . . but even virtue proves on examination to be too incomplete to be the end.[16]

After a long discussion which includes consideration of the theory of the Forms, Aristotle concludes that "happiness," *eudaimonia*, that is, "having good 'daimons,' being blessed with good 'genius,' prosperity, fortune, wealth," is *to ariston*, "the best (thing)."[17]

The emergence of the individual in lyric poetry is an extraordinary, even "world-historical" event in Western culture. Yet even as the individual becomes differentiated, emerges in his or her particularity in the aristocratic poetry of Sappho's day, the intellectual movements travel in an opposed direction, away from specificity and detail toward abstraction, in a movement that results in the physical speculation of the pre-Socratics, in the metaphysics of the Platonic dialogues, in Aristotelian logic. Sappho's poetry stands at a moment of transition, in which the specificity of the particular is still visible, in which a particular object, a headband, a field of flowers, exists in all its particularity, but in which at the same time that process of individualization that will allow for the equivalency among all citizens of ancient democracy is also being constituted. As the Homeric community changes, as aristocracy thrives, does its work, struggles with the revolutions of the tyrants in various ancient Greek cities, the aristocratic individual begins to serve as a

---

16. Aristotle, *The Nicomachean Ethics*, with an English translation by H. Rackham (Cambridge, Mass., and London, 1934), 1.v.1:60.

17. Ibid., 1.vii.8–9.

model for the democratic individual. The citizen of the democracy, putatively equal to all his fellows, is conceived first in aristocratic terms out of the material of Homeric culture, and in eros. It is the desiring self who emerges in the poems of Sappho and Ibykos, and who, as an "I," offers a paradigm to the individualism, the agonism and competitiveness of the ancient democratic city. Contemporary with the emergence of an individual who is first superior, then leveled, comes the philosophical tendency toward abstraction, toward impersonal, desituated definition. It is within the abstract definition of citizenship that the citizen takes his being, rather than in the name of his father and of his father's father. His mother was of necessity, eventually by law, the daughter of an Athenian citizen, but it is not his name, not her name, but rather this attribute, an abstract and general attribute, that defines his membership in the community of such a democracy as that of Athens. Aristotle's definition of "the best" is in this sense like a definition of "the citizen," who is an individual, specific yet abstract.

In Sappho's fragment 16 the transition from parataxis to hypotaxis, from parallel example to example as part of a general proof, joins an assertion of personal desire, of the celebration of an individual's erotic preference. Homer, Sappho, and Aristotle provide three points of reference along a trajectory, one that involves several different series of change, but that cannot usefully be described in terms of something like an essential human nature. We can see rhetorical change, the evolution of hypotactic logic, the production of new forms of selfhood or identity, and an effort toward a philosophical project, some definition of "the most beautiful." The history of philosophy must be rewritten to include work such as that of Sappho, which addresses questions even a philosopher in our sense might see as his or her province.

In the transition from tribal social structure to the ancient city, modes of thinking change. Sappho's ability to move toward abstraction, toward definition, and the positing of one term that subsumes a variety of examples, coincides, perhaps is even enabled, by contemporary phenomena in the culture she inhabits. One of the most striking of these is the invention in the eastern Mediterranean, in nearby Lydia, of coined money.

Herodotus reports of Lydia:

The country, unlike some others, has few natural features of
much consequence for a historian to describe, except the
gold dust which is washed down from Tmolus. (1.93)

The mountain Tmolus shared its name with a god and appears on
coins. Herodotus goes to characterize the culture of the Lydians,
remarking upon some peculiar practices:

Working-class girls in Lydia prostitute themselves without
exception to collect money for their dowries, and continue
the practice until they marry. . . . Apart from the fact that
they prostitute their daughters, the Lydian way of life is not
unlike our own. The Lydians were the first people we know
of to use a gold and silver coinage and to introduce retail
trade. (1.93ff.)

It is worth noting that Herodotus immediately after this assertion
attributes the invention of all games to the Lydians, who tried to
divert themselves from hunger pangs during a period of severe
famine. They invented dice, knucklebones, and ball games, eating
on one day and playing on the next, and survived in this way for
eighteen years. When the famine was not alleviated, they decided
instead to send a colony to Umbria under the direction of their
king's son, Tyrrhenus (1.96). Prostitution, the invention of gaming,
and the invention of coinage are all thus practices of the Lydians,
rendered roughly equivalent in this catalog of the peculiarities of
the inhabitants of Lydia.[18]

There is a vast literature on the invention of coinage, and a
growing dispute about the exact dating of the momentous event in
the West, which for these purposes must paradoxically include
Lydia, in Asia.[19] The first coins seem to have been made of elec-

18. On the invention of coinage, see Vincent Farenga, "La tirannide greca e la
strategia numismatica," in *Mondo classico: percorsi possibili*, ed. F. Buratta and F. Mariani
(Ravenna, 1985), 46ff. See also Marc Shell, *The Economy of Literature* (Baltimore, 1978).
19. On this issue, see Oswyn Murray, *Early Greece* (Stanford, Calif., 1983), 223–26.
Murray cites the later Herakleitos: "The exchange function of precious metals was
sufficiently widely recognized to be embodied in a philosophical analogy of Herakleitos, describing the characteristics of fire, the ultimate constituent of the universe: 'For
fire all things are exchanged, and fire for all things, as for gold goods and for goods
gold' (Frag. 90)" (226).

trum, "white gold," *leukos khrusos*, a natural alloy of gold and silver found on the slopes of Mount Tmolus. The temple erected in honor of Artemis at Ephesus contained coins, probably deposited around 600 B.C.E., that is, near the time of Sappho's "flowering," to use the ancient dating procedure. This deposit, which includes marked coins from the Greek cities of Ephesus and Miletus, also contains unmarked pieces of metal, and some scholars believe this indicates that coinage began at some time between 640 and 630 B.C.E. The practice seems to have spread from the practices of the Asian Lydians to the Asian Greeks, who participated in the foundation of the trading colony Naucratis in Egypt. Aegina, an island near Athens, was the only city-state from near the mainland to join in this foundation, and it too began to issue coinage in the last quarter of the seventh century. The coins of Lydia and Miletus seem to have retained a continuity with the standards of Mesopotamian weight; they show a ratio of 60:1, which is typical of Mesopotamian mathematical relations.

Aristotle, again in the *Nicomachean Ethics*, discusses the significance of coinage in enabling abstract thought, in permitting the recognition of abstract value:

> All commodities exchanged must be able to be compared [*symblēta*] in some way. It is to meet this requirement that men have introduced money [*to nomisma*]; money constitutes in a manner a middle term [*meson*], for it is a measure of all things [*panta metrei*]. (5.5.10)

> Money . . . serves as a measure which makes things commensurable and so reduces them to equality. (5.5.14)

(Aristotle later points out that the gods have no need for coins or currency of any sort [10.8.7].)[20]

The invention of money, of coinage, of a common denominator that renders things commensurable, is a great step forward from the simplest mechanisms of exchange, of barter, in which, say,

---

20. See also Karl Marx, *Capital*, vol. 1, trans. Eden Paul and Cedar Paul (London, 1957), 42–128. Marx says that Aristotle's understanding of value is limited because he fails to understand that all labor is identical, living as he does in a society based on slavery (31).

three cows are exchanged for a certain number of pieces of cloth. To establish a value in relation to a third term, a "middle" term, is to conceive of value as something separate from the objects themselves, and is to abstract it from use value and even exchange value, in the strictest sense. Cows and cloth are seen in light of money, that is, their relative value is calculated in terms of something which they are not, something that stands for abstract equivalency. It is not until money becomes purely symbolic, paper rather than metal, or metal which does not have equivalent value in its own right, that money assumes its purely abstract form. But the process of abstracting from objects their relative value, and conceiving of these in relation to the third term, coins, resembles the process of logical definition. Three cows and five pieces of cloth are equivalent to fifty drachmas; Helen, and Anaktoria, and ships, and chariots, and infantry are all equivalent to the abstract term *to kalliston*, "the most beautiful." It may be that these two processes of abstraction enable each other, that the abstraction of the notion of "the most beautiful" coincides with and allows for and profits from the invention of a mechanism for the measure of value.[21]

In *The Philosophy of Money*, Georg Simmel points out:

> Money is the representative of abstract value. From the economic relationship, i.e., the exchangeability of objects, the fact of this relationship is extracted and acquires, in contrast to those objects, a conceptual existence bound to a visible symbol. Money is a specific realization of what is common to economic objects. . . . Money is simply "that which is valuable." . . . Money is that divisible object of exchange, the unit of which is commensurable with the value of every indivisible object; thus it facilitates, or even presupposes, the detachment of the abstract value from its particular concrete context. The relativity of economic objects, which can be recognized only with difficulty in the exchange of indivisible objects—because each of the parties possesses, so to speak, an autonomous value—is brought into relief through the re-

21. See the fascinating essay by Jean-Joseph Goux, "Numismatics: An Essay in Theoretical Numismatics," in *Symbolic Economies: After Marx and Freud*, trans. Jennifer Curtiss Gage (Ithaca, N.Y., 1990), 9–63.

duction to a common denominator of value, of which money
is the most distinctive form.[22]

Sappho's "most beautiful" is like money in that it is the abstract, the
thing that allows for a relativism of value. Some value warriors, but
Sappho argues that all candidates for "the most beautiful" can be
reduced to a common denominator, all characterized as being, finally, abstractly, "whatsoever one loves." The invention of coinage
coincides historically with such protophilosophical efforts at definition; it allows things, even people, to be thought of in terms of a
common standard. Sappho measures men and women and things
not by setting them in a hierarchy, but as exemplifying a definition
in common, that "the most beautiful thing on the dark earth" is
equivalent to "whatsoever one loves."

Sappho's protophilosophical gesture in fragment 16 expresses
and helps to define the questions of her age, a period in which a
search has begun for absolutes, for ideas, for the one, for defini-
tions of what is, of being. In a context of praise, praise of Anaktoria, praise of eros, she asks what it is that unites human beings'
understanding of beauty, and answers that it is eros, desire. It is
remarkable that she answers this general question with a general
answer, while at the same time preserving the absolute particularity and specificity of her own answer to the question: What is
the most beautiful? A philosophical treatise, in the age of classical
philosophy, presents, although in the complex form of a dialogue,
an answer to this question that is highly abstract. Diotima, in Plato's *Symposium*, requires of the lover that he, and I use the pronoun
advisedly, not become fixated on the particular attributes of his
beloved, but that he rather use his erotic desire to move beyond a
particular body, beyond bodies, to the idea of beauty:

> And thus, by scanning beauty's wide horizon, he will be
> saved from a slavish and illiberal devotion to the individual
> loveliness of a single boy, a single man, or a single institution.
>
> And, turning his eyes toward the open sea of beauty, he
> will find in such contemplation the seed of the most fruitful
> discourse and the loftiest thought, and reap a golden harvest

22. George Simmel, *The Philosophy of Money*, ed. David Frisby, trans. Tom Botto-
more and David Frisby, 2d ed. (London and New York, 1990), 128.

of philosophy, until, confirmed and strengthened, he will
come upon one single form of knowledge, the knowledge of
the beauty I am about to speak of. (210 d)
It is an everlasting loveliness which neither comes nor goes,
which neither flowers nor fades. . . .

Nor will his vision of the beautiful take the form of a face,
or of hands, or of anything that is of the flesh. (211 a)

And if, my dear Socrates, Diotima went on, man's life is ever
worth the living, it is when he has attained this vision of the
very soul of beauty. And once you have seen it, you will
never be seduced again by the charm of gold, of dress, of
comely boys, or lads just ripening to manhood. (211 d)[23]

The voice in Sappho's fragment 16, on the other hand, while recognizing that human beings differ about what they find most beautiful, refuses to give up the radiance of Anaktoria's face, and her
lovely way of walking.

Having argued for Sappho's place in a possible history of philosophy, I look further at poem 16 in light of narratological questions and in light of the problems a female character poses for
traditional ideas of narrative. My argument focuses on the interpretation of the place of Helen in Sappho's poem, Helen who is for
Homer a reward from Aphrodite, for Aeschylus in the fifth century
a cursed cause of war.

Before the Lydian invention of coinage, men exchanged objects
of value. Scholars have characterized the Homeric world, that
vague temporal entity that stretches from the twelfth to the eighth
centuries B.C.E., as a culture of gift exchange.[24] The heroes of Homer exchange women also, as gifts, as guarantors of alliance, as
valuable prizes for excellence in battle. Menelaos, son of Atreus,
king of Mycenae or Argos, wins Helen as his wife against a multitude of rivals but, according to a late version of the story, Helen,
the most beautiful woman in the world, is awarded to Paris, son of

23. *Symposium*, trans. Michael Joyce, in *The Collected Dialogues of Plato*, ed. Edith
Hamilton and Huntington Cairns (Princeton, N.J., 1961). See David Halperin, "Plato
and the Erotics of Narrativity," in *Innovations of Antiquity*, ed. Hexter and Selden, 95–
126.

24. See, for example, Louis Gernet, *Anthropologie de la Grèce antique* (Paris, 1968),
344–59.

the king of Troy, as a prize for favoring Aphrodite in the contest for a golden apple inscribed *kallistēi*, "for the most beautiful woman." After Paris steals Helen from his host, Menelaos, Menelaos and his allies come to reclaim her. Thus the Trojan War itself is caused by a violation of the codes of exchange characteristic of heroic culture. The *Iliad* contains other such narratives of exchange and of its violation; the poem begins with the return of the war prize Chryseis to her father and with Agamemnon's subsequent seizure of Achilles' war prize Briseis. In the *Iliad* Helen is caught within the walls of Troy; we see her weaving a web that represents a battle like that before Troy, and pointing out the Greeks' heroes to the Trojan king Priam.[25] Aphrodite forces her to go to Paris' bed when the goddess snatches him from danger on the plain below the city. Helen mourns for the Trojan hero Hektor and laments her own arrival with Paris in Troy. Because of Aphrodite's promise to the shepherd Paris, Helen has been traded for the "apple of discord"; she is a thing, passively waiting to be reclaimed.

In the *Odyssey*, Helen greets the son of Odysseus, Telemakhos, when he visits Menelaos in search of his long-absent father. She seems, returned to her proper place in her husband's household, a contented queen, and there Homer alludes to her stay in Egypt. According to an alternate version of Helen's story, she herself never went to Troy. An *eidōlon*, an image or phantom, passed those years at Paris' side, while the real Helen was spirited away to Egypt. The poet Stesikhoros, blinded for singing abuse of her, wrote a famous palinode, which is recorded in Plato's *Phaedrus*:

> That story is not true, and you did not go on the well-benched ships and you did not reach the citadel of Troy. (243a)

Having written these lines, Stesikhoros immediately regained his sight, Plato reports (*Phaedrus* 243b). Yet in either version of this legend, Helen is moved by others, awarded as a prize, held as a captive, stolen away to Africa, fought over as a prize of war, returned to her rightful place at her husband's side.

Women in the Homeric world, especially such a woman as

---

25. On the description of Helen's weaving as an example of epic ekphrasis, see Page duBois, *History, Rhetorical Description and the Epic: From Homer to Spenser* (Cambridge, 1982).

Helen, immortal in memory for her beauty, are exchanged, given as prizes, stolen, sold as slaves. If they are moved about the land-scape of the Aegean by men, by divinities, as valuable objects, they also represent static points in that landscape, landmarks that sig-nify the immobility of most women, whose virtue is in their stasis, their fidelity. Like Hestia, the perfect, virgin daughter, divinity of the household hearth, good women stay where they are put.[26] The narrative of the *Odyssey* describes the passage of Odysseus from one woman to another, from the seductive and beautiful goddess Kalypso, who promises him immortality, to his faithful, waiting mortal wife Penelope. The hero moves across the epic landscape defining himself as he goes, encountering fixed female creatures of various sorts, and then moving beyond them. George Dimock, in a fine example of what Mary Ellman might have called "phallic criticism,"[27] says of the initial situation of the *Odyssey*:

> Leaving Calypso is very like leaving the perfect security of the womb; but, as the Cyclops reminds us, the womb is after all a deadly place. In the womb, one has no identity, no ex-istence worthy of the name. Nonentity and identity are in fact the poles between which the actors in the poem move.[28]

Odysseus, along with his son the only actor in sight, might be said from this point of view to be defining himself by leaving the "womb-Kalypso." The other boundary of his journey, from which he will depart again with his oar, is the bed of Penelope, another fixed, static place in the cartography of the poem, set like Kalypso's island as a landmark by means of which the hero marks out his position and charts his course.

The goddesses who inhabit the *Odyssey* act, but they too, with the exception of Athena the virgin warrior, not born of woman, are static figures. In their *Dialectic of Enlightenment*, Max Horkheimer and Theodor Adorno write of the sirens who tempt Odysseus and of the fixed, mythic creatures like them in the poem, figures be-

26. See Jean-Pierre Vernant, "Hestia-Hermès: Sur l'expression religieuse de l'espace et du mouvement chez les Grecs," in *Mythe et pensée chez les Grecs*, vol. 1 (Paris, 1965), 124–70.

27. Mary Ellman, *Thinking about Women* (New York, 1968).

28. George E. Dimock, Jr., "The Name of Odysseus," in *Homer*, ed. George Steiner and Robert Falges (Englewood Cliffs, N.J., 1962), 111.

longing forever to the past. Odysseus, in his "return," his *nostos*, passes and transcends these female beings in his trajectory through the epic landscape from Aia, Kalypso's island, to Ithaka, where Penelope waits:

> The mythic monsters whose sphere of power he enters always represent ossified covenants, claims from prehistory. Thus in the stage of development represented by the patriarchal age, the older folk religion appears in the form of its scattered relics: beneath the Olympian heavens they have become images of abstract fate, of immaterial necessity. . . . Scylla and Charybdis have a right to what comes between them, just as Circe does to bewitch those unprepared with the gods' antidote. . . . Each of the mythic figures is programed always to do the same thing. Each is a figure of repetition: and would come to an end should the repetition fail to occur.[29]

According to the Frankfurt School thinkers, these figures of repetition represent nature, from whom the hero, the figure of enlightenment, must free himself by denying his own part in nature. They are almost all female, marking the epic poem as the passage of the masculine hero through a potentially deadly and paralyzing series of female spaces. Odysseus moves away from Kalypso's island, where he is offered the ultimate immutability in exchange for marriage, immortality. He encounters Kirke, fends off her attempts to turn him into a captive animal, learns from her, and then moves on. He greets Nausikaa, seems to be considered a suitor for her hand, someone to be caught into the magical space of her home, but he leaves this space behind as well. He moves past the Sirens, past Scylla and Charybdis, leaves behind his mother and the other inhabitants in the land of the dead. Women remain rooted in the Odyssean landscape, landmarks in the hero's path. Odysseus, when he first encounters Nausikaa, seems to woo her as he supplicates her, using a simile that, while praising, emphasizes her immobility,

---

29. Max Horkheimer and Theodor W. Adorno, *Dialectic of Enlightenment*, trans. John Cumming (New York, 1972), 57–58. On the sirens, see also Pietro Pucci, "The Song of the Sirens," in *Odysseus Polutropos: Intertextual Readings in the Odyssey and the Iliad* (Ithaca, N.Y., 1987), 209–13.

even though he has first seen her playing with a ball, running with
her friends:[30]

> Yet in Delos once I saw such a thing, by Apollo's altar. I saw
> the stalk of a young palm [*phoinikos neon ernos*] shooting up. I
> had gone there once, and with a following of a great many
> people, on that journey which was to mean hard suffering for
> me. And as, when I looked upon that tree, my heart admired
> it long, since such a tree had never yet sprung from the earth,
> so now, lady, I admire you and wonder.[31]

When Odysseus finally proves to the patient and wily Penelope
that he is her husband, long gone and returned, she has tricked
him by saying that their marriage bed has been moved, while only
she and her husband know that it is made of a tree still growing in
the earth. The repetitive, natural, static, organic female characters
of the poem mark the landscape and cannot themselves move
within it. They wait for the heroes to come and go; Odysseus returns to Penelope and to his marriage bed and then moves past her
too, deeper inland, in fulfillment of the prediction made of his fate
by Teiresias. This pattern makes the mobility of the masculinized
Athena all the more remarkable. Mortal women and minor goddesses in the world of the Odyssey are trapped in cyclical, mythic
time; they belong to an age before history, which Odysseus leaves
behind as he discovers himself, establishes an identity, a history,
a name.

The study of narrative structure that has been a focus of some
recent literary theory often seems incapable of thinking beyond
the type of text exemplified by the Homeric epic. Female characters have been described as static, fixed entities in oral literatures,
and structuralists and their heirs, the semioticians, often generalize
from oral texts to describe women as objects, things to be exchanged, markers of place both geographically and textually.[32] In
a notorious passage Claude Lévi-Strauss once described the status
of women in kinship exchange relationships as resembling that of

30. I owe this observation to Carolyn Dewald.
31. *The Odyssey of Homer*, trans. Richmond Lattimore (New York, 1975), 6.162–68.
32. For an exception, see Nancy Felson Rubin, "Introduction: Why Classics and
Semiotics?" *Arethusa* 16, special edition on semiotics and classical studies (1983): 5–14.

words exchanged in a conversation among men.[33] In the analysis of narrative which Vladimir Propp began with his study of the folktale, woman is a princess, the object of the hero's quest, a prize.[34] A. J. Greimas, in presenting "elements of a narrative grammar," takes up the folktale once again:

> Now, the circulation of values, being seen as a series of transfers of object-values, can follow the two trajectories:
>
> 1. $F(d_1 \rightarrow O \rightarrow \bar{d}_1) \rightarrow F(\bar{d}_1 \rightarrow O \rightarrow d_2)$, which in the case of Propp's Russian folktales can be interpreted as follows: Society (d_1) experiences a lack, the traitor $(\bar{d}_1)$ kidnaps the king's daughter (O) and takes her elsewhere in order to hide her (d_2).
> 2. $F(d_2 \rightarrow O \rightarrow \bar{d}_2) \rightarrow F(\bar{d}_2 \rightarrow O \rightarrow d_1)$, which will mean: The hero $(\bar{d}_2)$ finds the daughter of the king (O) somewhere (d_2) and returns her to her parents (d_1).
>
> The Russian folktale thus shows a circular transmission of values by successively using two performing subjects and by valorizing one of the conformed spaces (that of the hero) at the expense of the other (that of the traitor).[35]

The king's daughter is an "O," an object, not a subject. The invisibility of the king's daughter's possible subjectivity to such models calls into question their presumed scientificity, striven for diligently through the use of pseudological formulae.

Women are not always "O"s, not always objects of value, stolen, traded, captured back, and returned to their rightful places. The diagram, the insistence of the subject-object duality, and the seemingly innocent assignment of gender to the two positions fail to take into account the possibility of women's status as subjects in their own right. Sappho's fragment 16, although not itself a narrative poem, contains a compressed narrative that in fact reverses the patterns of oral literature, of Homeric epic, Russian folktale, and

33. Claude Lévi-Strauss, *The Elementary Structures of Kinship*, ed. R. Needham, trans. J. H. Bell, J. R. von Sturmer, and R. Needham (Boston, 1969), 496.

34. Vladimir Propp, *Morphology of the Folktale*, ed. L. A. Wagner, trans. L. Scott (Austin, 1968).

35. Algirdas Julien Greimas, *On Meaning: Selected Writings in Semiotic Theory*, trans. Paul J. Perron and Frank H. Collins (Minneapolis, 1987), 78.

many myths of origin and universality, perhaps those of structuralism and semiotics themselves. She causes a problem at the origin of narrative and of the history of narrative by refusing to replicate the stories of masculine agency and feminine object status. In her poem men do not trade women, they do not move past static, fixed women who mark the landscape.

Sappho may be characteristic of her age in subverting the Iliadic interpretation of Helen's passivity in her sojourn in Troy, but she seems to lend it a particular evaluation. As she speaks of desire in new terms, circling down on a definition of it as an abstract force, she both renders the specificity of Anaktoria and sees Helen as an "actant" in her own life, a *subject* of eros, exemplary not only for her beauty but also for her desiring, for her movement toward that which she thought to be "the most beautiful thing on the dark earth." In the *Iliad* Helen remains the passive victim of Aphrodite, waiting for Paris, waiting perhaps for Menelaos to rescue her from captivity to the will of Aphrodite and of Paris. The *Odyssey* portrays her as a dispenser of narcotic drugs that ease pain and as the treacherous resident of Troy who stood outside the wooden horse containing the Greeks and imitated the voices of the Greek heroes' wives, trying to lure them to betray themselves. This representation of Helen, as scheming and responsible for her actions, receives greater elaboration in the post-Homeric age. Alkaios, Sappho's Lesbian contemporary, shares the view that Helen must be held accountable for the disasters of the Trojan people. He grants some limited agency to Helen; but in contrast to Sappho, he registers strong disapproval of the legendary beauty in two poems. In the fragment called N1 he calls her "maddened:"

> . . . and excited the heart of Argive
> Helen; maddened by the Trojan man,
> a traitorous guest, she followed him
> in a ship on the sea,
>
> leaving at home her child . . .
> and her husband's richly covered
>   bed . . .
> her heart persuaded by love . . .
> daughter of Zeus and Leda

*

> . . . many of his brothers . . .
> . . . the Trojan plain holds conquered
> because of that woman,
> many chariots in the dust . . .
> . . . and many lively-eyed men . . .
>   . . . slaughter . . .[36]

Diane Rayor's translation stays close to the Greek, translating *ek-maneisa* soberly as "maddened," while Denys Page's translation shades the poem further toward an negative assessment of Helen's shame:

> And fluttered the heart of Argive Helen in her breast; driven mad with passion [*ekmaneisa*] by the man from Troy, the traitor-guest, she followed him in his ship over the sea,

> Leaving her child at home forsaken, and her husband's richly-covered bed, since her heart persuaded her to give way to love, through the daughter of Dione and Zeus;

> . . . Many of his brothers the dark earth holds, laid low on the Trojan plain for the sake of Helen;

> And many chariots tumbled in the dust . . . and many dark-eyed . . . were trampled, and . . . Achilles . . . the slaughter.[37]

In another account of Helen's story Alcaeus compares her unfavorably to the more virtuous although no less unhappy Thetis:

> So the tale runs, that because of wicked deeds came bitter grief, Helen, from you upon Priam and his sons long ago, and Zeus made an end of holy Ilium in flames.

> Not such was the dainty maiden whom the noble son of Aeacus wedded, when he had summoned all the blessed gods to his marrying, and taken her from the halls of Nereus

---

36. *Sappho's Lyre: Archaic Lyric and Women Poets of Ancient Greece*, trans. Diane Rayor (Berkeley and Los Angeles, 1991). Rayor's fr. 6.

37. Page, *Sappho and Alcaeus*, fr. N1, 275.

To the house of Chiron: he unbound the pure maiden's girdle,
and thriving was the love of Peleus and the best of
Nereus' daughters; and in a year

A son she bore, mightiest of demigods, blest driver of bay
steeds. But they, the Phrygians, and their city perished
for the sake of Helen.[38]

Alcaeus insists on the destructive quality of Helen's deeds, her responsibility for the annihilation of the Trojans and their city; the obedient Thetis, in contrast, behaves passively, at least in Alcaeus' narration, transported virtuously from the house of her father Nereus to the house of her husband's Centaur comrade.

Sappho's poem does not condemn Helen, nor does she list the victims and suffering due to Helen's choice, nor does she make the epic heroine the victim of madness. Helen is one who acted, pursuing the thing she loved. For that action Sappho does not castigate her, but rather uses her example as part of her praise of Anaktoria, part of her proof that the most beautiful thing on the dark earth is what one loves. Helen's action is a result of the power of eros, and she, like all others on earth, follows what she loves. She is not a victim, not an object of exchange. The condensed, implicit Helen narrative of Sappho's poem cannot be satisfactorily addressed by such semiotic models as those of Propp and Greimas, which would categorize such elements of a narrative as Helen, daughter of a god, as "O," object of value. Perhaps the failure of women to write narrative, epic poetry, that silence which Sappho did not break, can be traced to the invisible pressure of models like theirs, patterns that insist on women's receptivity, passivity, their status as objects to be traded by the real "actants." In an essay entitled "Desire in Narrative," Teresa De Lauretis takes for granted a history that Sappho's poem belies:

If the female position in narrative is fixed by the mythical mechanism in a certain portion of the plot-space, which the hero crosses or crosses to, a quite similar effect is produced

38. Ibid., fr. B10, 278–79.

in narrative cinema by the apparatus of looks converging on
the female figure.[39]

Such views, often associated with contemporary film studies, con-
cede too much, in their ahistoricity and confidence in the universality of the Oedipus complex. Sappho's Helen is neither, in
De Lauretis' terms, following Lotman, "male-hero-human," nor
"female-obstacle-space."[40] Sappho, positioned very early in the
history of Western narrative and culture, sees Helen as motivated,
moving, mobilized by erotic desire.

It is even possible that in this poem Sappho celebrates Helen
for acting. The poem is so fragmentary at its heart that we cannot
know if the poet holds Aphrodite or eros responsible for Helen's
choice, but certainly the poem attributes movement to Helen herself. She is imagined "leaving," *kall[ipoi]s'*, "going," *eba*, "sailing,"
pleoi[sa, even though something may have "misled her," "led her
astray," *paragag,'* in lines now missing. And the voice in the poem
acts, as did Helen, in loving Anaktoria, in setting her above chariots and infantrymen; the poet acts, in thinking beyond the terms
of the epic vocabulary.

Sappho's rhetorical choices, in asking philosophical questions,
in imagining female subjectivity, constitute her as a poet of her
time as well as an extraordinarily privileged aristocratic woman.
The lyric age, the age of the tyrants, is a period of confusion, tur-
bulence, and conflict; it is from this moment, this break, that
Sappho speaks. Louis Gernet, in his essay "Mariage des tyrans,"
analyzes the anachronistic features of the marriages of the tyrants,
the elements of their alliances characteristic more of a legendary
past, the age of magical kings, than of a society moving toward
urbanization.[41] Jean-Pierre Vernant's study of Greek marriage also
helps to clarify the peculiar situation of women in the seventh and
sixth centuries:

> We can speak of a rupture between archaic marriage and that
> which is instituted in the frame of a democratic city, at the

---

39. Teresa De Lauretis, *Alice Doesn't: Feminism, Semiotics, Cinema* (Bloomington, Ind.,
1984), 139.

40. Ibid., 121.

41. Gernet, *Anthropologie*, 344–59.

end of the sixth century in Athens. In post-Clisthenes Athens, matrimonial unions no longer have as their object the establishment of relations of power or of mutual service between great sovereign families, but rather the perpetuation of houses, the domestic households that constitute the city.[42]

If the tyrants return to incestuous practices, as Gernet points out, their practices reveal a need, in the archaic, lyric age, the age of Sappho, to redefine and restructure the institution of marriage, so important in the lives of women in such cultures. The period of transition from one type of marriage to another, from a bride-price system to a dowry system, from a view of women as objects exchanged to bind distant families together to a view of women as placeholders of the *oikos*, of the father's household, requires the social labor of centuries. Sappho lives in between, in a historical period where aristocratic women seem to have had unusual power, neither still "value-objects" nor yet wards of their democratic citizen fathers, uncles, and brothers.

During the eighth and seventh centuries the institutions that had perpetuated the unquestioned dominance of the aristocracy— the system of noble households, law administered by aristocratic fiat, the dependence on rural economies, premonetary exchange— all were in a state of flux, challenged by growing mercantile, commercial, artisan groups clustering around the acropoleis, and at times finding allies among the aristocrats who ruled as tyrants. The conflict is documented by Alcaeus and other poets, who witnessed the establishment of new loci of power, and who frequently remained in the camp of the aristocrats, like Sappho, fighting for survival and for domination of the newly wealthy cities. The transitional nature of Sappho's society, the possibilities of new forms of social identity for her class and for women of her class, may have freed her from the rigidity of traditional conceptions of women as objects of exchange, conceptions that scholars inherit and still deploy as heirs of the Greeks. Sappho troubles some of these traditions, disrupting the narrative of narratives at its origin, displacing

42. Jean-Pierre Vernant, "Le mariage," *Mythe et société en Grèce ancienne* (Paris, 1974), 62–63.

the narrative of the history of philosophy. Sappho belongs in these narratives, in the histories of philosophy and in the histories of narrative. Her situation allowed for poetry like the Anaktoria poem, a love poem that is at the same time an extension of the potential for abstract thinking, and a rewriting, a turning of narrative formulae. If Sappho's poem 16 is, in Adorno's terms, "a philosophical sundial telling the time of history," it enabled her to see Helen as a subject, as hero of her own life.

SIX

Sappho in the History of Sexuality

I mean the title of this chapter in a double sense, one of which I might correct the other. In one sense I refer to the absence of the ancient Greek poet Sappho in the contemporary discourse of what after Michel Foucault is called "the history of sexuality." In another sense, I mean to participate in the writing of another history of sexuality, especially of ancient Greek sexuality, one in which Sappho does figure, and in which she figures so definitively as to trouble and disrupt the other, the received ideas current and derived from Foucault's description of the Greeks' use of their pleasures.

Although classicists have tended to dismiss Foucault's work in general, and in particular the second volume of The History of Sexuality, *The Use of Pleasure*, Foucault has become a seminal figure for many scholars in other fields in the humanities.[1] His work on madness and punishment has defined later work in the field of history, and many feminists are much influenced by his historical model. Although the first volume of the History of Sexuality does not deal in detail with questions of gender, although Foucault's

---

1. On Foucault and on classicists who use Foucault's work, see Amy Richlin, "Zeus and Metis: Foucault, Feminism, Classics," *Helios* 18 (1991): 160–80, and Bruce Thornton, "Constructionism and Ancient Greek Sex," in ibid., 181–93. See also the review by Martha Nussbaum, "The Bondage and Freedom of Eros," *Times Literary Supplement* 4548 (17 June 1990), 573, and Bruce Thornton, "Idolon Theatri: Foucault and the Classicists," *Classical and Modern Literature* 12.1 (1991): 81–100.

work in fact rarely addresses the woman question, many scholars who work on the history of women depend on his notions of *episteme*, of discourse, of disciplinary genealogies. It is possible to construct in particular an account of early modern, modern, and postmodern culture in Europe and North America based on his argument concerning the relationship between power and knowledge; Foucault suggests that power, enacted through disciplinary knowledge, is expressed at multiple and various sites in modern culture, and is now internalized in institutions, through forms of power and knowledge such as psychoanalysis. His has been an unquestionably enabling account for many discontented with Hegelian, post-Hegelian, Marxist master narratives, in part due to its episodic, discontinuous qualities. I have difficulties with Foucault's work on post-Renaissance European culture, in particular because gender as a category does not seem to figure in his narrative, even as a historically produced category, because although he sees psychoanalysis and sexology as purely instrumental discourses, enacting power as they claim knowledge, they seem to me to have been part of women's gaining a voice and a right to sexual pleasure in the twentieth century. But I am concerned here with his move into the field of classical studies, because I think it curiously merges with the views of a scholar like Allan Bloom and represents for those interested in the history of sexuality in general a troublingly and ideologically reduced view of the Greeks.

I want to use the figure of Sappho to disrupt Foucault's narrative, to challenge his hegemony as the authority on the history of sexuality. Foucault's version of the history of ancient sexuality will be relied on by many in early modern, modern, and postmodern cultural studies. But his reading of this history carries with it assumptions about the original, ubiquitous, and inevitable primacy of masculine subject-formation, of women's subjection and submission. To rewrite the beginning of Foucault's story of Western culture is to put into question the whole. If his account of the Greeks forms part of his implicit and historicist narrative about the whole of the history of sexuality, that story perpetuates some of the worst features of the most traditional views of classical culture, that it is an austere, philosophical, Apollonian, Platonic, pederastic symposium.

Foucault argues in *The Use of Pleasure*, following his work on sexuality in the nineteenth and twentieth centuries in the first volume of the History of Sexuality, that the very notion of sexuality as a category must be interrogated and historicized. What is needed, he says, rather than a history of "sexuality," is a genealogy of the desiring subject, and he means to trace the slow formation, in antiquity, of a "hermeneutics of the self."

> The accent was placed on the relationship with the self that enabled a person to keep from being carried away by the appetites and pleasures, to maintain a mastery and superiority over them, to keep his senses in a state of tranquility, to remain free from interior bondage to the passions, and to achieve a mode of being that could be defined by the full enjoyment of oneself, or the perfect supremacy of oneself over oneself.[2]

Such mastery entails a careful "use of the pleasures." Foucault formulates "several recurrent themes of austerity that could center on four great axes of experience: the relation to one's body, the relation to one's wife, the relation to boys, and the relation to truth."[3]

This account of classical culture troubles me because it takes for granted the subordination and subjection of women. In the passage I cited above, Foucault writes of a "person," of "his senses," the possessive adjective not gendered in French. I read along believing he is discussing "persons," until I come upon, with a slight shock, "one's wife." Not everyone possesses a wife. Such a move is typical of Foucault's histories. There is an imagined "we," a community of "one"s. And a woman reader is not part of that "we." Women are objects of this gaze, of this analysis, of this community to which "one" belongs. Foucault begins the history of sexuality, of subjectivity, with the anti-erotic, misogynist discourse of ancient philosophy, a discourse I read as partial, interested, aristocratic, polemically pederastic, and antidemocratic. The "quadri-thematics of austerity" Foucault describes assume that the anti-erotic strain

---

2. Michel Foucault, *The Use of Pleasure*, vol. 2 in the History of Sexuality, trans. Robert Hurley (New York, 1985), 31.

3. Ibid., 32.

dominated ancient culture, and that women, like boys, diet, and philosophy, were always merely occasions for the philosophical subject's mastery of himself.

Of course, Foucault disregards not only much literary evidence, from Greek tragedy, from lyric poetry, that once placed women more at the center of Greek cultural debate, but he also ignores the only female poet whose work we have, Sappho, a poet like many lyricists focused on the senses, on a voluptuous erotic universe. He ignores her writings, as do many others who work on the history of sexuality, among them some of his followers, with the important exception of John J. Winkler.[4] Of course, before the field of "the history of sexuality" per se existed, classicists like K. J. Dover and Eva Stehle were doing important work on Sappho and on Greek sexuality. But even in the fascinating book *Before Sexuality: The Construction of Erotic Experience in the Ancient Greek World,* Sappho is almost invisible.[5] She is portrayed on a vase, along with her fellow Lesbian poet Alkaios, illustrating an essay on figural ambiguity by Françoise Frontisi-Ducroux and François Lissarrague,[6] and mentioned by Froma Zeitlin as a source for imitation by Longus in *Daphnis and Chloe.*[7]

How can Sappho not figure in the history of sexuality? It is remarkable that given the renewed interest in ancient sexuality, so valuable a body of evidence as Sappho's corpus should be overlooked by contemporary critics. It may be because she is not Athenian and therefore deviant from the norm of the ancient *polis* culture about which we know most. It may be because her work comes not from the classical age, but from the so-called lyric age, and therefore cannot be measured against the substantial other evidence concerning the classical period, from historians, comic poets, philosophical writers like those consulted by Foucault, orators and such. Of course archaic, lyric culture is very different from

---

4. See the important essay of John J. Winkler, "Double Consciousness in Sappho's Lyrics," in *The Constraints of Desire: The Anthropology of Sex and Gender in Ancient Greece* (New York and London, 1990), 162–87.

5. *Before Sexuality: The Construction of Erotic Experience in the Ancient Greek World,* ed. David M. Halperin, John J. Winkler, and Froma I. Zeitlin (Princeton, N.J., 1990).

6. Ibid., 219, 239.

7. Ibid., 438.

classical culture, dominated as it was by the struggle between aristocrats and tyrants, between tyrants and their subjects. There is
radical change, particularly in Athens, between the seventh and the
fifth centuries B.C.E. But, and I believe this is a very important issue,
the methodological decision to discuss only classical culture is significant, not inevitable, self-evident. It turns "the Greeks" into our
ancestors, within the terms of a certain narrative trajectory origi-
nally, visibly, obviously devoted to misogyny and the control of
women, and to a program of philosophical self-mastery. To begin
the history of the West with classical Greece and with the philosophers is a polemical choice that determines the subsequent course
of the narrative of Western civilization, and the place of "the
Greeks" in that narrative: In the beginning were men. These
Greeks exemplify certain virtues, and do not indulge in erotic excess, the pursuit of pleasures, luxury and longing. See, for example,
the portrait of the Greeks that emerges in William Bennett's *Book
of Virtues*, in which the Greeks appear as exemplars of the virtues of
"self-discipline," "responsibility," "friendship" (male-male, Damon
and Pythias), "work," "courage," "perseverance," and so on.[8] Sappho, needless to say, does not appear. Sappho is absent from the
history of sexuality, as from many other histories, in part because
she is a woman, because she writes about sex between women and
about female desire. Her desire is transgressive but not destructive.
Sappho cannot be scapegoated as antithetical to civilization; yet
her subjugation is at the foundation of the narrative of austerity.
She is the truly heterogeneous, beneath the homogeneous, against
which the homogeneous is forcibly asserted. Her desire is assym-
metrical to that of the male subject and incompatible with the reputed passivity of the female object. These features of Sappho's
work make her difficult to assimilate into the narrative told by
Foucault and his followers, a narrative that posits a continuity of
masculine subjective centrality and that cannot incorporate the
troubling ambiguity registered in the work of a poet who is a
woman, and who exhibits neither a neat, symmetrical, and virtuous
willingness, the modest complement to masculine desire, nor an

8. See William J. Bennett, ed., *The Book of Virtues: A Treasury of Great Moral Stories*
(New York, 1993).

absence of desire, nor the lustful indiscriminate but distinctly heterosexual hedonism of Aristophanes' comic women.

Lyric poetry is a particularly valuable source for attitudes con-
cerning sexuality, not least because of its rhetorical situation, what
Northrop Frye calls "the radical of presentation." In his *Anatomy of
Criticism*, Frye says:

> The fourth possible arrangement, the concealment of the
> poet's audience from the poet, is presented in the lyric. . . .
> The lyric is . . . preeminently the utterance that is over-
> heard. . . . The radical of presentation in the lyric is the
> hypothetical form of what in religion is called the "I-Thou"
> relationship. The poet, so to speak, turns his back on his lis-
> teners, though he may speak for them, and though they may
> repeat some of his words after him.[9]

Sappho's lyrics, like those of the other lyric poets of her age, often
have this quality of discourse overheard, of a privacy temporarily
made visible to the listener. Her audience, her readers, have a tran-
sient access to domains of archaic life usually protected from
strangers. I am reminded of the scene in Herodotos' *Histories* in
which the Lydian king Candaules, having remarkably conceived a
passion for his wife, invites his trusted subordinate Gyges to view
her naked.

> Gyges, since he was unable to avoid it, consented, and when
> bedtime came Candaules brought him to the room. Presently
> the queen arrived, and Gyges watched her walk in and put
> her clothes on the chair. Then, just as she had turned her
> back and was going to bed, he slipped softly out of the room.
> But the queen saw him.[10]

The queen calls Gyges to her and tells him he must either kill
Candaules and seize the throne, with her as his wife, or die himself.

> Night came, and he followed her into the bedroom. She put
> a knife into his hand, and hid him behind the same door as

---

9. Northrop Frye, *Anatomy of Criticism: Four Essays* (Princeton, N.J., 1957), 247–48.
10. Herodotus, *The Histories*, trans. Aubrey de Selincourt (Harmondsworth, England, 1954), 44.

before. Then, when Candaules was asleep, he crept from behind the door and struck.

The power seems to lie with the one seeing and hearing the other,
unbeknownst to her. The power in this scene begins with Candaules, who owns both the woman and the man, and forces the man
to view his wife. But finally, in this story, power lies in the hands
of his wife, who effects his murder in vengeance for his display of
her. She controls not only Candaules, but also the viewer, Gyges.[11]
The rhetorical situation of Sappho's lyrics is that of an overheard
internal dialogue, speech recalled by the poet. The audience is
given access to a private world, the world of the poet's inner
thoughts, her memories, sometimes an intimate scene between
herself and her lover, or between herself and the goddess Aphrodite, now recalled and overheard by Sappho's audience. The
speaker seems vulnerable in this situation; she is giving access to
her most private thoughts to strangers. Like Candaules' wife, she
seems vulnerable, but it is she who finally dominates.

This is Sappho's fragment 94 (L.-P.), in Denys Page's translation:

Honestly I wish I were dead! Weeping she left me

With many tears, and said "Oh what unhappiness is ours;
    Sappho, I vow, against my will I leave you."

And this answer I made to her: "Go, and fare well, and
    remember me; you know how we cared for you.

If not, yet I would remind you . . . of our past happiness.

Many wreaths of violets and roses and . . . you put around
    you at my side,

And many woven garlands, fashioned of flowers, . . . fit for a
    queen, you anointed . . .

And on soft beds . . . you would satisfy your longing . . .

---

11. See also the discussion of this scene in *Games of Venus: An Anthology of Greek and
Roman Erotic Verse from Sappho to Ovid*, ed. and trans. Peter Bing and R. Cohen (New York,
1992).

And no . . . holy, no . . . was there, from which we were
  away,

No grove . . .

What follows is a traditional explication of this poem, with the
concomitant claim that it should, after all, form part of a history of
ancient sexuality. This is a poem about privacy, about opening up
privacy to view; the play of persons is the terrain of this exploration. The issues of privacy, of women's space, of their accessibility
are crucial to Greek notions of sexuality, although they do not
enter into Foucault's descriptions of the philosophical subject's
drive for austerity and self-mastery.

I frame my reading of this poem through the shifting of grammatical persons it undergoes and undertakes. In an essay on
pronouns, Emile Benveniste makes a distinction that serves to characterize Sappho's work, to distinguish it from Homeric epic and
from the philosophical treatises that form the basis for Foucault's
notions concerning the Greeks. Benveniste says:

> A linguistic text of great length—a scientific treatise, for
> example—can be imagined in which "I" and "you" would not
> appear a single time; conversely, it would be difficult to con-
> ceive of a short spoken text in which they were not
> employed.[12]

The lyric poetry of Sappho is different from most of the philosophical treatises examined by Foucault, in its use of pronouns, in
its mode of address. Sappho addresses particular people, names
them, insists on the specificity of her desire, and on its dyadic setting. Even Plato, who writes dialogues purporting to represent
conversation, records long, pronoun-free dissertations, lectures on
philosophical matters interrupted only by the monosyllabic assent
of his interlocutors. Unlike the austere, self-mastering Greek philosopher privileged by Foucault, Sappho's subject is determined
not by austerity, by the will to self-mastery, self-containment, self-
absorption, abstraction, but rather by specificity, naming, the address of an other. And there is a resolutely nonnarrative, nondev-

---

12. Emile Benveniste, "The Nature of Pronouncs," *Problems in General Linguistics*, trans.
Mary Elizabeth Meek (Coral Gables, Fla., 1971), 217–18.

elopmental insistence in Sappho's lyric address. It refuses to unify and develop into epic, even as it will not be assimilated into the impersonality and abstraction of philosophical discourse.

Benveniste points out further that third person pronouns are entirely different from "I" and "you"; the third person stands for, replaces or "relays" another part of an enunciation, rather than indicating person. The third person can indicate any object as its reference, does not depend on the instance of the discourse, includes an often large number of variants, while the first and second persons are linked to the exercise of language and point to the speaker as such.

> *I* can only be identified by the instance of discourse that contains it and by that alone . . . the form of *I* has no linguistic existence except in the act of speaking in which it is uttered. . . . By introducing the situation of address, we obtain a symmetrical definition of *you* as the "individual spoken to in the present instance of discourse containing the linguistic instance *you*." [13]

In effect, one characteristic of the persons "I" and "you" is their specific "oneness": the "I" who states, the "you" to whom "I" addresses himself are unique each time. But "he" can be an infinite number of subjects—or none. . . . A second characteristic is that "I" and "you" are reversible: the one whom "I" defines by "you" thinks of himself as "I" and can be inverted into "I," and "I" becomes a "you." There is no like relationship possible between one of these two persons and "he" because "he" in itself does not specifically designate anything or anyone. [14]

The "I" and "you" are opposed, correlatives of one another, possessing the marks of personhood, while the third person, "he," "she," "it," "they" are impersonal, not personal. The "I"-"you" correlation is very specific:

> When I get out of "myself" in order to establish a living relationship with a being, of necessity I encounter or I posit a

---

13. Ibid.
14. Benveniste, "Relationships of Person in the Verb," ibid., 199.

"you," who is the only imaginable "person" outside of me. These qualities of internality and transcendence properly belong "I" and are reversed in "you." One could thus define "you" as the *non-subjective* person, in contrast to the *subjective* person that "I" represents; and these two "persons" are together opposed to the "non-person" form (= he).[15]

Sappho's poetry works through these shifting oppositions, staging an encounter between an "I" and a singular "you," representing a scene of intimacy recovered through memory. Fragment 94 in particular also plays on the oppositions between "I," "you," and various "we"s, reconstituting and recodifying a female space.

Discussing the plural forms, Benveniste points out the peculiarities of the first person plural:

It is clear, in effect, that the oneness and the subjectivity inherent in "I" contradict the possibility of a pluralization. If there cannot be several "I"s conceived by an actual "I" who is speaking, it is because "we" is not a multiplication of identical objects but a *junction* between "I" and the "non-I," no matter what the content of this "non-I" may be. This junction forms a new totality which is of a very special type whose components are not equivalent.[16]

Benveniste discusses the form "we" in languages differentiating between an inclusive and an exclusive "we," that is, distinguishing between an "I + you" "we" and an "I + they" "we." In Indo-European languages, this distinction is not marked. The presence of the "I" in such languages is, he argues, very strong, and sometimes the "we" can stand for a singular subject. "The reason for this is that 'we' is not a quantified or multiplied 'I'; it is an 'I' expanded beyond the strict limits of the person, enlarged and at the same time amorphous." The "we" of majesty is a more massive, more solemn person. "On the other hand, the use of 'we' blurs the too sharp assertion of 'I' into a broader and more diffuse expression: it is the 'we' of the author or orator."[17]

What does all this have to do with Sappho, and with the poem

15. Ibid., 201.
16. Ibid., 203.
17. Ibid.

I cited earlier? This is a poem peculiarly concerned with relations of persons, not just the recollection of persons now absent, as are many of Sappho's poems, but especially here with questions of grammatical persons, and with the changing lines and boundaries between the "I" and others. It seems to me that this poem begins with the "I," moves to an "I-you" dialogue, employs a shifting form of "we" that accommodates first Sappho and her lover, then Sappho and other women. This "we" then partakes of pleasures, becomes embodied, allows room for the explication of the pleasures of the "you," and is returned to and finally defined as a "we" through negation, in absentia, through the irrecoverability of past shared experience.

The question of reading thus becomes: who is the "we" of this poem? I mean this not in the sense of the old questions concerning Sappho's actual environment, the debate about her circle of women, her possible status as a schoolmistress, as a mistress of the muses for young girls. I mean this question in a strictly formal sense. What is the intersubjectivity being posited here? Who speaks? To whom? What is the status of layers of persons here, the voices in the poem, the poet behind them, the audience to whom they are addressed?

The poem comes from a sixth-century parchment and is, of course, fragmented. So much the better; I read it as it stands, not imagining what might have been there once. The meter is "two glyconics followed by a glyconic with dactylic expansion."[18] The poem begins in the middle of something, with the first line absent, fragmented away; so we lack the first part of the couplet.[19] The first line we have resounds with delta and tau; *tethnakēn adolōs thelō.* The theta of the first word is echoed in that of the last, lambda and omega of the middle word repeated in the last word. Campbell points out that *adolōs* is a word "used in treaties"; it also recalls that master of *dolos*, Odysseus, expert in *mētis*—ruses, guile, trickery. Jean-Pierre Vernant and Marcel Detienne call him "the very em-

18. David A. Campbell, *Greek Lyric Poetry: A Selection of Early Greek Lyric Elegiac and Iambic poetry* (Basingstoke and London, 1967), 278.

19. On this poem, see Thomas McEvilley, "Sappho, Fragment 94," *Phoenix* 25 (1971): 1–11; W. Schadewalt, "Zu Sappho," *Hermes* 71 (1936): 366, and *Sappho* (Potsdam, 1950), 115–19; Anne Pippin Burnett, *Three Archaic Poets: Archilochus, Alcaeus, Sappho* (Cambridge, Mass., 1983), 290ff.

bodiment of cunning."[20] This speaker refuses the tricks of *mētis*, but nonetheless invokes their presence through the use of the alpha privative, the prefix of negation in Greek.

The voice of the poem is an "I"; it is unclear whether the first line extant, the line translated as "Honestly, I wish I were dead," emerges from the "person" who stands for the poem itself, as the voice of the narrator of the poem.[21] This is a fruitful and productive ambiguity, an accident of transmission, since we, whoever we are, cannot know who utters this line. Is it the voice of the poem, or of the lover? The first line of this poem means something quite different if it is the overheard utterance of the voice of the poet, the so-called narrator's voice. If it is she whom we overhear, in a private speech to herself, no dialogue except with the assumed but invisible listener, then the words are those of someone either in great despair or exaggerating for effect, pretending to despair in order to emphasize rhetorically the love she bears for the absent one. This poem seems to create a mood of possible exaggeration, of emphatic stress on the pains of love, that after all serve as a foil, as dramatic contrast to the pleasure remembered. In any case, the ambiguity of the source of the first line is productive, since it produces an indeterminacy between "Sappho" and the parting lover. They are fused, indistinguishable from one another; the poem then proceeds to separate them out, to distinguish them one from another, and then to recount a situation of fusion once again in the life of pleasures now lost to them.

The next line introduces the theme of departure, leaving, abandonment. "She, weeping, left me behind"; the *kata* of the compound verb emphasizes the negative aspects of the departure. *Katalimpanō*, "leave," like *kataleipō*, is used of people dying, or of going far away. Dying is going into a far country, to which one can jour-

---

20. Marcel Detienne and Jean-Pierre Vernant, *Cunning Intelligence in Greek Culture and Society*, trans. Janet Lloyd (Hassocks, England, 1978), 22.

21. McEvilley, "Sappho, Fragment 94": "The wish to die, as often in Sappho, is a metaphor for the rejection of present time, and memory, that tomb where the present lies when it has died, may serve as a surrogate for physical death" (8). He implies that it is not memory, but poetry, that "eases the pain" of the present, "the healing imagination entering to soothe pain of life" (9). The poem, after the fourth strophe, represents the world in which Sappho wants to be: "The unbalancing fourth strophe is the striving against the bonds: as the poem, in this strophe, breaks loose from static form, so it breaks free from the grip of the world" (9).

ney only once, never to return; to join a companion who has gone to that far country can mean only to die oneself. She was weeping greatly (*polla*); she reminds her interlocutor *ōs deina peponthamen*, "What unhappiness is ours." The participle, *psisdomena*, "weeping," indicates that the second speaker within the poem, being cited, is feminine; the repetition of the first person pronoun stresses the dialogical quality of this opening sequence; the voice in the poem recalls a woman, a girl, weeping, leaving, speaking, all in the past. Then the second speaker, whom the first voice recalls, breaks into the second person plural with *peponthamen*. A "we" is created; the sufferings of the first voice, who wishes to die, generates weeping and leaving, the second voice who creates a new hybrid, an inter-subjectivity, a new "person." This "person," like the first who wishes to die, has suffered or experienced extraordinary things, this time in the perfect tense. It is as if the sufferings endured, complete in the past, have brought into being this new first person plural. The verbal ending of *peponthamen* echoes in its sound, though not in sense, the ending of *katelimpanen*, and stresses the creation of a "we" from the "she" who abandoned Sappho. But this is a retrospective gaze, time receding as we observe it; sufferin gs in the remoter past brought forth this state, this lament in a less remote past; someone now wants to die.

The lover addresses Sappho by name, says that she leaves her unwillingly. *Apulimpanō*, "I leave," picks up and emphasizes the theme of departure and abandonment; *apoleipō* means "lose," "leave behind," "distance," "surpass," "forsake" "abandon" (of places one ought to defend). The *me* (accusative first person pronoun) and *moi* of the first lines become *s'* (second person pronoun) here. This is a complex moment in the shifting of pronouns, in which the referent Sappho, or the voice speaking the poem as a whole, is indicated first by omega, the ending of the verb, then by *me* and *moi*, the first person pronouns, then by *se*, for the second person, depending on who is addressing her.

Sappho reclaims her own voice in the next lines, emphasizing her return by pronouncing the pronoun *egō*, "I." The poet rhetorically dramatizes the interstitial, intersubjective dynamic of desire, with a sort of "call and response." She returns the utterance to herself, recalling her answer to the other woman. She bids her farewell, tells her to go and to remember her, Sappho, again with the first person pronoun as object. *Kamethen* "and [remember] me" is almost echoed verbally in the next line, which begins with *memnais'*. "For you know that we followed you closely, sought after you, pursued, attended to you." Hers is a move of consolation for the voice of Sappho herself. Because of the ambiguity in the first person plural, as described by Benveniste above, the poet both assembles around her, with this "we," a company, and extends her own being, assumes a sort of majesty. The first use of the first person plural seems to suggest a dyad, the lover and the poet, together having suffered terrible or wonderful things, *deina*. Here Sappho turns to the lover and asserts another reality, the continuity of her own existence, and perhaps her continuing association with others who were there before her lover came, will be there after her lover departs, are present as someone says she honestly wants to die. The poet extends her compliments to the absent lover; she is so loved that she is loved by many, but these others are Sappho's allies, too, in her moment of recollection and loss.

Sappho turns to further consolidation, saying if her lover does not remember, that she, Sappho, wishes to recall things to her. Her words, *alla s' egō thelō*, "but I wish," recall not only the first line of the stanza above, *egō . . . ameiboman*, "I answered," but also the first line we have, *tethnakēn adolōs thelō*, "Honestly I want to die," strengthening the attribution of this first extant line to the voice of the poet in the poem. Here Sappho wants to remind, to recall to memory something. This strophe is quite fragmentary, breaking off and resuming with "and beautiful things we experienced, suffered," with the first person plural verb this time in the imperfect. The verb recalls the perfect verb of the second strophe, where the lover speaks of the terrible things "we" have suffered. Sappho is answering her by countering her experience of pain with the recollection of mutual experiences of pleasure. This time the reference of the first person plural is extended, no longer Sappho and her others posed against the lover, but perhaps all of them together subsumed into a new company. *Deina* are directly challenged with *kala;* the terrible, awesome things are matched by "beautiful things."

With this preparation, the poem enters a new scene, in which the *kala*, these "beautiful things," are described in detail. In part as an effect of the fragmentation of the text, the physical beauties of this next section of the poem seem slightly diffuse or dislocated, as if the whole world were turned to flowers. There are crowns of violets, roses, perhaps little crocuses. There are repeated forms of *polus*—*pollois, pollais, polloi*, "much, many"—a sense of abundance and repetition, many occasions on which abundance flowed. The other, the one to whom Sappho speaks, performs various actions in the midst of a wealth of flowers. Next to Sappho, she places something around something or someone. She casts many garlands, braided together, of flowers. The word *apala*, "tender," recurs later; here it is used to characterize the neck around which these flower garlands are thrown, so that the neck itself comes to resemble a flower's stem, or the crowns of violets, roses, and little crocuses of the stanza before. The *upothumis*, a garland worn around the neck, contains reference to the *thumos*, the soul, breath, life of the human being. It is as if the very life of the lover were being fettered by these beautiful, tender bonds of flowers.

This whole section of the poem partakes of the luxury and sensuousness of the archaic world, discussed in an important essay by Barbara H. Fowler.[22] Thomas McEvilley discusses the three temporal planes of the poem, the present, the time of the departure, and what he calls "the early life": "The emotions of all three times are involved in the moment of speaking." In the last time, the time of the most remote past, mood and language change. "Stark and harsh in the present, formal and drab with weeping in the direct past, the language now becomes free and ornamental. Images of beautiful objects abound in what has been up to now an imageless poem."[23] Sappho is an aristocrat, living a life of luxury and pleasure, recalling sensuous life led within an aesthetic that values such pleasures. She mentions *muron*, the sweet juice extracted from plants, sweet-oil, unguents, balsam, and says it is *brentheiōi*, probably "precious and costly." She says: "you . . . anointed" with something

---

22. Barbara H. Fowler, "The Archaic Aestheitc," *American Journal of Philology* 105 (1985): 142.

23. McEvilley, "Sappho, Fragment 94," 9. He further suggests that the world of the end of the poem is an "imagined life." "It is a ghost city where Sappho and her friend may wander, as through a 'forest of symbols' that suggest the condition of their hearts. . . . Or, again, the supposed events can be seen as an entire symbolic lifetime, based on suggestions of courtship and marriage" (11). This life, a life in which a lover of the beautiful "is wedded to it through an inner rite," is shared with her readers in the poems.

"royal," "queenly," *basilēiōi.* All the verbs are in the aorist, suggesting an occasion in the past saturated with a mood of luxury, indulgence, wealth. Although the flowers may be products of nature, precious unguents imported from the East and royal ointments are the possessions of the rich, of the privileged class to which Sappho herself belonged.

Fragment 81, discussed in the next chapter as well, reads:

> . . . reject . . . (as quickly as possible) . . . and you, Dica, put lovely garlands around your locks, binding together stems of anise with your soft [*apalaisi*] hands; for the blessed Graces look rather on what is adorned with flowers and turn away from the ungarlanded.[24]

Like fragment 96, these lines recall a mood of pleasure and luxury, and a companionship shared with female divinities.

The next strophe of fragment 96 speaks of sexual longing and satisfaction and enters definitively into the history of sexuality and of its concomitant subjectivity, that vexed area of cultural studies oriented at present in such a way as to disregard such scenes of female desire. Sappho recalls a *strōmnan molthakan,* a "soft bed" or couch; Page makes clear that *strōmnē* means not a couch for reclining, or dining, or sitting, "but a bed, a place where you lie down for the night." Something here, unclear because of the fragmentary state of the manuscript, is feminine, tender, soft, delicate. Then comes the phrase *exiēs pothon,* "you would satisfy your longing." A similar phrase is used in Homer to describe the desire for food and drink which feasters put away from themselves, satisfying their bodily desires. But here *pothos* is sexual longing, yearning, love or desire. Denys Page remarks drily that "there are obvious indications that it [this stanza] contained matter incompatible with the modern theory of Sappho's character. . . . No useful purpose would be served by reporting the desperate shifts by which some modern scholars have attempted to eliminate those indications."[25] He re-

---

24. David A. Campbell, *Greek Lyric I: Sappho and Alcaeus* (Cambridge, Mass., and London, 1982), 108–9.

25. Denys Page, *Sappho and Alcaeus: An Introduction to the Study of Ancient Lesbian Poetry* (Oxford, 1955), 80. By "modern theory" he means the Sappho-as-schoolmistress view espoused by Wilamowitz.

fers to his own argument considering the scholarship on Sappho, which disparages this view:

> Appreciation of the quality of her art and judgement of her sentiments have often been distorted by prejudiced opinions about her social background and moral character. The prestige of Wilamowitz gave new and lasting dignity to the old theory that Sappho was a paragon of moral and social virtues.[26]

Page clearly believes that this passage proves that Sappho was *not* a paragon of moral and social virtues, indeed because of this very description of this soft bed and the longing satisfied there.

In Sappho's verse, the *pothos* is a longing for what is absent, for what is lacking, and thus it reintroduces the mood of regret and melancholy that began the poem. If the woman is reminded of the beautiful things she and Sappho shared—wreaths of flowers, garlands, precious and queenly oils—as well as the satisfaction of longing on a soft bed, then this recollection entails not only consolation but also a bittersweet recognition of the beauties now lost to them.

The fragments that make up this poem trail off in the last stanza remaining to us. The broken quality of the last lines intensifies the atmosphere of pathos they connote. Even the careful, literal, philological translation of the Macmillan editor David Campbell conveys the tone of regret and loss embodied in these fragmentary lines: "The sense seems to have been, 'There was neither . . . nor shrine . . . from which we were absent, no grove . . . nor dance. . . .'"[27] Sappho turns from the lush sensuality of the scene between women, the flowers, garlands, unguents, and soft bed, to another scene, a more public space of holy shrines, of sacred groves, of dances, performed perhaps in honor of Aphrodite, as in other poems. By including the contrasts in the motion of dances, the stasis of shrines, the sounding of music and song, the stillness of holy groves, she includes all public space, all private space. The mention of these sites represents a return to another kind of devotion, not that conveyed by the word of *pedēpomen*, "we cared for

26. Ibid., 110–11.
27. Campbell, *Greek Lyric Poetry*, 279.

you," but in some way consistent with such attentions. The intimate pleasures and satisfactions of these women are of a piece with
worship at shrines, groves, choral performances. They are the private side of a public life; the poem recalls all these beauties, private
and public, as an effort at consolation that, in the poem as we have
it, stresses the union of Sappho and her addressee in loss. Sappho
is drawn into the memories of pleasures, seeking to console, and
ends in a mood of regret. The negatives of the last two stanzas,
koute, oudu, ouk, although they express the *presence* of Sappho and
her lover at shrine, grove, dance, allow us to see that they will no
longer be together at shrine, grove, dance, that the days of pleasure and celebration are no more.

Like other poems of Sappho's corpus, this poem begins by establishing a dialogue between the poet and another woman. It
evokes a moment of intense presence and then moves out again
into a wider world. Its portrait of desire and its satisfaction are far
from the farcical representations of lustful women in such come-
dies as Aristophanes' *Ecclesiazousae*. They are far too from the inad-
vertent destructiveness of Sophocles' Deianeira in the *Trachiniae*,
from the pain and revenge of Euripides' Phaidra in the *Hippolytus*,
the queen's desire for her stepson never satisfied, a longing that
results in the woman's suicide, the youth's destruction. In the classical period women's desire is described only by men, and it is always encoded as dangerous, destructive to the order of things.

In Michel Foucault's version of the classical age, consideration
of female desire does not even enter the scene. Women are the occasion of men's self-mastery, one site of men's exercise of authority:

> The husband's self-restraint pertains to an art of governing—
> governing in general, governing oneself, and governing a
> wife who must be kept under control and respected at the
> same time, since in relation to her husband she is the obedi-
> ent mistress of the household.[28]

> The wife's virtue constituted the correlative and the proof of
> a submissive behavior; the man's austerity was part of an
> ethics of self-delimiting domination.[29]

28. Foucault, *The Use of Pleasure*, 165.
29. Ibid., 184.

To juxtapose these pronouncements, based on the works of Xenophon and Plato, with Sappho's fragment, is to see how prejudicial and interested is the view of ancient sexuality represented in Foucault's work. Sappho is unthinkable in such a system. She is the woman who is not a wife. She is not defined by her integration into a social system in which she is traded by her father to her husband. She has not been socialized by her husband, not instructed in the ways of household management. She is not virtuous, mastered, and obedient; she is not submissive to the governance of a masculine authority. She exhibits neither the insatiable lust of an Aristophanic comic character nor the obsessive, destructive, reckless eros of Clytemnestra, Deianeira, and Phaidra, those tragic heroines whose actions bring down noble men. Sappho's desire and memory are directed elsewhere. Although Foucault ignores the tragic heroines and their desire, and this omission in itself reduces the force of his portrait of the classical age, it seems even more significant that he fails to recognize the only voice of female desire in classical culture, that of Sappho, its power and its object conforming not at all to the thematics of austerity he describes.

Although we can know almost nothing about the performance of Sappho's poems, about the immediate environment of her production of them, it is clear from the language she uses that she writes at least some of the time as a woman "narrator," in a feminine voice, desiring other women. Reading her poetry must transform our view of antiquity as an exclusively masculine domain, one in which women had no voice, served only as the occasions of masculine self-mastery. Sappho's poems present a powerful challenge to what has sometimes been seen as a monolithically phallic economy, an untroubled history of masculine subjectivity triumphant through all of Western culture. Sappho celebrates not household labor and fertility, not the role of the good wife, but rather memory and yearning, the amorous pleasures women share on soft beds. We, whoever we are, cannot leave Sappho out of the history of sexuality. We must come to terms with this woman who troubles the stable origin of Western civilization and the history of sexuality, even the genealogy of the desiring subject, this woman who speaks of her desire.

SEVEN

Michel Foucault, Sappho, and the Postmodern Subject

In an interview given to the French newspaper *Le Monde* in 1980, an interview in which he insisted he not be named, Michel Foucault said, against judgment:

> I can't help but dream about a kind of criticism that would not try to judge, but to bring an oeuvre, a book, a sentence, an idea to life; it would light fires, watch the grass grow, listen to the wind, and catch the sea-foam in the breeze and scatter it. It would multiply, not judgements, but signs of existence; it would summon them, drag them from their sleep.[1]

I consider here the kinds of things that Michel Foucault has allowed me to think, the signs of existence his work summons for me. He produces in the cultural historian a new curiosity, curiosity which he says evokes

> the care one takes of what exists and what might exist; a sharpened sense of reality, but one that is never immobilized before it; a readiness to find what surrounds us strange and

---

This chapter had its origin in a paper delivered at a conference on Michel Foucault and the History of Sexuality at Texas Tech University.

1. Michel Foucault, *Politics Philosophy Culture: Interviews and Other Writings, 1977–1984*, ed. Lawrence D. Kritzman, trans. Alan Sheridan et al. (New York and London, 1990), 326.

odd; a certain determination to throw off familiar ways of thought and to look at the same things in a different way.[2]

I have found much to criticize and judge as I have read Foucault, in the previous chapter as indeed I have over the years, but here I explore, with appropriate curiosity, what his work has helped me to see, especially in the domain of the sexuality of the ancient Greeks, with particular reference to the figure of Sappho.

I find it difficult rhetorically to lay out the ways in which Foucault's work has mattered to me without acknowledging the fragmented, disparate, split nature of my sense of self, a self produced in late capitalism, with gender, class, all those markers that locate one tenuously and ambiguously in the world. All of these affect the encounter with the great man.[3] I am a psychoanalytic female subject, an academic, a Marxist historicist feminist classicist, split, gender-troubled, in the midst of a book about Sappho. And I realize as I write that I could not have written this book without Michel Foucault. So how can that be? I have to take these various elements of whom I think myself to be, and look at them in relation to the work of Foucault. And I will illustrate them, as he says, "watch the grass grow," reading Sappho.

For a historicist, that is, someone that believes there is such a thing as history, Foucault is a revelation. He takes for granted the existence of historical difference. Given the tenets of deconstruction, the exposure of the binary opposition between "now" and "then," between present and past, and the pastiche and ahistoricity of postmodernism, it has become difficult recently to think the problem of historical difference. Foucault affirms that difference, radically, absolutely. He regards the organization of past cultures with a tense curiosity, defamiliarizing the past, pointing out its otherness in a way distinctly liberating for the historicist. For me, in relation to the question of Sappho, whom as I have complained at length he does not discuss, the defamiliarization of the past allows for a fresh view of the archaic world in which she lived. From

---

2. Ibid., 328.
3. Judith Butler, "Contingent Foundations: Feminism and the Question of 'Postmodernism,'" in *Feminists Theorize the Political*, ed. Judith Butler and Joan W. Scott (New York and London, 1992), 14–15.

his point of view, one cannot innocently sustain a belief in the essence of the family, of gender, of sexuality, essences that we are encouraged to take for granted. Nor can we assume a comforting continuity between antiquity and the present. In a way Foucault offers a radical critique of what we used to call "bourgeois ideology," that belief that the organization of our own culture is right, inevitable, and according to immutable laws of human nature.

What does this do for my reading of Sappho? It opens my eyes to features of her poetry that might not be visible without this defamiliarization. For example, take again these lines from one of Sappho's fragments:

> I have a beautiful child, her form
> like golden flowers, beloved Kleis
> whom I would not trade for all of Lydia
> or lovely . . .[4]

As Diane Rayor points out in her note to this, her fragment 45 (L.-P. 132), "Kleis is thought to be the name of Sappho's mother and daughter."[5] The translation of *pais* as "child" avoids the difficulty of whether or not this child is a member of Sappho's family; the word could refer just as well to a slave, someone belonging to Sappho, at her mercy sexually, as were all slaves in this economy in which some people owned others. The modern tendency to turn Kleis unquestioningly into a daughter may be a sign of the ways in which the family as a social structure of our universe occludes our reading of the past, and also of an attempt to de-eroticize the relationship between the *persona* in the poem and this girl whose form is "like golden flowers."

Another of the nineteenth-century tropes of Sappho scholarship was the attempt to domesticate Sappho by making her a schoolmistress, someone who was training pupils in the ways of the muses. The history of classical scholarship on this author abounds in attempts to assimilate her into the cozy world of nineteenth- and twentieth-century academic life, to apply criteria

---

4. *Sappho's Lyre: Archaic Lyric and Women Poets of Ancient Greece*, trans. Diane J. Rayor (Berkeley and Los Angeles, 1991), 72; Eva-Maria Voigt, *Sappho et Alcaeus: Fragmenta* (Amsterdam, 1971), 132.

5. *Sappho's Lyre*, trans. Rayor, 166.

of the present to her very distant past. Although Foucault says nothing useful, in my view, about archaic Greek life, his work lays the ground for the assumption that life in her world was different, that Sappho's culture was constituted differently from our own. So I see with different eyes the situation produced by Sappho's poetry, a situation in which social existence, the separation between public and private, the family are put into question, in which Sappho's desire must be rethought, neither as "musical," nor as a class desire on the model of aristocratic culture of early modern Europe, nor as lesbian, homosexual desire, the kind of desire described and produced by nineteenth-century sexology. Something else, something different, something historically other happens in Sappho's poetry, something that emerges before the birth of the author. Foucault's work opens up the possibility that we don't yet know what happens, and that if we are lucky, patient, and curious in his sense, we might be able to see it. Foucault allows me to think about history otherwise, not just as the ideologically produced "then" to our "now," but as a different series of categories. This is not a trivial point in a world in which people still often rely on a belief in "common sense" and "human nature" in dealing with historically and geographically distant cultural phenomena.

For a Marxist, what does Foucault let one think in a new way? Foucault and Marxism have had a troubled history, as we learn not only from his work, but from the two recent biographies by Didier Eribon and James Miller.[6] Foucault seems always to be setting himself against the tradition of Hegel and Marx, a tradition of progress, of inevitable class struggle and the victory of the proletariat. In an interview with Duccio Trombadori, he recalls the Hegelian legacy of postwar French education:

> "It's clear, then, that the Hegelianism . . . which was proposed as an answer for us at the university with its model of 'continuous' intelligibility, wasn't capable of responding to our needs. . . . What did one find instead in Nietzsche? The idea of discontinuity, the announcement of a 'Superman' who would surpass 'man.' And then in Bataille, the theme of the

---

6. Didier Eribon, *Michel Foucault (1926–1984)* (Paris, 1989); and James Miller, *The Passion of Michel Foucault* (New York, 1993). See also David Macey, *The Lives of Michel Foucault: A Biography* (New York, 1993).

'limit-experiences' in which the subject reaches decomposi-
tion, leaves itself, at the limits of its own impossibility."[7]

Foucault says further, "an interest in Nietzsche didn't represent a
way of distancing oneself from Marxism or communism. Rather, it
was almost the only path leading to what we, of course, thought
could be expected of communism."[8] Foucault was a member of the
French Communist Party for a time in the 1950s, although he left
after the so-called doctors' plot against Stalin in 1952. And the
French party's role in the events of May 1968 convinced him that
European communism was unable to think outside of determinis-
tic, nineteenth-century forms of thought. He seems to have been
at times more sympathetic to Maoism, at least at the period when
other French intellectuals saw Mao as the answer to their dreams
of liberation. But, although Foucault often appeared in demonstra-
tions and on picket lines with communists, his intellectual assumptions led him in very different, Nietzschean directions from what
most people assume to be Marx's views. So what can Foucault offer
to Marxists? Here again, I think his willingness to rethink fossilized
categories of historical thought can bring something to Marxism.
When one considers the relationship of so-called vulgar Marxism
to classical history, to its assumptions about the transparency of
the economy and of class struggle in antiquity, Foucault's example
can be very useful. It may be that other forms of power, other
forms of social relation, define the culture in which Sappho lived,
and that to project modern ideas of class on archaic society may
be to misunderstand those forms of power. Sappho says, in Rayor's
fragment 34:

> What country woman bewitches your mind . . .
> wrapped in country clothes . . .
> not knowing how to draw her skirts around her ankles?

Perhaps class power was expressed in terms of sexual domination,
and Sappho best understood as one of those who had the right of
pursuit in sexual relations, the power to read, to write, to lay out
her desire in literary forms of seduction.

---

7. Michel Foucault, *Remarks on Marx: Conversations with Duccio Trombadori*, trans. R. J.
Goldstein and James Cascaito (New York, 1991), 48.
8. Ibid., 51.

What does it mean for a classicist to come to terms with the work of Foucault? The discipline of classics is peculiarly marked with assumptions of an ahistorical nature. The philological tradition stresses common sense, empiricism. The transparency of the past is for many scholars a given; one employs philological method not to uncover the strangeness of antiquity but rather to dwell in a culture assimilated to our own, still most usefully illuminated by textual scholarship or by New Critical techniques of literary interpretation.

Although the tradition of hermeneutics, of interpretation of the past through our investments in a present, grows out of biblical and classical scholarship, classics as a discipline, in the Anglo-Saxon world at least, has in recent years exhibited little interest in hermeneutics as a theoretical tradition.[9] And Foucault as well as Gadamer and his followers, acknowledging their interests in the present, in the relations between present and past, can unsettle the placid contemplation of the classicist. Foucault acknowledges quite definitively at the beginning of his work on classical culture that his interest in the ancient world grows out of his work on nineteenth- and twentieth-century scholarship. In *The Use of Pleasure*, he says:

> It seemed that by starting from the modern era, and proceeding back through Christianity to antiquity, one would not be able to avoid raising a question that was at the same time very simple and very general: why is sexual conduct, why are the activities and pleasures that attach to it, an object of moral solicitude?[10]

His labor on antiquity is thus motivated, interested. Even more, his desire, never expressed explicitly, seems to find in antiquity a site for the "arts of existence," of an ascetic and aesthetic of the self, as well as a historical encouragement of pederasty, that lead him to draw an unfamiliar portrait of the world of the Greeks, one, I might

9. But see Charles Martindale, *Redeeming the Text: Latin Poetry and the Hermeneutics of Reception* (Cambridge, 1993), and Daniel L. Selden, "*Ceveat lector:* Catullus and the Rhetoric of Performance," in *Innovations of Antiquity,* ed. Ralph Hexter and Daniel Selden (New York and London, 1992), 461–512.

10. Michel Foucault, *The Use of Pleasure,* vol. 2 of the History of Sexuality, trans. Robert Hurley (New York, 1986), 9–10.

add, that has infuriated many classicists.[11] Yet very few scholars in the field of the classics, with the notable exceptions of John J. Winkler and David Halperin, have seriously entertained Foucault's ideas about the Greeks, let alone thought with Foucault, allowed their thinking to be enriched by his remarkable insights into historical difference. Some critics of Foucault, and thus of Winkler and Halperin, seem to believe that there is no historical difference, that we are the Greeks, and that if we are homophobic, for example, so must they have been.

Furthermore, Foucault's writing has allowed me, as a classicist, to insist on the historicity of the Greeks, for example on their particular role in the history of subjectivity. Not simply in relation to what we now call sexuality, that is, but in terms of a historical difference that must be registered in every facet of life, in which forms of knowledge and power operate together, in which surveillance and punishment take their place, in which what seems natural to us in reading a historically distant culture must be interrogated scrupulously. Of course, for example, it is possible to find the condemnation of pederastic acts in ancient Greek texts; but what do they mean? How do they work in the configuration of multiple discourses about social existence? Might they be read not as absolute and unanimous forms of interdiction, but rather as invective expressed within a political forum, where enmities of tribe and family and city excite multiple forms of insult? Foucault has made it more possible to think the otherness of the Greeks, the ways in which they may be our ancestors, but not ourselves, in a way immensely liberating to historical speculation, a speculation that classicists are sometimes reluctant to grant to themselves or to others.

As a person interested in the history of sexuality, I have found much of interest in Foucault's work. One cannot claim that studies in ancient sexuality were founded by him; K. J. Dover and Jeffrey Henderson preceded him in work on the Greeks, Amy Richlin and others in studies in Latin culture.[12] The greatest interest for me in

---

11. For discussion on these points, see n. 1 of the chapter entitled "Sappho in the History of Sexuality."

12. Jeffrey Henderson, *The Maculate Muse: Obscene Language in Attic Comedy* (New Haven, Conn., 1975); K. J. Dover, *Greek Homosexuality* (Cambridge, Mass., 1978); Amy Richlin, *The Garden of Priapus: Sexuality and Aggression in Roman Humor* (New Haven, Conn., 1983).

his work on ancient Greek sexuality lies in its attempt to move beyond simple description, beyond empiricism, to an analysis of the otherness of the Greek relationship to the *aphrodisia*, to their setting within a social context, to the production of the philosophical subject. Foucault, as I have said, wanted to look at the production of desiring persons, the hermeneutics of the self, and considered the *aphrodisia* just one of many sites of self-mastery in ancient Greek culture. He also set his analysis of ancient Greek practices in relation to contemporary issues of sexuality, power, the status of homosexuality, sexology, and psychoanalysis by conceiving of his research on the Greeks within an extended history, the "genealogy of desiring man."[13] Although the term "sexuality" came to him to seem anachronistic, a product of sexology and nineteenth-century efforts at internalization of the policing of the self, still his work came to matter very much for many readers as part of a narrative describing the evolution of Western culture, as I argued in the previous chapter. By occasional comparatist gestures, it pointed up the peculiarity of Western culture in its neglect of amatory arts, in contrast to ancient Hindu culture, for example.

Foucault's work on the history of sexuality can profitably be brought to bear on Sappho. Even though, regrettably, he ignores her existence, Foucault requires me to interrogate my ideas about her accessibility, the transparency of her desire, its facile translation into desire familiar in the twentieth century. I think he is right in arguing that there is no such ahistorical constant as "sexuality."[14] Therefore, it is necessary to look harder at what is going on in ancient society, to try to see what Sappho's strategies and words and rhetoric mean in an unfamiliar world. Is she the agent of power, the privileged aristocrat whose desire can be expressed because of her social position, desire that most significantly is directed at someone subjected by that desire? Is this a more important feature of her poetry than the fact that her desire is directed at another female? What about such lines as these, from Hephaistion's *Handbook on Metre*, preserved because they demonstrate the "antispastic tetrameter catalectic":

13. Foucault, *The Use of Pleasure*, 12.
14. Ibid., 4.

Sweet mother, I cannot weave—
slender Aphrodite has overwhelmed me
with longing [pothōi] for a boy [paidos, thus perhaps "child"].[15]

Lines fragmentary, indeterminate, undecidable. We cannot know
who speaks these lines, how they fit into a larger poetic whole,
what narrative they enable. But they trouble received ideas about
Sappho's assumed lesbian identity and essence, in ways that might
prove fruitful for any history, especially one that interrogates and
puts into question fixed entities such as sexuality and homosexuality. For all this, we owe a great deal to Foucault, Halperin, Winkler. If contemporary lesbians have sought an ancestor in Sappho, a
source of poetic inspiration in antiquity, might she be seen, as well
as an ancestor, as well as an essentialized lesbian of the past, as
someone struggling with self-mastery, for whom poetry is a site
for that mastery, a space of memory and recollection?

As well as a historicist, Marxist, classicist, historian of sexuality,
I am also a feminist. And here I find the greatest problem with the
work of Foucault. He does not see that the discourses of sexuality
and sexology in the nineteenth and twentieth centuries may ac-
company and enable women's liberation, that they are not only
forms of power and knowledge that govern. He is not interested in
gender, he does not see women in ancient Greece except as wives
in the household, another occasion for the master's self-mastery.
And he leaves Sappho out of the history of sexuality. So what can
Foucault offer a feminist? He can keep me from reifying the category woman, keep me from making ahistorical, essentialist assumptions about women. The work of someone like Judith Butler,
immensely energizing to queer theory and feminism, would not be
possible without Foucault. He allows us to recognize that we may
all just be performing gender, and we can perform it differently, as
Butler says in *Gender Trouble*:

Just as bodily surfaces are enacted as the natural, so these
surfaces can become the site of a dissonant and denaturalized
performance that reveals the performative status of the natural itself.[16]

15. *Sappho's Lyre*, trans. Rayor, L.-P. 102, 18.
16. Judith Butler, *Gender Trouble: Feminism and the Subversion of Identity* (New York and
London, 1990), 146.

And when we do historical work on women, we may just be producing woman as a category *for ourselves*, for ourselves to inhabit as we continually produce it in discourse. Maybe—and this is something I continue to speculate about—maybe there is no such thing as gender binarism in ancient Greece until the time of Plato and Aristotle.[17] Maybe male and female bodies are best understood otherwise, in terms of other kinds of opposition, as different species, or, as David Halperin has suggested, in terms of the penetrated and the penetrators. Halperin argues, speaking of ancient Greek society:

> Sex . . . is conceived to center essentially on, and to define itself around, an asymmetrical gesture, that of the penetration of the body of one person by the body—and, specifically, by the phallus—of another. Sex is not only polarizing, however; it is also hierarchical. For the insertive partner is construed as a sexual agent, whose phallic penetration of another person's body expresses sexual "activity," whereas the receptive partner is construed as a sexual patient, whose submission to phallic penetration expresses sexual "passivity." Sexual "activity," moreover, is thematized as domination.[18]

The fact that Sappho is an aristocrat, dominant if not "phallic," may be more significant than the fact that in her discourse, the adjectives that modify the "I" in her poetry have feminine endings.

Perhaps we should be interrogating further, historically, what feminism means here and now. Do women really want to hold on to a historically specific idea of woman, an idea of woman particular to our historical horizon, and project it back into history, forward into the future? Women as passive, victims of male sexual aggression, hidden by history, or visible implicitly only as the logically inevitable binary opposites of men? Sappho sings:

> Night. . .
> Virgins . . .
> celebrate all night . . .

17. See Page duBois, *Sowing the Body: Psychoanalysis and Ancient Representations of Women* (Chicago, 1988), 183ff.

18. David Halperin, *One Hundred Years of Homosexuality and Other Essays on Greek Love* (New York and London, 1990), 30.

may sing of your love and
the violet-robed bride.
But once roused, go [call]
the unwed men your age
so we may see [less] sleep
than the clear-voiced
[bird].[19]

It may be that struggles for certain rights, like reproductive rights, rights to women's bodies, rights for equal pay for equal work, need to be fought out within our own, historical horizon of gender difference. But that does not necessarily mean that when we look at Greek antiquity, we see two genders, symmetrical or asymmetrical, recognizable as identical to our own, with the same patterns of misogyny and masculinity/femininity. Many of us have come to see even the recognition of such a simple pair as reductive and impossible in the present as well. So why should we insist on the constancy of gender binarism in the past?

So this is what Foucault has to offer feminism, a feminism that might want eventually to self-destruct—a historical perspective on what the alliance among women means, and a recognition that we need to interrogate the category of gender, the reading of the body, the naming of women, as much as any other category. This will sound like heresy to many feminists, and I bring it up here partly to be provocative, but also because I think we do need to recognize that an ahistorical commitment to feminism is as ahistorical as any other essentialism. It may be a strategic necessity, but I think we should let the interrogation of the category play itself out.

As someone interested in psychoanalysis, I again find myself stimulated and disturbed by Foucault's work. In the first volume of the History of Sexuality, Foucault argues that psychoanalysis is not a discourse of the lifting of repression, of the throwing off of Victorian prudery, but rather that it is another example of what he calls "the deployment of sexuality."[20] Psychoanalysis is one of the mechanisms by which knowledge produces power, and power

19. *Sappho's Lyre*, trans. Rayor, 61; Voigt, *Sappho et Alcaeus*, 30.
20. Michel Foucault, *The History of Sexuality*, vol. 1, *An Introduction*, trans. Robert Hurley (New York, 1980).

knowledge. Freud's speaking cure is, in Foucault's view, not a path toward greater freedom for psychoanalytic patients; it is an institution produced historically as part of the discourse system, or *episteme* of the late nineteenth and early twentieth centuries, a system through which we are called into existence, called upon to speak, inhabited by power. The institution of psychoanalysis continues the project so brilliantly explicated in *Discipline and Punish*, through which we become modernist subjects, convinced that sexuality is our truth, our deepest secret, who we are. Foucault's analysis, along with Deleuze and Guattari's *Anti-Oedipus*, allows for the historicizing of psychoanalysis, a resistance to the view that psychoanalysis offers a final, absolute, and true schema for the interpretation of psychic life for all ages.[21] Foucault's account of how the discourses of sexology work permits a certain ironic distance on claims of interpretation based on psychoanalytic theory. So, for example, a reading of a Sappho poem that confirmed the tenets of Lacanian psychoanalysis would be problematized in a new way, as not only ahistorical but also as part of a mechanism of socialization in the present, one that seeks to produce and enact power over the ancient Greek object through the deployment of psychoanalytic knowledge, seeks to confirm the hegemony and universality and ahistorical truth-value of psychoanalysis as a discipline.

Foucault was exemplary in his inconsistency. He changed his mind with every book, with every new object of study. This has been a point of criticism for many, but in fact it can be seen as an inspiring paradigm of the Nietzschean individual unconcerned by appeals to absolute logic or some divine truth. At the end of his life Foucault was particularly interested in what the Greeks called *parrhēsia*, "free, frank speech," addressed to a social superior by someone powerless. He was interested in the ancient Cynics, and in particular in the figure of Diogenes. In his 1983 seminar at Berkeley, he lectured on Cynic *parrhēsia* and its various techniques:

> Cynic parrhesia in its scandalous aspects also utilized the practice of bringing together two rules of behavior which seem contradictory and remote from one another. For example, regarding the problem of bodily needs. You eat.

21. Gilles Deleuze and Felix Guattari, *Anti-Oedipus: Capitalism and Schizophrenia*, trans. Robert Hurley, Mark Seem, and Helen R. Lane (New York, 1977).

There is no scandal in eating, so you can eat in public. . . .
Since Diogenes ate in the agora, he thought that there was
no reason why he should not also masturbate in the agora;
for in both cases he was satisfying a bodily need (adding that
"he wished it were as easy to banish hunger by rubbing the
belly").[22]

Foucault himself took political stances not unlike those of the Cynics, always oppositional, temporary, engaged, often working collectively, moving from one stance to another without anguish and
without guilt, seeming to believe that his role as an intellectual
could be defined without reference to personal absolutes or some
principle that transcended historical, local situations. In some ways
he offers us the model of the postmodern intellectual, striving always to realize himself by carving out a career of multiple political
positions. He wrote at the beginning of the second volume of the
History of Sexuality:

The "essay"—which should be understood as the assay or
test by which, in the game of truth, one undergoes changes,
and not as the simplistic appropriation of others for the purpose of communication—is the living substance of philosophy, at least if we assume that philosophy is still what it was
in times past, i.e., an "ascesis," askesis, an exercise of oneself in
the activity of thought.[23]

These words of implicit self-criticism, characterizing a great turn
in his work, after a period of reflection and reorientation, demonstrate an admirable capacity for changes of mind.

How does this model of the cynical intellectual bear on a possible reading of Sappho? The example of Foucault, poststructuralist
Diogenes, leads me to rethink, shamelessly, things I once said and
to revise my views. Although at times he seems to have changed
his mind without notifying his devoted readers, at the end of his
life, in his work on ancient sexuality, he is modest, self-critical, and
at least rhetorically humble in claiming to know little about his

22. Michel Foucault, Discourse and Truth: The Problematization of Parrhesia: Notes to the
Seminar Given by Foucault at the University of California at Berkeley, 1983, ed. Joseph Pearson
(1985), 80.
23. Foucault, The Use of Pleasure, 9.

subject. Even though he retains a somewhat magisterial stance throughout his career, the lyrical, oracular tone of *Madness and Civilization* could not be more different from the modest, relatively affectless voice of the History of Sexuality.

This assessment of ways in which Foucault's thinking has enabled my own seems necessary because of my sense in recent years that his work has come under increasingly polemical attack, in the context of an unfortunate assault on theory in our time. One of the attackers suggests that we should not be reading French theory because the "frogs" groveled under the Nazi jackboot during the Second World War.[24] This sort of attack is of course easily dismissed, but such work can be read within a strain of American xenophobia and antiintellectualism that is seeking ascendance at the moment. We have the dismissal of Continental theory on many fronts. Paul DeMan was a Nazi sympathizer, Martin Heidegger a Nazi himself, Jacques Derrida a reader of Heidegger and friend of DeMan, and Michel Foucault a gay man interested in sadomasochism. Now I myself have been troubled by the Nazism of Heidegger, which I have written about, and I think it important to try to assess the ways in which Heidegger's political affiliations affected his intellectual labors.[25] But I don't think we should dismiss his work or, worse, not read it because of those affiliations. His work and life are part of the historical record, and people who work on the history of culture should be studying both.

To dismiss Foucault's work because of his sadomasochism, or his queer politics, or its theoretical difficulty, is an attitude that is highly suspect and needs to be interrogated. It is perhaps interesting to think about the life of Foucault and to see the connections

24. Camille Paglia, "Junk Bonds and Corporate Raiders: Academe in the Hour of the Wolf," reprinted from *Arion* (Spring 1991), in *Sex, Art, and American Culture: Essays* (New York, 1992), 170–248. For example: "By what retrograde lace-curtain shrinking from reality did our academics look to spinsterish French notions of the 'decentered subject'? Of *course* the French felt decentered: they'd just been crushed by Germany. American G.I.'s (including my uncles) got shot up rescuing France when she was lying flat on her face under the Nazi boot. Hence it is revolting to see pampered American academics down on their knees kissing French buns" (211). And: "He was a Herod without a Salome. . . . if what I have reliably heard about his public behavior after he knew he had AIDS is true, then Foucault would deserve the condemnation of every ethical person" (230).

25. Page duBois, *Torture and Truth* (New York and London, 1991), 127–47.

between that life and his historical and theoretical positions. But in his recent biography of Foucault, James Miller recounts the beginning of his engagement with the life of Foucault in a disturbing anecdote, leading me to conclude that theory-bashing can converge with gay-bashing in a deeply destructive way, which pragmatist, empiricist, antitheoretical common-sense Americans can take to heart with a vengeance.

> Miller says, in a postscript to his biography of Foucault: One evening in the spring of 1987, an old friend who teaches at a university in Boston, where I live, relayed a shocking piece of gossip: knowing that he was dying of AIDS, Michel Foucault in 1983 had gone to gay bathhouses in America, and deliberately tried to infect other people with the disease.

He asks himself, "What if the story were true?"

> In ways that were unfamiliar and therefore interesting to me, I began to think about the meaning of death and the human capacity for cruelty, about the tractable character of pain, and the possible implications of embodying an ethos of deliberate irresponsibility.[26]

That is to say, he begins his biography with the question of whether Foucault deliberately infected others with AIDS. He skirts around this issue with maddening indirection, citing Daniel Defert on the "limit-experience," and saying to himself in conclusion: "I now had to wonder whether the rumor that had gotten me started was closer to the truth than I had come to think possible."[27] The biography is structured around this question, as if Miller's project had been to construct a portrait of a man for whom this was a plausible narrative, a Nietzschean utterly without responsibility, committed to the "limit-experience." The question for Miller is not first of all what Foucault offers to the intellectual tradition of the West, but whether or not he was a Typhoid Mary, or a patient Zero, a carrier of infection. His is the most modest and generous version of a view that at its extremes is consistent with the right's violent, gay-bashing patriotism. Foucault is bringing a foreign vi-

---

26. Miller, *The Passion of Michel Foucault*, 375, 376, 377.
27. Ibid., 380.

rus into America. He infected good American boys not only with the deadly HIV virus, but also with the dangerous, boot-licking tendencies of post-'68 French theory, theories contaminated with Nazism, communism, and the dangerous effeminacies of Paris. Eve Kosofsky Sedgwick, in the *Epistemology of the Closet*, argues powerfully, as a gay-loving, gay-affirmative person, about the need to counter our culture's homophobia. She says:

> The number of persons or institutions by whom the existence of gay people—never mind the existence of *more gay people*— is treated as a precious desideratum, a needed condition of life, is small, even compared to those who may wish for the dignified treatment of any gay people who happen already to exist. Advice on how to make sure your kids turn out gay, not to mention your students, your parishioners, your therapy clients, or your military subordinates, is less ubiquitous than you might think.[28]

This is the last point—that as a gay person Foucault has been the target of antitheoretical, anti-French, that is, xenophobic criticism, that his work has become, in the eyes of some, suspect and dangerous because it too is infected with sadomasochism and the AIDS virus.

What I recall, for my own sake, about the life of Foucault, as a gay-loving, gay-affirmative person, is the example of many post-Stonewall gay people in America, who offered a new paradigm of sexuality, one perhaps never seen before in the history of the world. In San Francisco, New York, and other cities of the 1970s, an extraordinary sexual experiment took place, in which pleasure often broke loose from the paradigm of the conjugal couple, the bourgeois family, the asymmetrical dyad based on hierarchical heterosexuality. This was an extraordinary moment in the history of the West, new geographical and psychic territory inhabited by people who refused to capitulate to the modern ideal of the family, of Beaver Cleaver normality, of the demand that we all live our sexuality in the same way.

And to rewrite it now as immoral, irresponsible, dangerous be-

28. Eve Kosofsky Sedgwick, *Epistemology of the Closet* (Berkeley and Los Angeles, 1990), 42.

cause of AIDS, is to participate in the most banal of puritanical narratives about crime and punishment, is to affirm unquestioningly the internal policing, surveillance, and disciplining of bodies enacted in our culture. Part of the venom and jubilation about Foucault's death, part of the demonizing of theory and of his impact on American cultural studies, has to do with gay-bashing, with fear of infection, with xenophobia and the crudest sorts of antiintellectualism. So I will continue to look to Foucault as an exemplar a certain utopian model of eroticism.

I of course have my difficulties with the work of Foucault, difficulties I have discussed elsewhere.[29] In his earliest work, he seems to describe violent ruptures in the worldviews of early modern and modern culture, without any sense of unevenness in cultural formations, or of the remotest possibility of gradual change. The world was informed by the Renaissance *episteme*, then suddenly the classical. Foucault uses peculiar, eccentric, unrepresentative examples to prove immense generalizations. He speaks in an often arrogant, oracular tone, rarely interrogates his own power. He often leaves women out of his stories, or he takes for granted their object status, as he does in the *The Use of Pleasure*. He is never concerned about the causes of the phenomena he describes, never sees the economic or indeed any motor of change. It was rarely clear what politics followed from Foucault's example; he seemed determined not to offer an example, not to present principles, but to act always locally, atomistically although sometimes collectively, and at least temporarily, to be a cynic.

In the end, I am still a feminist and a Marxist. But I find myself determined by the work of Foucault much more than I am always willing to recognize, and moved by his example.

29. See, e.g., duBois, *Sowing the Body*, 2, 181, 189–91.

EIGHT

Asianism and the Theft of Enjoyment

Once upon a time we thought of cultures as homogeneous, coherent entities, with shared ideologies about all things. We talked about the Renaissance worldview, about Dogon views of nature and culture, even about people we confidently called "the Greeks." But things have changed, in part because of the political struggles that have defined recent history in North America. We acknowledge not only that the "American way of life" includes fissures of gender, class and ethnicity, but that these fissures have fissures of their own, that to speak of "women," for example, is to erase much difference, differences of regionalism, class, ethnicity, sexual preference. Various sorts of Americans, and of course others around the world, have fought for recognition of multiplicity—people of color, Lesbians and gay people, women. And Americans' understanding of their culture as a whole has come to accommodate a recognition of complexity, contestation, and real difference that has affected the way historians do their work as well. Social historians have subverted the traditional historical project, looking at realms of existence once ignored by diplomatic, military, or intellectual history, kinds of history that, obliterating difference, focused on representative great men or spoke only of world-historical events. We now read about women's history, working-class history, the history of everyday life, about the illiterate and

This chapter had its origin in a paper written for a conference on rhetoric at the University of Tennessee.

the obscure, and about the workings of power and sexuality in producing cultural difference.

The field of classical studies has long been slow to respond to the changes in the wider world. It has often prided itself on holding a certain line against the tides of trendiness, or of maintaining an oasis in the midst of wholesale surrender to contemporary concerns. Some within the field conceive their mission as the maintenance of standards of objectivity and historical science in the face of a mounting demand for relevance, for engagement in the social concerns of the present. Some classicists are reluctant to recognize the historicity of their own methodology, which is not itself without ideological dimensions. For many it is in fact an Anglo-Teutonic empiricism, motivated by a desire to emulate the verifiability of the physical sciences in this founding field of the humanities; scholars confident in such methods, I believe, often don't recognize that the position they assume in relation to their data does make ideological assumptions, does choose a type of interpretation against other types.[1] It is not the absolute and final truth of the text that philology, for example, produces, but a certain reading of the text, one that focuses on correctness, on legibility, on fidelity to the earliest text—a reading that often readily and infinitely defers interpretation because the text can never be established absolutely, surely, satisfactorily, must always be labored over further. Of course we all depend on philological work; we need it to read at all the texts of fragmentary poets like Sappho, for example. But philology itself is not enough, and its arrogance in relation to efforts of interpretation, what it regards as scandalous speculation, is regrettable. It might be argued that this representation of certain tendencies in the field of classical studies falls prey to exactly the sort of assumption I was damning earlier, insofar as it treats the discipline as monolithic, without internal contradiction. It is true of course that there are countercurrents in classical

---

1. See, e.g., the hilarious essay by Steve Nimis, "Fussnoten: das Fundament der Wissenschaft," *Arethusa* 17 (1984): 105–34. See also Martin Bernal's crucial work on the foundation of the discipline of classics in *Black Athena: The Afroasiatic Roots of Classical Civilization*, vol. 1: *The Fabrication of Ancient Greece, 1785–1985* (New Brunswick, N.J., 1987).

studies: investigations of women's history and of sexuality in particular. Nonetheless, there seems to be a lag in the discipline in relation to other fields in the humanities. Even the most advanced, progressive and exciting work in the field has until very recently been informed by the methodological paradigms of structuralism, perhaps with some poststructuralism sprinkled in, without much recognition of the work of Michel Foucault in the study of power and sexuality, and with almost no recognition of new work on the internally contradictory, contestatory, and heterogeneous nature of most cultures.

Classical historians have been more ready than philologists to see the periods they study as marked by internal difference. Although our picture of the classical *polis* remains relatively unaffected by currents of intellectual change in the wider world, such an important book as Josiah Ober's *Mass and Elite in Democratic Athens* allows us to see the project of fifth-century orators as the production of consensus, an ambition that must take for granted differences to be overcome if the city is to understand itself as a whole. Equally significant, however, is recent study of such a strikingly heterogeneous entity as Hellenistic culture.[2] While it may be possible to accept the Athenians' ideological representation of themselves as homogeneous, autochthonous sons of Ion, the cultural diversity of the Hellenistic city of Alexandria is unmistakable. In fact, among students of Greek culture, it has often been the case that only the classical age of Athens appeals; studies have focused on rhetoric, on the Athenian legal system, on Athenian tragedy, as if other sites of Hellenic culture did not exist, as if Alexandria, for example, precisely because of its contamination by other peoples, other geographies, were not really Greek, need not figure in one's education and research about the ancient Greek world. Such historians as Sarah Pomeroy have long been trying to call classicists' attention to the richness of evidence about everyday life available from papyrus fragments of ancient Hellenic Egypt, but there has been a distinct parochialism in Hellenists' view of this perhaps dangerously non-Hellenic outpost of Hellenic civilization, even

---

2. See, e.g., *Images and Ideologies: Self-Definition in the Hellenistic World*, ed. Anthony W. Bulloch, Erich S. Gruen, A. A. Long, and Andrew Stewart (Berkeley and Los Angeles, 1993).

though its scholars mediated, sometimes ruthlessly, our own access to pure Attic thought.[3] Alexandria was a vast megalopolis, with a polyglot population of Greeks, Egyptians, Syrians, and Jews, and many of these different peoples maintained social, political forms and institutions that were never remotely assimilated into anything resembling a classical polis. Yet Alexandria was a Greek city, of Macedonian-Greek foundation, the first and largest city of the Hellenistic world, far more important culturally in some terms than Athens, Pergamum, or Antioch.

Martin Bernal's work in Black Athena has had significant impact on classical studies.[4] He has pointed out first of all that the discipline was constituted as an intervention in a highly charged field in the eighteenth and nineteenth centuries. It staked out a claim, in an atmosphere of anxiety about origins, for the Aryan beginnings of Western civilization and supported, in his view, an erasure of the African and Semitic roots of much that Enlightenment culture held dear. The discipline of classics thus constituted itself through a position on questions of racial purity, looking backward at the Greeks as our purely Aryan, miraculously alphabetic and philosophical and democratic ancestors. This part of Bernal's work seems especially valuable to me, in that it poses for students of the classical world the necessity to interrogate their discipline, its formation, and the unexamined assumptions that form its unconscious.

But there is a further, much more ambitious aim in Bernal's work, one I am less qualified to evaluate, concerning the actual, true historical origins of classical civilization, one that attempts to rectify the eugenicist rewriting of ancient history in the eighteenth and nineteenth centuries. Bernal claims not only that what was to become Greece, or the miscellany of ancient city-states that came to see itself provisionally and intermittently as the Hellenes, came into contact with Egyptian and Semitic cultures throughout their

---

3. See Sarah B. Pomeroy, Women in Hellenistic Egypt from Alexander to Cleopatra (New York, 1984).

4. Martin Bernal, Black Athena: The Afroasiatic Roots of Classical Civilization, vol. 1, The Fabrication of Ancient Greece, 1785–1985 (New Brunswick, N.J., 1987), and vol. 2, The Archaeological and Documentary Evidence (New Brunswick, N.J., 1991). On classicists' response to Bernal, see, e.g., the special issue of Arethusa devoted to the first volume, "The Challenge of Black Athena," Arethusa 22 (1989).

history, but that the influence was earlier and more profound than some scholars have recognized.[5] Bernal contends, for example, that the Egyptians colonized Greece in remote antiquity, and that we, heirs of the Athenians, are also descended culturally from Egyptian ancestors. We must wait for the archaeologists and linguists to sort out the value of Bernal's hypothesis, but I admire his willingness boldly to rewrite all of ancient history, to make speculative leaps, valuing ancient evidence against the grain of received wisdoms. What his work does for me at this point in my own argument is to strengthen my sense that we have paid too little attention to difference, diversity, and heterogeneity in the ancient world, and that our view of poetry, rhetoric, and literary texts, as well as all other phenomena and institutions of antiquity, must change in light of his and others' critical eye on this and all other political and social communities.

We might look at rhetoric, for example, as an institution, through the lens of difference. It has been easiest to see rhetoric as an institution with its own history, one linked in unspecified ways to the evolution of the city-state, empire, and nation, but without focusing on it as part of culture as a whole, as internally divided and as a terrain of cultural struggle. We have seen it as an instrument of argument, as a tool enabling opponents in a law court, for example, or in a political debate, to state their views, persuade, and conquer. It has been easy to personify rhetoric, to see it developing almost anthropomorphically, emerging from infancy, stretching its limbs, blooming eventually into arthritic, formulaic atrophy.

I will look at just one issue in the history of rhetoric before considering one of the fragments of Sappho in relation to that history, in order to try to think about rhetoric both as a contested field and as a language in which social conflicts are being staged, contested, negotiated, and managed. If we see rhetoric as an agent of social negotiation, and rhetorical discourse, that is meta-rhetoric, discourse about rhetoric, as itself bearing social-historical weight, then rhetoric can no longer be treated as an autonomous intellectual domain, with a completely separate decline and fall. It

5. Some ancient historians have taken account of these relations; see, e.g., Oswyn Murray, *Early Greece* (Stanford, Calif., 1983), 72–73.

is working in culture, doing cultural labor, providing pleasures, reinforcing and negotiating relations of power.

I return to the old debate concerning Asiatic and Attic styles in part because this opposition illuminates the position of Sappho the poet in relation to a Western, European, Atticizing tradition. The rhetorical theorists in ancient Rome, meta-rhetoricians, more often than not, when distinguishing between Attic and Asian styles, deprecate the Asian, associating it with luxury and effeminacy, just as Vergil implies the threat Dido represents to Aeneas by portraying Aeneas dressed in luxurious, Asianizing clothing in book 4 of the *Aeneid*. Asianism is diseased, contaminating, effeminate, and slavish, while Atticism is sound, virile, bracing and masterful. Tacitus associates Attic style with political liberty in his *Dialogues on Orators* (c. 100 C.E.); the aristocratic nostalgia for classical Athenian democracy is a constant feature of Roman imperial rhetorical theory, even though it frequently accompanies contempt for contemporary, vanquished Greeks. The Romans characterized the Athenians of the classical age as proto-Roman aristocrats, in their denunciations of imperial luxury and impotence; the classical Athenians exemplified all that had been lost by the time of empire. Classical Athenians were seen as spare, austere, manly, philosophically virtuous and virginal like the goddess Athena.

Let me begin by citing two passages from ancient writers on rhetoric. The first comes from Dionysius of Halicarnassus, a Greek writer who arrived in Rome around 30 B.C.E., and who shared Roman Augustan views in the following observations about the corrupting power of what he deems "nonphilosophical" rhetoric, rhetoric associated with "the East":

> Unnoticed and undetected by the ignorant vulgar, this rhetoric not only enjoyed an abundance, luxury, and elegance unknown to its predecessor, but attached to itself the honours and political supremacies which belonged by right to its philosophical sister. With its crudeness and vulgarity, it ended by making Greece like the household of some desperate roué, where the decent, respectable wife sits powerless in her home, while some nitwit of a girl, there only to ruin the property, thinks she has a right to rule the roost, and bullies the wife and treats her like dirt. Just so, in every city,

even—worst of all—in the highly cultivated, the old, native Attic muse was in disgrace, cast out from her inheritance, while another, sprung from some Asian sewer the other day—some Mysian or Phrygian or, God help us, Carian plague—claimed the right to govern the cities of Hellas, and, in her ignorance and madness, to drive out her sane philosophical rival.

. . . This generation has restored to the old, respectable rhetoric her just honour. . . . Apart from some few cities in Asia, where ignorance makes good learning slow to penetrate, the liking for the vulgar, frigid, and tasteless in literature has ceased. Those who formerly took pride in such things are becoming ashamed and gradually deserting to the other side. . . .

The cause and beginning of this great change lies in Rome. The mistress of the world makes all other cities look to her.[6]

There is much to remark on here. The virtuous Attic philosophy is compared to the virtuous Attic wife, while the new rhetoric is a slut. Not only a slut, but an Asian slut. And all of Hellenic rhetoric has been contaminated by this creature from the sewer. The bad rhetoric is associated with the East and with the eroticized and promiscuous female. Dionysius looks for salvation to the West, to Rome—Halicarnassus fell into Roman hands in 129 B.C.E.— Rome, whose transforming effect on the world is happily described as a "penetration." As a Greek, Dionysius exhibits an unfortunate identification with his Roman oppressor, even as he strives to celebrate the revival of Attic style. As a Greek of Asia Minor, he might be expected to have been contaminated with the Asian virus, being himself a Carian, but like Herodotos of Halicarnassus before him, although perhaps more of an ironist, he believes himself an Athenian at heart. Dionysius is writing at the very moment of Augustus' consolidation of power; the empire thrives, pushing out its borders even further, incorporating new populations, and rhetoric is invigorated, made potent, as Rome swells.

In later periods, identification with the proud masculinized goddess Athena, figure for Attic rhetoric and for a potent Rome,

6. Dionysius of Halicarnassus, *De antiquis oratoribus*, preface, 5.306.

gives way to anxiety about the polluting effeminacy of Asianizing rhetoric, encountered outside, uncovered within. Difference
among women, the difference between the Athenian virgin and the
Carian girl, becomes difference discovered within, within the masculine state, within the male citizen; differences become threaten-
ingly fluid. This second passage comes from Quintilian, a rhetorician of the first century C.E. Quintilian shares Dionysius' concerns
about the dangerous effects of Asiatic contamination. And he discovers a disturbing effeminacy of bad rhetoric, which he compares
to the effeminacy of decadent Roman youth:

> The Attic people, smooth and correct, would put up with
> nothing empty or redundant, while the Asians, in general a
> more bombastic and boastful race, puffed themselves out
> with vainglory in oratory also.
>
> Healthy bodies, sound of blood and strengthened by
> exercise, get their beauty from the same source as their
> strength—for they are of good complexion, spare, muscles
> showing. But suppose these bodies were to be plucked and
> rouged and effeminately prinked; they would become hide-
> ous just because of the trouble taken to make them beautiful.
> Legitimate and splendid dress gives a man authority . . . ; but
> when it is womanish and luxurious it does not beautify the
> body—it lays bare the mind. In the same way, the diapha-
> nous and multi-coloured way of expression that some affect
> takes the manhood from the matter which they clothe in
> such verbal costume.[7]

The good rhetoric is phallic—spare, unadorned, masculine; the
bad, Asiatic rhetoric is womanish and puffed up.

The complex dialectic of positions is instructive. Dionysius the
Greek tries to "abject" his own Hellenism, writing in Greek and
praising Roman potency, Roman Atticism. Quintilian names Asiatic weakness and finds it horribly visible among the youths of his
own society. As both cases show, rhetorical theory desires to
found itself on opposition, to use gender and ethnic, geographical
markers, as well as generational ones, to mark itself off from what
precedes, and to claim that its new perfected style restores a lost

7. Quintilian, *Institutio oratoria* 8, preface, 19–21 (375); and 12.10.16–17 (407).

perfection. The apparent disquiet, even anxiety, about contamination, gives passion to the debate concerning language and style. In Rome, a sense of imperial mission sustains these claims of the restoration of virginity and austerity. The empire is consuming new peoples, but fears poisoning of its own body. The conquered, defined as weak by virtue of conquest, and therefore slavish and feminine, are entering the privileged, patriarchal space of greater Rome. At the very moment when territory is being expanded and new colonies incorporated, old frontiers must be defended against incursion. When barbarian populations with strange tongues, strange habits, threaten to produce the dissolution of the ancient ways, the rhetorical body is seen as in danger of effeminacy and contamination, as in need of a purge, of the erection of discrete boundaries.

In this Roman tradition, such vigilance toward sexual activity is dispersed through the body politic. Michel Foucault, in his work on this period, *The Care of the Self*, discusses a new intensity about the body, the practices elaborated in a concern for the preservation of corporeal health. He recalls Galen, who

> recommends a doubly cathartic cure to one of his friends who has given up sexual activity but finds that he is in a state of constant excitation. Galen advises him first to relieve himself physically by excreting the accumulated semen; then— once the body is purified—to let nothing enter the mind that might deposit images there: "to refrain completely from spectacles, not to tell stories or recall memories which could stimulate his sexual desire."[8]

Foucault describes the new regimes of vigilance toward sexual activity almost exclusively in terms of the individual and without attention to Galen's rhetoric of the spectacle. In fact, as we have seen, the relationship between the boundaries of empire and between the individual, rhetorical, and imperial bodies allows a social reading of the predominant fears of contamination by excess sexual desire, effeminacy, and Asiatic corruption.

The Roman debates on rhetoric were reinscribed in seven-

8. Michel Foucault, *The Care of the Self*, vol. 3 of the History of Sexuality, trans. Robert Hurley (New York, 1986), 136–37.

teenth-century England, another moment of expanding empire. We find similar rhetorical categories reproduced and to some extent reinterpreted. The Renaissance reinscription involves a coding of earlier styles in English as Asianizing and feminized. The ancients' rejection of certain styles as Asiatic and effeminate formed the basis for arguments that a new perfected rhetoric must and would emerge from a contaminated feminine origin, tainted with Ciceronian Asianisms and voluptuous Euphuism. The Roman rhetoricians' condemnation of effeminate, degenerate, pleasurable style is read into the transfer of power from Elizabeth to James. Richard Flecknoe describes the historical narrative concerning style in this way:

> That of Queen Elizabeths dayes, *flaunting* and *pufted* like her Apparell: That of King *Jame's*, *Regis ad exemplum*, inclining much to the *Learned* and *Erudite*. . . .[9]

The learned Francis Bacon, rhetorician, proto-scientist, and servant of the Jacobean state, in his rhetorical works contrasts the more Asiatic Ciceronian style with the Senecan by calling the former "spread and dilated." He is often anti-Ciceronian, admiring the styles of Seneca and Tacitus, those defenders of republican Rome, a lost paradise, and the even further removed Athenian democracy that produced Atticism. He deprecates what he calls "concinnity," from the Latin *concinnitas*, "elegance," a noted feature of the Ciceronian style, as *non ornamentum virile*, not a manly ornament of style. Bacon says in the preface to *De Augmentis*, addressed to King James, that he prefers a manner of delivery that is "active and masculine, without digressing or dilating." The adjectives he used to describe Ciceronianism and Euphuism are "round" and "sweet." Bad stylists are accused of "delicacies and affectations"; they follow the Asiatic Adonis rather than Hercules.[10] Although Bacon condemns the excesses of the plain style, practiced by extreme followers of Seneca, who break knowledge into "sticks," his sympathies often lie with the Atticizing "philosophical style."

---

9. Richard Flecknoe, *Miscellania* (London, 1653), 77, cited by George Williamson in "Pointed Style after Bacon," in *The Senecan Amble* (Chicago, 1966), 211.

10. Francis Bacon, *Of the Advancement of Learning* 4.4, ed. W. A. Wright (Oxford, 1920), 31.

As Morris Croll put it at the beginning of the twentieth century, "Bacon's great service to English prose was that he naturalized a style in which ingenious obscurity and acute significance are the appropriate garb of the mysteries of empire."[11] Although scholars have differed concerning Croll's description of Bacon's style, it seems to me most valuable in pointing to the *social meaning* of the reform of style. The burden of empire stimulates concern about internalized effeminacy, which is first recognized in the moment of expansion; as the imperialist rhetorician looks outward, he sees that which must be purged from within. Heirs and symbolic descendants of a female prince, ruled by a king with male favorites, rhetoricians of the early seventeenth century in England make their own the meta-rhetorical discourses of Rome. In the service of a new empire, a rhetoric is forged that casts off the effeminacy of the past, that combines accuracy with persuasiveness without indulging in "pufted" ornament.

So we return to my earlier proposition. It would be possible to trace the history of this figure, the rise of Asianism, its naming, its cultivation, its ramifications and turns, its loss and reinscription in the rhetoric of the Renaissance. I would like however to see what it is doing in the first century, and then how a poet like Sappho lies somewhere at the beginnings of this tradition, Asianizing and effeminate herself. In this case I am concerned less with the rhetoric of these passages, more with the way in which rhetorical discourse, discourse about rhetoric, functions within a social text.

The work of the Slovenian philosopher Slavoj Žižek illuminates how discourse about Asianism functions in the immensely complex social, economic, and cultural worlds of the Roman empire. Žižek, writing about contemporary Eastern Europe, including his own country, the former Yugoslavia, uses Hegelian and Lacanian theory to account for the rise of nationalism in formerly socialist countries. In so doing, he points to the psychic roots of xenophobia. He argues first of all that nationalism is produced when a

11. Morris Croll, "Attic Prose: Lipsius, Montaigne, Bacon," in *"Attic" and Baroque Prose Style: The Anti-Ciceronian Movement* (Princeton, N.J., 1969), 195. On Bacon, see Page duBois, "Subjected Bodies, Science and the State: Francis Bacon, Torturer," in *Politics and Culture I, Body Politics—Disease, Desire and the Family,* ed. Michael Ryan (Minneapolis, 1994).

people attributes to another a "theft of enjoyment" that is right-fully their own.

> We always impute to the other an excessive enjoyment; s/he wants to steal our enjoyment (by ruining our way of life) and/or has access to some secret, perverse enjoyment.[12]

The paradoxical nature of such xenophobia, or racism, or hatred of the other, is that somehow national identity, our "Thing," as Žižek calls it, is both inaccessible to the other, who could never know what it was to be authentically a member of our community, and at the same time absolutely threatened by the others' enjoyment. Žižek mentions as examples the alleged excessive enjoyment of black people, of Jews; he calls up the example of the Japanese, who have assumed for Americans the status of "other" once held by Russian communists.[13] The American media represent the Japanese as incapable of enjoying themselves; their economic superiority is due to the fact that they don't consume enough, that they assemble too much wealth and take an improper enjoyment in that wealth.

If we look closely at the logic of this accusation, it is clear that what American "spontaneous" ideology really reproaches the Japanese for is not simply their inability to take pleasure, but the fact that their very relationship between work and enjoyment is strangely distorted. *It is as if they find enjoyment in their excessive renunciation of pleasure*, in their zeal, in their inability to "take it easy," to relax and enjoy; and it is this attitude that is perceived as a threat to American supremacy.[14]

The Roman rhetorical writers' descriptions of Asianism exhibit features of this same dynamic. The organization of enjoyment of both Asian rhetoricians and of their audiences is flawed, and dangerous. Not only do they enjoy excessively, but they are stealing Roman enjoyment by ruining the Roman way of life and demonstrating access to some "secret, perverse enjoyment." These crea-

---

12. Slavoj Žižek, "Eastern Europe's Republics of Gilead," *New Left Review* 183 (1990): 54.

13. For another view on the other inside, also inflected by psychoanalytic theory, see Julia Kristeva, *Strangers to Ourselves*, trans. Leon Roudiez (New York, 1991).

14. Žižek, "Eastern Europe," 56.

tures, like the whore from the Carian sewer, take pleasure in unspeakable acts that fascinate and horrify the ideologue of Roman or Atticizing rhetoric. The very fact, of course, that the good rhetoric, the faithful wife of Rome, is really the faithful wife of Athens, already a bit too far East, contaminated with association with Asia by definition, suggests some displacement, some anxiety at the heart of the denunciation.

And in fact Žižek discusses a further feature of nationalism that casts light on how rhetorical discourse works in the context of empire. He points out that the hatred of the enjoyment of the other is always really hatred of one's own enjoyment. Roman writers, even especially these writers, are already Asian, effeminate, are fearful of the other inside, the actor, the transvestite, the performing whore. Žižek says:

> The fascinating image of the Other personifies our own innermost split—what is already "in us more than ourselves"—and thus prevents us from achieving full identity with ourselves. *The hatred of the other is the hatred of our own excess of enjoyment.*[15]

Although I recognize the dangers of applying wholesale a Hegelian-Lacanian-Slovenian theoretical schema to these phenomena of antiquity, I see affinities between the xenophobia described by Žižek, anti-Semitism, racism, homophobia, sexism in our culture and in the cosmopolitan atmosphere of ancient Rome, and contemporary philologists' fear of the erotic pleasure represented in the female Sappho's work. Žižek's work allows one to discern the fear at the heart of the rhetorical passages I read above, the fear that within the Roman self, the Stoic, resolute, military self, there is always already rhetoric, that is, something effeminate, pleasurable, degenerate, something that must be abjected, projected unto others, onto the Asianists, the Asians, the Carian whores, even the virtuous Athenian wives, if the Roman way of life in its perfection is to be preserved.

What is most remarkable about the anti-Asianist discourse is that it allows us to see the original instability of any discourse about rhetoric. Just as there is debate about the founding moment

15. Ibid., 57.

of rhetoric, about its temporal origin, so there is debate about its spatial point of origin, its geographical beginnings. And Roman rhetoric is not Roman, it is Attic. And Attic rhetoric is not Greek; it is Italian, or Sicilian.[16] Rhetoric is said to have been invented by Homer, an Asian Greek, or by the Sicilians Corax and Tisias, from Syracuse, or by Gorgias, from Leontini in Southern Italy. There is no stable point of origin, certainly no Attic origin, no moment at which rhetoric begins; it is always and already contaminated, foreign, unstable, loose, and already inside the body politic, which can never abject it, can never succeed in seeing it only outside.

The meta-rhetorical passages I cited above are doing social work. They contribute to xenophobia, to the constitution of proper Englishness and *Romanitas* through the castigation and rejection of others who enjoy themselves otherwise, improperly. The Romanized, Atticized rhetoricians attempt to disguise but nonetheless betray the uneasy status of rhetoric, the anxious posture of the rhetorician who fears effeminacy and dangerous, creeping degeneracy. We need to look not just at the ways in which rhetoric operates in the history of social relations but also at the ways in which meta-rhetorical discourses do cultural work in our own social field, in the disciplines we practice and reproduce. We might consider such questions as why classical studies, and especially philology and epigraphy, are coded as British, Teutonic, and manly. Rhetorical studies mediate between this hard historical field and another, constituted differently, a sort of subjugated, instrumentalizing pedagogy, composition studies that are ideologically feminized, within universities rendered equivalent to nursing or child care, coded as "women's work."

What has all this to do with Sappho? First of all it is possible to discern in the work of Sappho a kind of luxuriousness that is already foreign, *avant la lettre,* to pure Atticism, to the cold clear light of classical prose and poetry. The pure and tragic utterances of Sophocles' characters, the logic of Demosthenes' periods, models for rhetorical perfection in later days, epitomize the Greek style

16. See Vincent Farenga, "Violent Structure: The Writing of Pindar's *Olympian* 1," *Arethusa* 10 (1977): 197–218.

for those who follow. The interested representation of Atticism, which survives to our own day not only in the conservatism of Bloom and Bennett but also in the History of Sexuality of Michel Foucault, fails to recognize the stained voluptuosity of Aeschylean choral odes, the erotic play in Hellenistic verse, as authentically Greek. But already, at the origins of Greek literary history, we find Sappho, who disturbs the paradigm of classical order by offering another kind of pleasure. In fragment 81, taken from Athenaeus' *Deipnosophistai* and supplemented by a papyrus fragment, we find a characteristically Sapphic celebration of luxury and decoration that upsets the paradigmatic forms of Atticism, even of Pindaric high-mindedness, at the very beginnings of the poetic tradition:

> . . . reject . . . (as quickly as possible) . . . and you, Dica, put lovely garlands around your locks, binding together stems of anise with your soft hands; for the blessed Graces look rather on what is adorned with flowers and turn away from the ungarlanded.[17]

The ungarlanded, *astephanōtoisi*, are not pleasing to the gods. We might read this brief fragment, cited by Athenaeus apropos of the wearing of garlands, as a poetics. Sappho writes, and prefers, a style of writing that rejoices in the flowery, in the adorned, as opposed to a more austere, decorous, restrained style, of the sort that was praised and imitated in the works of the great Attic orators, by their Roman and early modern descendants.

This stylistic choice is evidence in many poems among Sappho's works, most of which have been lost, perhaps indeed because of their aesthetic, which contradicts the principles of "the classical" in the view of the many editors who pass along the tradition to us.[18] Among the fragments exhibiting a nonclassical aesthetic is fragment 94, discussed earlier in this book, in which Sappho speaks of the adornment of her friends, lovers, companions, in diction and poetic form that imitate the flowery atmosphere established by her words:

17. David A. Campbell, *Greek Lyric I: Sappho and Alcaeus* (Cambridge, Mass., and London, 1982).

18. See W. R. Johnson, *The Idea of Lyric: Lyric Modes in Ancient and Modern Poetry* (Berkeley, 1982).

> You put on many wreaths of violets and roses and
>   (crocuses?)
> together by my side, and round your tender neck you put
>   many
> woven garlands made from flowers and . . .
> with much flowery perfume fit for a queen, you anointed
>   yourself . . .

The words in Greek twine around each other, adjective modifying noun in such a way as to imitate the braiding of flowers, words plaited and wound together, creating a poem that is itself a garland, a crown for the recipient, for the reader.

Stobaeus, in his anthology, writing of "folly," cites Sappho in a fragment number 55; she is probably engaging in invective against a rival:

> But when you die you will lie there, and afterwards there
> will never be any recollection of you or any longing for you
> since you have no share in the roses of Pieria; unseen in the
> house of Hades also, flown from our midst, you will go to
> and fro among the shadowy corpses.[19]

Pieria, birthplace of the Muses, offers its roses, roses that appear in the crowns adorning the lovers of fragment 94. It may seem facile or inappropriate to equate Sappho's naming of roses and other flowers with what is now called a "flowery" style, but in fact the appearance of roses, crocuses, honey-lotuses, chervil, anise, and violets in Sappho's lines bespeak her love of luxury, her pleasure in proliferating, lush multiplicitous detail; her language is flowery in both senses of the term, denoting flowers, and furthermore suggesting richness, not austerity, pleasure, not profit.

I cite one more poem recalling the adornment of the body of the woman, exhibiting an aesthetic far from that imagined by the stern critics of Roman luxury, and the ascetic philosophical tradition dear to Plato and to Michel Foucault:

> For my mother (once said that) in her youth, if someone had
> her locks bound in a purple (headband), that was indeed a
> great adornment; but for the girl who has hair that is yellower

---

19. Stobaens 3.14.12 (iii 221 S. Wachsmuth-Hense).

than a torch (it is better to decorate it) with wreaths of flowers in bloom. Recently . . . a decorated headband from
Sardis . . . (Ionian?) cities . . .[20]

Such lines are exactly the sort of thing that have led severe classicists to condemn Sappho for triviality. A. R. Burn, author of *The
Lyric Age of Greece*, for example, notes that Sappho's poetry does not
"travel." Sappho's interest in feminine beauty, in the adorning and
enrichment of feminine beauty, in clothing and flowers and perfumes and items of luxury betrays, in their view, an ignorance or
lack of interest in higher matters of state and exemplifies the feminine character through the ages. In Sappho's case such themes are
addressed in poetry of great and controlled beauty; she uses the
case endings of her dialect with skill and delicacy, embroidering
stanzas in which adjectival and nominal word-endings echo and
interplay with each other to superb effect, creating a tapestry or
mosaic of densely concentrated effects.

Fragment 98 stands as a particularly rich example of Sappho's
"Asianism." It suggests the ways in which the conventional map of
Greek poetry must be re-drawn, in which Atticism itself must be
re-oriented. If we tend to see Athens, Athenian tragedy, Athenian
prose, as the foundation of Western civilization, the work of such
writers as M. L. West and Martin Bernal are reconfiguring the ancient world, forcing a new cartography of antiquity that takes account of the Greeks' situation in the eastern Mediterranean, bor-
dering on the Persian Empire, on the ancient Middle East, on
Egypt, on ancient North Africa.[21] Although many classicists, especially those who work on Homer, the Archaic Age, and the ancient historians and philosophers, have long stressed the interrela-
tions of the Greeks and their neighbors, the dependence of Greek
thinking and social relations on models presented to them by
nearby, highly evolved civilizations, it has taken longer for this
understanding to be incorporated into the broader culture's vision
of the Greeks.

It seems particularly important to understand how Sappho, resident of Mytilene, on the island of Lesbos, is closer to Asia in many

20. Campbell, *Greek Lyric* I, fr. 98.
21. See, e.g., in addition to Bernal's *Black Athena*, Hesiod, *Theogony*, ed. with commentary by M. L. West (Oxford, 1966).

ways than she is to Attica. Not just geographically, although of
course the proximity of Lydia and Sardis, the presence of the
Lydian empire, of the Persians nearby, affected the Lesbians' sense
of their Greekness, their belonging to a wider Hellenic community, their participation in such pan-Hellenic rituals, ceremonies,
gatherings as the Olympic games, the worship of Apollo at distant
Delphi. Their distance from these sites of common devotion may
have created a strong sense of Greek identity, of their shared linguistic bonds with mainland Greece, of a common heritage in the
poems of Homer, in the legends of gods and heroes.

Also crucial, however, was their sense of vulnerability as well as
attraction to the huge empires that bounded them. From the end
of the eight century, the kingdom of Lydia became a powerful
neighboring presence.[22] During his reign, from about 687 to 652,
the Lydian Gyges threatened the Greek cities of Asia Minor. In
more pacific periods, Greeks began trading with the city of Sardis.
In the sixth century the settlements of Asiatic Greeks lost their
independence to the expanding Lydian state, their cities made subject to the ruler in Sardis. And later, when Lydia succumbed in 546,
these same cities fell under the domination of the Persians; it was
their resistance to Persian domination that led eventually to the
wars between the Persians and the Greeks at the beginning of the
fifth century. Psammetichus I (663–609), ruler of Egypt, used mer-
cenary troops from Ionia and Caria in his army and founded settlements for these soldiers in Egypt. Naucratis, a trading settlement
at the Nile delta, was founded by Milesians about 610, and the
settlement became a center for the importation of Greek ceramic
ware. The later Egyptian ruler Amasis (569–526) was particularly
well-disposed to the Greeks, as Herodotos recounts:

> Amasis favoured the Greeks and granted them a number of
> privileges, of which the chief was the gift of Naucratis as a
> commercial headquarters for any who wished to settle in the
> country. He also made grants of land upon which Greek
> traders, who did not want to live permanently in Egypt,
> might erect altars and temples. Of these latter the best

22. Jeffery notes the existence of "cheap barbarian slave-labour" on Lesbos and the
geographical setting of Mitylene, facing east to Asia and the Troad. L. H. Jeffery, Archaic Greece: The City-States, c. 700–500 b.c. (New York, 1976), 240.

known and most used—and also the largest—is the Hellen-
ium; it was built by the joint efforts of the Ionians . . . of the
Dorians . . . and of the Aeolians of Mytilene.[23]

The links between the Greeks of Asia Minor and Egypt were particularly strong in this period, and Sappho's brother was reported
to have engaged in trade with the Egyptians, as Herodotos tells us.
He describes a pyramid said to have been built by the Egyptian
ruler Mycerinus, son of Cheops, predecessor of Psammetichus and
Amasis, and implicates Sappho herself in its story:

> There are people in Greece who say that this pyramid was
> erected by the courtesan Rhodopis. They are quite wrong,
> and I do not think they even know who Rhodopis was. . . .
> She was by birth a Thracian, the slave of Iadmon, son of
> Hephaestopolis of Samos, and fellow-slave of Aesop the
> fable-writer. . . .
>   She was brought to Egypt by Xanthus the Samian, to fol-
> low her trade, and Charaxus of Mytilene, son of Scam-
> andronymus and brother of Sappho the poetess, paid a large
> sum to redeem her from slavery. Having in this way obtained
> her freedom, she remained in Egypt and succeeded by her
> great beauty in amassing a fortune which—for her—was a
> considerable one, but certainly not sufficient for building a
> pyramid. There is no sense in pretending she was excessively
> rich, for the tenth part of her property can be seen to-day by
> anyone who cares to go and look at it: for wishing to be
> remembered in Greece by some sort of temple-offering such
> as nobody had ever thought of before, she spent a tenth of
> her money on as many iron roasting-spits as it would buy,
> and sent them to Delphi. They still lie in a heap behind the
> altar which the Chians dedicated, opposite the actual shrine.
> The prostitutes of Naucratis seem to be particularly attrac-
> tive. . . . When Charaxus returned to Mytilene after purchas-
> ing Rhodopis' freedom, he was ridiculed by Sappho in one
> of her poems.[24]

23. Herodotus, *The Histories*, trans. Aubrey de Selincourt, rev. A. R. Burn (Harmondsworth, England, 1972), 2.178.
    24. Ibid., 2.133–37.

This anecdote, possibly constructed by Herodotos from poems attributed to Sappho of which only fragments remain, suggests not only that someone of notoriety in Egypt would desire to be known and recognized for her wealth back in mainland Greece, in the pan-Hellenic shrine of Delphi, but also that the ties between the eastern Greeks, especially the Lesbians, with Egypt, were quite strong.[25]

And Sappho enters the text of Herodotos, implicated in this eastern Aegean network of commerce and aphrodisiac expenditure, figured as the chastiser of her besotted brother. Their father's name, Scamandronymus, contains the name of the river Scamander, near Troy, and may reflect Asian origins or a military success of an ancestor in Asia. Fragments 5 and 15b tell another story; Sappho wishes for the release of her brother from enslavement to a prostitute, called by her Doricha; the poem's reconstruction begins: "Grant, Cyprian and Nereids, that my brother come hither unharmed, and that all his heart's desire be accomplished." And it concludes: "Grant that she, Doricha, be not proud to tell how he came the second time to her longed-for love (*pothennon eron*)."[26]

Sappho lived in a period in which the eastern Greeks enjoyed great prosperity in large measure because of their ties with the rest of Asia and with Africa. Their great commercial expansion accompanied the deployment of Ionian mercenaries and Ionian fleets. Her ties with the East, with Lydia, Sardis, and with Africa, with Naucratis, enter into Sappho's poetry, setting her into a different cartography from that of Pindar, who looks most often to the West, to the tyrants and heroes of Sicily and Magna Graecia, and to the heroes and sons of heroes of the mainland, a different cartography from that of the tragic poets, who return again and again to Thebes, Mycenae, Argos, Athens, and to a Troy transfigured by its resemblance to the everyday life of the classical city. The precious objects of Sappho's world come from the East, and she uses them in establishing an atmosphere of luxury, of pleasure and the ornamentation of life. I look at these objects in order to trace the

25. On Naucratis and Rhodopis, see Murray, *Early Greece*, 215–18.
26. Denys Page, *Sappho and Alcaeus: An Introduction to the Study of Ancient Lesbian Poetry* (Oxford, 1955), 45–46.

presence of the East, of the wealth and exoticism of the garments and objects with which Sappho furnishes her erotic universe.

Fragment 98 refers, in an atmosphere of comparison, to a "decorated headband from Sardis." A girl with golden hair should adorn her hair with flowers; Sappho then recalls a *mitranan poikilan apu Sardian*, "a decorated headband from Sardis," an object that entered the scene *artiōs*, "recently." In a later stanza, which seems to be from the same poem, she again uses the phrase *poikilan . . . mitranan*, this time perhaps complaining, perhaps apologizing to Kleis that she has "nowhere" from which such an object might be obtained. The line goes on to refer to Mytilene, her city, and then trails off into fragments. Is she apologizing because Lesbia cannot boast the exquisite work of such craftsmanship? The word *poikilan* recalls the beginning of another poem, perhaps the only complete poem from the works of Sappho that we now possess. The first word of this poem, fragment 1, is *poikilothron'*, which probably means "ornate-throned," referring to the goddess Aphrodite. John J. Winkler says: "*Poikilophron* means 'having a mind (*-phron*) which is *poikilos*,' a notion usually translated by words like 'dappled,' 'variegated,' 'changeful,' 'complex.' It designates the quality of having many internal contrasts, whether perceived by the eye or by the mind."[27]

The *mitra*, a "snood," or headband, remarkable for its dappled beauty, is a piece of adornment brought from the nearby Lydian city of Sardis. This city is cited several times in Sappho's poetic corpus as a figure for luxury, for distance, for longing. Phocaea, an Ionian city, the northernmost in Asia Minor, also furnished cloths for adornment. Athenaeus cites Sappho, in a fragment culled from his work and numbered by modern scholars 101:

> And when Sappho says in Book 5 of her lyric poems, addressing Aphrodite,
> " . . . and handcloths . . . purple, perfumed (?), (which Mnasis) sent (to you) from Phocaea, expensive gifts . . . ,"

---

27. The word may have been *poikilophron*, "of varied mind." See John J. Winkler, "Double Consciousness in Sappho's Lyrics," in *The Constraints of Desire: The Anthropology of Sex and Gender in Ancient Greece*, (New York and London, 1990), 167; see 162–87, esp. 166–67.

she means handcloths as an adornment [*kosmon*] for the head.[28]

The Phocaeans are said by Herodotus to be "the first Greeks to make long sea voyages; it was they who showed the way to the Adriatic, Tyrrhenia, Iberia, and Tartessus."[29] The Phocaeans showed the way for trade from east to west.

Sappho's word *poikilos*, "many-colored," "dappled," "manifold," "intricate," "artful," "changeable," recurs in her fragment 39, in association with Lydia:

and a gay leather strap [*poikilos maslēs*] covered (her?) feet, a fine piece of Lydian work.

This line is cited by a scholiast, commenting on Aristophanes' *Peace*, to demonstrate the superiority of Lydian dyes. Another frustratingly, mysteriously, beautifully, fragmentary poem, of which only the line beginnings remain, reads:

> . . . robe . . .
> saffron . . .
> purple robe . . .
> cloak . . .
> garlands . . .
> (beauty?) . . .
> (Phrygian?) . . .
> purple . . .[30]

Here too we find richness, luxurious garments, crowns, adornment, color, and (perhaps) the part of Asia Minor known as Phrygia drawn together to suggest the exotic stuffs of the East, perhaps even the fabulous wealth of the Phrygian king Midas. These broken lines are particularly evocative of an aesthetics of the fragment.

In another fragment, number 99, Sappho may refer to women who use the dildo, *olisb'*, or to a plectrum striking strings, and then calls to Apollo, son of Leto and Zeus, who is invited to come to rites in his honor, leaving woody Gryneia, an Apollo shrine in Asia Minor.[31] It is possible that Sappho's own family had roots in the

---

28. Athenaeus 9.410e; Campbell, *Greek Lyric I*, fr. 101.
29. Herodotus, *The Histories*, 1.169.
30. From a sixth-century parchment; Campbell, *Greek Lyric I*, fr. 92.
31. This text is particularly uncertain.

mainland of Asia Minor, in the part of the Aegean now known as
Turkey. Her father's name, as noted earlier, was said to be either
Skamander or Skamandronymos; the river near Troy, city famed
from the *Iliad*, was the Skamander. And Sappho's own name may
have been Asiatic.[32]

There are other signs that Sappho's gaze was directed elsewhere, not toward the Hellenic homeland of Athens, Attica, Mycenae and Argos, Delphi, and Olympia, but eastward toward Lydia
and Sardis, south toward the Lebanon and Egypt. Sappho refers
several times to the worship of Aphrodite's lover Adonis, who was
associated with Asia Minor. Marius Plotius Sacerdos attributes the
invention of the metrical unit the "adonius," or "sapphic," to Sappho, citing her line *ō ton Adōnin*, "Alas for Adonis" (fr. 168). And
Hephaestion, quoting Sappho in his handbook on meters:

> "Delicate Adonis is dying, Cytherea; what are we to do?"
> "Beat your breasts, girls, and tear your clothes." (fr. 140a)

Adonis was the son of the king of the island of Cyprus, Kinyras,
and always associated with the East:

> For the Greeks it was well known that he was an immigrant
> from the Semitic world, and his origins were traced to By-
> blos and Cyprus. His name is clearly the Semitic title *adon*,
> Lord. . . . What can be identified is the spread of the Meso-
> potamian Dumuzi-Tammuz cult. Old Testament prophets
> speak of it as an abomination: women sit by the gate weeping
> for Tammuz, or they offer incense to Baal on roof-tops and
> plant pleasant plants. These are the very features of the
> Adonis cult.[33]

Of course Adonis was mourned elsewhere in the Greek world. But
Sappho's particular devotion to the cult of Aphrodite suggests that
in this case as in others she was oriented toward the East. Hers is
the earliest mention of the Adonis cult in Greek.

32. See G. Zuntz, "On the Etymology of the Name Sappho," *Museum Helveticum* 8
(1951): 12–35.

33. Walter Burkert, *Greek Religion*, trans. John Raffan (Cambridge, Mass., 1985), 177;
see also Marcel Detienne, *The Gardens of Adonis: Spices in Greek Mythology*, trans. Janet
Lloyd (Atlantic Highlands, N.J., 1977); Murray, *Early Greece*, 85–86; and Winkler, *Constraints*, 189, 199, 201, 205, 208 on Detienne's work.

In the post-Homeric age all poets looked to the *Iliad* and the *Odyssey* and other poems of the epic cycle, and sang of the wonderful feats of the Homeric heroes. Sappho's poem 44, written possibly for a wedding, although not in the meter associated with *epithalamia*, touches on the heroic context but characteristically stresses the wealth and abundance of Troy, the city of Asia Minor that held for a time Helen, wife of Menelaus, and refused to surrender her, precipitating the Trojan War.

> the herald came . . . Idaeus . . . swift messenger, . . . "and of
> the rest of Asia . . . imperishable renown. Hector and his
> comrades are bringing a dark-eyed girl from holy Thebe and
> the streams of Placia, dainty Andromache, in ships over the
> salt sea. Many golden bracelets and purple robes . . . trinkets
> of curious pattern [*poikil'athurmata*], and silver cups innumerable, and ivory."

The celebration continues in Troy, Ilium itself:

> and maidens sang clearly a holy song, and a wondrous echo
> reached the sky, . . . and everywhere in the streets was . . .
> bowls and chalices . . . myrrh and cassia and frankincense
> [*murra kai kasia libanos t'*] were mingled.[34]

Denys Page, whose translation I have cited, says dourly of this poem: "It displays for the first time the talent of Sappho (for I shall continue doubtfully to suppose that she is the author) in the art of story-telling. That talent is of a high, though by no means the highest, order."[35] It nonetheless exhibits a delight in the abundance of an ancient, Asian world.[36]

The word translated as "frankincense," *libanos*, itself suggests the East; in one of the most evocative of her poems, fragment 2, discussed elsewhere in this book, Sappho calls Aphrodite to her from Crete, and promises to her the altars of Lesbos "smoking with incense" (*tethumiamenoi libanōtōi*). Denys Page comments:

> This is the earliest extant mention in Greek of *frankincense*,
> small whitish globules of hardened aromatic resin, intro-

---

34. Page, *Sappho and Alcaeus*, 63–64.
35. Ibid., 70–71.
36. On epic diction in this poem, see R. L. Fowler, *The Nature of Early Greek Lyric: Three Preliminary Studies* (Toronto, 1987), 47.

duced to Greece probably little if at all earlier than the seventh century B.C. There is no mention in Homer of the burning of incense; in Egypt it was a common practice long before the Mycenaean era. Frankincense was presumably an article of the Phoenician trade, the ultimate source in Sappho's day being the Hadramaut in South Arabia.[37]

Frankincense is mentioned in Herodotos' *Histories*, and is thought to come from the distant East:

> It would seem to be a fact that the remotest parts of the world have the finest products. . . . the most southerly country is Arabia; and Arabia is the only place that produces frankincense, myrrh, cassia, cinnamon, and the gum called ledanon. All these, except the myrrh, cause the Arabians a lot of trouble to collect. When they gather frankincense, they burn storax (the gum which is brought into Greece by the Phoenicians) in order to raise a smoke to drive off the flying snakes; these snakes, the same which attempt to invade Egypt, are small in size and of various colours, and great numbers of them keep guard over all the trees which bear the frankincense, and the only way to get rid of them is by smoking them out with storax.[38]

He describes various features of the collection of cassia and cinnamon, and concludes that "the whole country exhales a more than earthly fragrance."[39] In *The Gardens of Adonis*, Marcel Detienne discusses the role of spices in classical culture, and describes how the Greeks of the classical period understood marriage, domestic life, and sober, reproductive sex to stand in stark contrast to an erotic hedonism bound up with the heat of the sun, aphrodisiac perfumes, unguents, and exotic aromatics. Spices represent a danger to the classical city and to the household, united around a marriage:

> Aromatic substances by-pass marital relations either by emitting the irresistible appeal of perfume which brings to-

37. Page, *Sappho and Alcaeus*, 36.
38. Herodotus, *The Histories*, 3.106.
39. Ibid., 3.112.

gether the most distant of beings or else by provoking pre-
cocity in the sensual adolescent, or extreme sexual potency
in the seducer or hyper-sexuality in women—all of which
are forms of excess.[40]

These potent substances, which carry with them the possible dis-
ruption of all order, at least in the minds of the classical age, con-
taminate Greece from the East. Sappho seems to revel in them.

In two of Sappho's most complete fragments, the East figures as
a crucial compass point, in one case marking a site of difference, of
comparison between the place where she finds herself and an elsewhere, in another fragment signifying distance and creating the
familiar mood of longing for an absent woman, whose absence
generates the poem itself. In poem 16, discussed earlier, the poet
sets "whatsoever one loves" against the background of the military.

Some say a host of cavalry, others of infantry, and others of
ships, is the most beautiful thing on the black earth, but I say
it is whatsoever a person loves.

The poet goes on to recall Helen, who was led, perhaps by eros or
Aphrodite, to Troy, and the memory of Helen leads her to Anaktoria. What remains of the poem concludes with the walk and
sparkle of the face of Anaktoria, which the poet prefers to "the
Lydians' chariots and armed infantry" (*ta Ludōn armata k'an oploisi/
pesdomakhentas*). In this first part of the poem we are firmly situated
in the past, in the world of epic heroes. In an important turn, however, after the story of Helen is invoked, the poet looks to Anaktoria, who is "not present," *ou pareoisas*. The woman, who is set in
the place of "whatsoever" one loves, replaces not only the horsemen, infantry, and ships of the first two lines of the poem, but also
Helen herself, the fabled beauty of the past. With the mention of
Anaktoria, we enter another time, the present of the poem, from
which Anaktoria's living presence is excluded. But she is present in
Sappho's invocation of her, vividly realized not through epic epi-
thets of conventional beauty such as "white-armed," but with the
recollection of her step, of her face's *amarugma*, its "sparkle, twinkle,

40. Marcel Detienne, *The Gardens of Adonis*, 127.

changing color and light." And accompanying this specification of the beloved, her invocation, her production in the poem, comes a specification concerning the military forces that began the poem turning it, in a sort of anamorphosis, away from the Homeric past and toward the present. These are Lydian chariots and armed infantry, forces in the contemporary scene.[41] David Campbell points out that "Lydians are mentioned as a particularly powerful and splendid race,"[42] and recalls fragment 132:

> I have a beautiful child who looks like golden flowers, my darling Cleis, for whom I would not (take) all Lydia or lovely . . .[43]

Lydia was wealthy (Xenophanes speaks of the corrupting effect of Lydian luxury on his own people, the Colophonians)[44] and belligerent. After Gyges took over its throne, he sent military expeditions against the Greek cities of Miletus and Smyrna and captured Colophon; his son Ardys took Priene and attacked Miletus. Lydia's chariots are a signifier not just of splendor, perhaps equal to that of ancient Troy, but also of aggression.[45] Herodotus says of the Lydians at the time of Croesus: "In those days, by the way, there were no stouter or more courageous fighters in Asia than the Lydians. They were cavalrymen, excellent horsemen, and their weapon was the long spear."[46] Beyond this invocation of Lydia as a point of comparison and rejection, the chariots of poem 16 affect the temporal quality of the poem, as I have said, pulling it into the present,

---

41. Although there is some dispute about the deployment of the chariot in war at this date, Denys Page states, concerning these lines: "I see no reason to doubt that Sappho is speaking of things within her own knowledge: the picture of Lydians setting out to *war* in *chariots* can still be drawn a century (and more) later" (*Sappho and Alcaeus,* 55.) He cites Aeschylus' *Persians,* lines 45ff.

42. *Greek Lyric Poetry: A Selection of Early Greek Lyric, Elegiac and Iambic Poetry,* ed. David A. Campbell (Basingstoke and London, 1967), 270.

43. Campbell, *Greek Lyric I,* 149.

44. Fr. 3, DK 21 B 3.

45. On the affinities of the weapons in the armory described in Alcaeus' fr. 357 with the near East and Egypt, see Anthony J. Podlecki, *The Early Greek Poets and Their Times* (Vancouver, 1984), 77.

46. Herodotus, *The Histories,* 1.78; on Lydia, see Murray, *Early Greece,* 232ff.

away from the mythic universe of Helen and Troy, and arguing for attention to that present. The distant Lydians, like the absent Anaktoria, gain significance as the contemporary equivalents of the legendary Trojans and mythical Helen, who also lived in Asia Minor; Sappho ends her poem with Anaktoria and with the Asiatic soldiers, with a focus on a contemporary beauty and on contemporary militarism, that constant presence to the East that is Lydia.

It is possible that Anaktoria, "not present," is herself far away in Lydia, like another of the women Sappho remembers in poem 96. I have discussed this poem elsewhere, in another light; I would like here to stress its orientation toward Asia.[47] I cite the translation of Diane Rayor:

> . . . Sardis . . .
> often holding her [thoughts] here
>
> *
>
> you, like a goddess undisguised,
> but she rejoiced especially in your song.
>
> Now she stands out among
> Lydian women as after sunset
> the rose-fingered moon
>
> exceeds all stars; light
> reaches equally over the brine sea
> and thick-flowering fields,
>
> a beautiful dew has poured down,
> roses bloom, tender parsley
> and blossoming honey clover.
>
> Pacing far away,[48] she remembers
> gentle Atthis with desire,
> perhaps . . . consumes her delicate soul;

47. See Page duBois, *Sowing the Body: Psychoanalysis and Ancient Representations of Women* (Chicago, 1988), 26–27.

48. R. L. Fowler argues that *zaphoitaisa* should be translated "going through," *Nature*, 68–69.

to go there . . . this not
knowing . . . much
she sings . . . in the middle.

It is not easy for us to rival
the beautiful form of goddesses,
. . . you might have . . .

*
*

And . . . Aphrodite

        . . . poured nectar from
a golden . . .
    . . . with her hands Persuasion.[49]

As always, Denys Page feels compelled to deprecate Sappho's lines: "Sappho sings to comfort Atthis, who is separated from a favorite companion. . . . So simple is the theme, and it is doubtful whether there are more subtle undertones to be detected."[50]

I earlier argued about this poem that it seems to represent a celebration of the unplowed earth, the terrain spontaneously yielding up flowers rather than the life-sustaining grains of cultivated fields. In contrast to discourses that honor the earth as lit up by Homer's "rosy-fingered Dawn," that make an analogy between the plowed furrows in the earth and women's bodies, and that see agriculture as a crucial and sustaining practice of life in the ancient city, Sappho seems to privilege the female moon (*a brododaktulos mēna*) and feminine dew (*a d'eersa kala*), and the flowers that bloom in the night. Burnett reminds us:

according to ancient belief, it was the moon that brought plants to their perfection, and it was by moonlight that flowers were gathered for beneficent magic and for medicines. The moon's light and the moon's moisture were thought of as the source of all that was cool, fresh, round and soft, in con-

49. *Sappho's Lyre: Archaic Lyric and Women Poets of Ancient Greece*, trans. Diane J. Rayor (Berkeley and Los Angeles, 1991), 61–62.

50. Page, *Sappho and Alcaeus*, 93. See Anne Pippin Burnett, *Three Archaic Poets: Archilochus, Alcaeus, Sappho* (Cambridge, Mass., 1983), 300ff, with extensive bibliography.

trast to the heat, salt and hardness produced by the sun. The moon was feminine, and it controlled not just fecundity, but ripeness in general.[51]

As often, Sappho in this fragment takes up the discourses of Homer, Hesiod, myth and ritual, and while alluding to them, constructs another reality of nocturnal freshness, beauty, and yearning.

What interests me especially here is that way in which the moon, rising in the night sky, with its rosy fingers, connects the site of the poem's utterance with Lydia. If the conjecture about line 1 is correct, and Sardis is to be read out from the letters *sard*, then this poem twice refers to Asia Minor, where the woman described remembers Atthis. That woman resembles the moon, standing out preeminent among Lydian women as the moon stands out among the stars. The particular, specific, Asianizing geography seems significant here, although Anne Pippin Burnett, one of the best readers of Sappho, points to the universal time/space dimensions of this poem:

> In its geography, a She who is There is divided from a We who are Here by an intervening track of traversable sea, but this map can also be read as showing a Now that means pain and cries of grief, divided from a Then that meant songs and joy by a stretch of time that is untraversable.[52]

From another orientation, considering the geography of the ancient Greek world, taking account of its position at the edge of Asia, it matters as well that the moon, after the sun sets, rises and shines out over both Sardis, with its Lydian women, and the place from which Atthis, and the poet, remember the absent woman. Here too we have the complex interplay of pronouns of address; the addressee of the poem, presumably Atthis, is "you," *se*, but most vividly realized is the absent one, far away in Sardis, standing out among Lydian women. The poet and Atthis gaze toward the Aegean shore, eastward, focused on Sardis and Lydia, where their absent friend goes through fields of flowers, where the light of the

51. Burnett, *Three Archaic Poets*, 308.
52. Ibid., 303–4.

common moon illuminates both Asia and this nearby island so closely linked to it.

It is not only rhetoric, that Sicilian art, which is contaminated from its beginnings with Asianism. If Asianism is effeminacy, floridity, luxuriousness, then we must see Sappho as well, at the very beginnings of Western poetry, as an Easterner. Her poetry looks to the East, she dwells on the objects of great luxury and beauty that Lydian Sardis provides, on Atthis' friend now lost to her in Sardis. Her poetics of loss and rememoration focus on precious, ornate objects, on the pleasures of daily life, and on yearning for the absent friends who shared those pleasures. Hers is not precisely the Asianism of Gorgias, Demosthenes, and those later orators condemned by the Romans, yet she nonetheless, along with all the other lyric poets who rejoice in sensuality, contaminates the strain of Greek poetry at its source, with luxury, with "Asianist" longings.

The great epinician poet Pindar, more than a hundred years later, an aristocrat in a democratizing age, looks instead to the West, toward the Italy which will contain Rome and its fearful discourses about the Asian menace. He writes of the heroic games in which the Greeks from many cities competed, and he can stand here for another kind of poetics, ornate and triumphant, visible in this beginning to the first Olympian ode:

> Water is preeminent and gold, like a fire
> burning in the night, outshines
> all possessions that magnify men's pride.
> But if, my soul, you yearn
> to celebrate great games
> look no further
> for another star
> shining through the deserted ether
> brighter than the sun, or for a contest
> mightier than Olympia—
> where the song
> has taken its coronal
> design of glory, plaited
> in the minds of poets

as they come, calling on Zeus' name,
to the rich radiant hall of Hieron
who wields the scepter of justice in Sicily,
reaping the prime of every
distinction.[53]

Sappho, who looks East, remembering friends and not victors, celebrating lovers not tyrants, remembering pleasure not victories, disrupts the origins of Western civilization by her eccentric stance at the very farthest edge of the West, between Europe and Asia.

53. *Pindar's Victory Songs*, trans. Frank J. Nisetich (Baltimore and London, 1980), 82.

SELECT BIBLIOGRAPHY

Adorno, Theodor. "On Lyric Poetry and Society." In *Notes to Literature*. Vol. 1. Translated by Shierry Weber Nicholsen. New York, 1991.

Andrewes, A. *The Greek Tyrants*. London, 1956.

Aloni, A. "Eteria e tiaso: i gruppi aristocratici di Lesbo tra economia e ideologia." *DArch* 3.1 (1983): 21–35.

Armstrong, Timothy J., trans. *Michel Foucault Philosopher*. New York, 1992.

Austin, Norman. *Helen of Troy and Her Shameless Phantom*. Ithaca, N.Y., 1994.

Balmer, Josephine, trans. *Sappho: Poems and Fragments*. Newcastle upon Tyne, 1992.

Barnard, Mary, trans. *Sappho: A New Translation*. Berkeley, Calif., 1958.

Barstone, Willis, trans. *Sappho and the Greek Lyric Poets*. New York, 1988.

Benjamin, Walter. *Illuminations: Essays and Reflections*. Edited by Hannah Arendt. Translated by Harry Zohn. New York, 1969.

Benveniste, Emile. *Problems in General Linguistics*. Translated by Mary Elizabeth Meek. Coral Gables, Fla., 1971.

Bernal, Martin. *Black Athena: The Afroasiatic Roots of Classical Civilization*. Vol. 1, *The Fabrication of Ancient Greece, 1785–1985*. New Brunswick, N.J., 1987. Vol. 2, *The Archaeological and Documentary Evidence*. New Brunswick, N.J., 1991.

Bing, Peter, and R. Cohen. *Games of Venus: An Anthology of Greek and Roman Erotic Verse from Sappho to Ovid*. New York, 1992.

Boedeker, Deborah. "Sappho and Acheron." In *Arktouros: Hellenic Studies Presented to Bernard M. W. Knox*, edited by G. W. Bowersock, W. Burkert, and M. C. J. Putnam. Berlin, 1979.

Bremmer, Jan, ed. *From Sappho to De Sade: Moments in the History of Sexuality*. London and New York, 1989.

Brown, C. "Anactoria and the Chariton-Amarygmata, Sappho Fr. 16, 18 Voigt. *Quaderni Urbinati di Cultura Classica*, n.s. 2 (1989): 7–15.

Burkert, Walter. *Greek Religion*. Translated by John Raffan. Cambridge, Mass., 1985.

Burn, A. R. *The Lyric Age of Greece*. New York, 1960.

Burnett, Anne Pippin. *Three Archaic Poets: Archilochus, Alcaeus, Sappho*. Cambridge, Mass., 1983.

Butler, Judith. *Gender Trouble: Feminism and the Subversion of Identity*. New York and London, 1990.

———. "Contingent Foundations: Feminism and the Question of 'Postmodernism.'" In *Feminists Theorize the Political*. Edited by Judith Butler and Joan W. Scott. New York and London, 1992.

———. *Bodies That Matter: On the Discursive Limits of "Sex."* New York and London, 1993.

Calame, Claude. *Les choeurs de jeunes filles en Grèce archaïque*. Vol. 1, *Morphologie, fonction religieuse et sociale*. Vol. 2, *Alcman*. Rome, 1977.

———. "Sappho immorale?" *Quaderni Urbinati di Cultura Classica* 28 (1978): 211–14.

Campbell, David A. *The Golden Lyre: The Themes of the Greek Lyric Poets*. London, 1983.

———. *Greek Lyric Poetry: A Selection of Early Greek Lyric, Elegiac and Iambic Poetry*. Basingstoke and London, 1967.

———, trans. *Greek Lyric I: Sappho and Alcaeus*. Cambridge, Mass., 1982.

Carey, C. "S. fr.96LP." *Classical Quarterly*, n.s. 28 (1978): 366–71.

Carson, Anne. *Eros the Bittersweet: An Essay*. Princeton, 1986.

———. "Putting Her in Her Place: Woman, Dirt, and Desire." In *Before Sexuality: The Construction of Erotic Experience in the Ancient World*. Edited by David M. Halperin, John J. Winkler, and Froma I. Zeitlin. Princeton, 1990.

Cassin, Barbara, ed. *Nos Grecs et leurs modernes: Les stratégies contemporaines d'appropriation de l'antiquité*. Paris, 1992.

Chatterjee, Partha. *The Nation and Its Fragments: Colonial and Postcolonial Histories*. Princeton, N.J., 1993.

Dane, J. A. "Sappho fr. 16: An Analysis. *Eos* 69 (1981): 185–92.

Davison, J. A. *From Archilochus to Pindar*. London, 1968.

DeJean, Joan. *Fictions of Sappho, 1546–1937*. Chicago and London, 1989.

Detienne, Marcel. *The Gardens of Adonis: Spices in Greek Mythology*. Translated by Janet Lloyd. Atlantic Highlands, 1977.

Detienne, Marcel and Jean-Pierre Vernant. *Cunning Intelligence in Greek Culture and Society*. Translated by Janet Lloyd. Hassocks, England, 1978.

Devereux, George. "The Nature of Sappho's Seizure in Fr. 31 LP as Evidence of Her Inversion." *Classical Quarterly* 20 (1970): 17–31.

Dews, Peter. *Logics of Disintegration: Post-Structuralist Thought and the Claims of Critical Theory*. London, 1987.

Dodds, E. R. *The Greeks and the Irrational*. Berkeley, 1951.

Donlan, Walter. "The Social Groups of Dark Age Greece." *Classical Philology* 80 (1985): 293–308.

Dover, K. J. *Greek Homosexuality.* Cambridge, Mass., 1978.

duBois, Page. *Sowing the Body: Psychoanalysis and Ancient Representations of Women.* Chicago, 1988.

Eribon, Didier. *Michel Foucault (1926–1984).* Paris, 1989.

Farenga, Vincent. "La tirannide greca e la strategia numismatica." In *Mondo classico: percorsi possibili.* Edited by F. Buratta and F. Mariani. Ravenna, 1985.

Felman, Shoshana, ed. *Literature and Psychoanalysis: The Question of Reading: Otherwise.* Baltimore and London, 1982.

Finley, J. H. "Sappho's Circumstances." In *Arktouros: Hellenic Studies Presented to Bernard M. W. Knox.* Berlin, 1979.

Foley, Helen, ed. *The Homeric Hymn to Demeter: Translation, Commentary, and Interpretive Essays.* Princeton, N.J., 1994.

Foster, Hal, ed. *Postmodern Culture.* London, 1985.

Foucault, Michel, *The Use of Pleasure.* Vol. 2 of the History of Sexuality. Translated by Robert Hurley. New York, 1986.

———. *Politics Philosophy Culture: Interviews and Other Writings 1977–1984.* Edited by L. D. Kritzman. Translated by Alan Sheridan et al. New York and London, 1990.

———. *Remarks on Marx: Conversations with Duccio Trombadori.* Translated by R. J. Goldstein and James Cascaito. New York, 1991.

———. *The Care of the Self.* Vol. 3 of the History of Sexuality. Translated by Robert Hurley. New York, 1986.

Fowler, Barbara Hughes. "The Archaic Aesthetic." *American Journal of Philology* 105 (1984): 119–49.

Fowler, R. L. *The Nature of Early Greek Lyric: Three Preliminary Studies.* Toronto, 1987.

Frankel, H. *Early Greek Poetry and Philosophy.* Translated by M. Hadas and J. Willis. Oxford, 1975.

Gentili, Bruno. *Poetry and Its Public in Ancient Greece: From Homer to the Fifth Century.* Translated by A. Thomas Cole. Baltimore and London, 1988.

Gerber, D. E. "Studies in Greek Lyric Poetry: 1975–1985." *Classical World* 81 (1987/88): 73–144, 417–49.

Giacomelli, A. "The Justice of Aphrodite in Sappho Fr. 1." *Transactions of the American Philological Association* 110 (1980): 135–42.

Giangrande, G. "Sappho and the 'olisbos'." *Emerita* 48 (1980): 449–50.

———. "A che serviva l' 'olisbos' di Saffo?" *Labeo* 29 (1983): 154–55.

Goux, Jean-Joseph. *Symbolic Economies: After Marx and Freud.* Translated by Jennifer Curtiss Gage. Ithaca, N.Y., 1990.

Grahn, Judy. *The Highest Apple: Sappho and the Lesbian Poetic Tradition.* San Francisco, 1985.

Greimas, A. J. *On Meaning: Selected Writings in Semiotic Theory.* Translated by P. J. Perron and F. H. Collins. Minneapolis, 1987.

Gubar, Susan. "Sapphistries." *Signs* 10 (1984): 43–62.

Hague, R. "Sappho's Consolation for Atthis, fr. 96 LP." *American Journal of Philology* 105 (1984): 29–36.

Hallett, Judith P. "Sappho and Her Social Context: Sense and Sensuality." *Signs* 4 (1979): 447–64.

———. "Beloved Cleis." *Quaderni Urbinati di Cultura Classica*, n.s. 10 (1982): 21–31.

Halperin, David M. *One Hundred Years of Homosexuality and Other Essays on Greek Love.* New York and London, 1990.

Harvey, David. *The Condition of Postmodernity.* Oxford, 1989.

Horkheimer, Max, and Theodor W. Adorno. *Dialectic of Enlightenment.* Translated by John Cumming. New York, 1972.

Howie, J. G., "Sappho Fr. 16 (LP): Self-Consolation and Encomium." In *Papers of the Liverpool Latin Seminar 1976.* Liverpool, 1977.

———. "Sappho Fr. 94 (LP): Farewell, Consolation, and Help in a New Life." In *Papers of the Liverpool Latin Seminar 2.* Liverpool 1979.

Jameson, Fredric. *Postmodernism, or, The Cultural Logic of Late Capitalism.* Durham, N.C., 1991.

Jeffery, L. H. *Archaic Greece: The City-States c. 700–500 B.C.* New York, 1976.

Jenkyns, R. *Three Classical Poets: Sappho, Catullus, and Juvenal.* Cambridge, Mass., 1982.

Kirkwood, Gordon M. *Early Greek Monody: The History of a Poetic Type.* Ithaca, N.Y., and London, 1974.

Lacan, Jacques. *Ecrits: A Selection.* Translated by Alan Sheridan. New York and London, 1977.

Lanata, Giulia. "Sul linguaggio amoroso di Saffo." *Quaderni Urbinati di Cultura Classica* 2 (1966): 63–79.

Lardinois, Andre. "Lesbian Sappho and Sappho of Lesbos." In *From Sappho to De Sade: Moments in the History of Sexuality.* Edited by Jan Bremmer. New York and London, 1989.

Latacz, J. "Realitat and Imagination. Eine neue Lyrik-Theorie und Sapphos *phainetai moi kenos*-Lied." *Museum Helveticum* 42 (1985p: 67–94.

Lefkowitz, Mary. *The Lives of the Greek Poets.* Baltimore, 1981.

———. "Critical Stereotypes and the Poetry of Sappho." *Heroines and Hysterics.* New York, 1981.

Lobel, E., and D. L. Page. *Poetarum Lesbiorum fragmenta.* Oxford, 1955.

Loraux, Nicole. *Les Expériences de Tirésias: Le féminin et l'homme grec.* Paris, 1989.

Macey, David. *The Lives of Michel Foucault: A Biography.* New York, 1993.

Marcovich, M. "Sappho Fr. 31: Anxiety Attack or Love Declaration?" *Classical Quarterly* n.s. 22 (1972): 19–32.

Marry, J. D. "Sappho and the Heroic Ideal: *erotos arete.*" *Arethusa* 12 (1979): 71–92.

Martindale, Charles. *Redeeming the Text: Latin Poetry and the Hermeneutics of Reception.* Cambridge, 1993.

Marzullo, Benedetto. *Studi di Poesia Eolica.* Florence, 1958.

McEvilley, Thomas. "Sapphic Imagery and Fragment 96." *Hermes* 101 (1973): 257–78.

———. "Sappho, Fragment Thirty-One: The Face behind the Mask." *Phoenix* 32 (1978): 1–18.

———. "Sappho, Fragment Two." *Phoenix* 26 (1972): 323–33.

———. "Sappho, Fragment Ninety-Four." *Phoenix* 25 (1971): 1–11.

Merkelbach, Reinhold. "Sappho und ihr Kreis." *Philologus* 101 (1957): 1–29.

Miller, James. *The Passion of Michel Foucault.* New York, 1993.

Miller, P. A. "Sappho 31 and Catullus 51: The Dialogism of Lyric." *Arethusa* 26 (1993): 183–99.

Most, G. "Sappho Fr. 16.6-7 L.-P." *Classical Quarterly* 31 (1981): 11–17.

Murray, Oswyn. *Early Greece.* Stanford, Calif., 1983.

Nagy, Gregory. "Phaethon, Sappho's Phaon, and the White Rock of Leukas." *Harvard Studies in Classical Philology* 77 (1973): 137–77.

Ober, Josiah. *Mass and Elite in Democratic Athens: Rhetoric, Ideology, and the Power of the People.* Princeton, N.J., 1989.

O'Higgins, D. "Sappho's Splintered Tongue: Silence in Sappho 31 and Catullus 51." *American Journal of Philology* 111 (1990): 156–67.

Page, Denys. *Sappho and Alcaeus: An Introduction to the Study of Ancient Lesbian Poetry.* Oxford, 1955.

Paglia, Camille. *Sex, Art, and American Culture: Essays.* New York, 1992.

Parker, Holt N. "Sappho Schoolmistress." *TAPA* 123 (1993): 309–51.

Podlecki, Anthony J. *The Early Greek Poets and Their Times.* Vancouver, 1984.

Pomeroy, Sarah B. *Women in Hellenistic Egypt from Alexander to Cleopatra.* New York, 1984.

———, ed., *Women's History and Ancient History.* Chapel Hill, N.C., 1991.

Privitera, G. A. *La rete di Afrodite, Studi su Saffo.* Palermo, 1974.

Pucci, Pietro. *Odysseus Polutropos: Intertextual Readings in the Odyssey and the Iliad.* Ithaca, N.Y., 1987.

Race, W. H. "Sappho fr. 16 (L-P) and Alkaios fr. 42 (L-P): Romantic and Classical Strains in Lesbian Poetry." *Classical Journal* 85: 1 (1989): 16–33.

Rauk, J. "Erinna's 'Distaff' and Sappho fr. 94." *Greek, Roman and Byzantine Studies* 30: 1 (1989): 101–16.

Rayor, Diane, trans. *Sappho's Lyre: Archaic Lyric and Women Poets of Ancient Greece.* Berkeley and Los Angeles, 1991.

Rissman, L. *Love as War: Homeric Allusion in the Poetry of Sappho.* Konigstein/Ts., 1983.

Rivier, A. "Observations sur Sappho 1, 19 sq." *Revue des Etudes Grecques* 80 (1967): 84–92.

Robbins, E. "Who's Dying in Sappho Fr. 94?" *Phoenix* 44: 2 (1990): 111–21.

Rubin, Nancy Felson. "Introduction: Why Classics and Semiotics?" *Arethusa* 16, special issue on semiotics and classical studies (1983): 5–14.

Rubin, Nancy Felson, and William Sale. "Meleager and Odysseus: A Structural Study of the Greek Hunting Maturation Myth." *Arethusa* 16, special issue on semiotics and classical studies (1983): 137–41.

Russo, J. "Reading the Greek Lyric Poets." *Arion* 1·(1973–74): 707–30.

Saake, H. *Sapphostudien: Froschungsgeschichtliche, biografische und literarasthetische Untersuchungen.* Munich, 1972.

Schadewalt, Wolfgang. *Sappho.* Potsdam, 1950.

Schneider, M. "Sappho Was a Right-on Adolescent—Growing up Lesbian." *Journal of Homosexuality* 17: 1–2 (1989): 111–30.

Sedgwick, Eve Kosofsky. *Epistemology of the Closet.* Berkeley and Los Angeles, 1990.

Segal, Charles. "Eros and Incantation: Sappho and Oral Poetry." *Arethusa* 7 (1974): 139–60.

———. "Otium and Eros: Catullus, Sappho, and Euripides' *Hippolytus.*" *Latomus* 48 : 4 (1989): 817–22.

Shell, Marc. *The Economy of Literature.* Baltimore, 1978.

Skinner, Marilyn. "Sapphic Nossis." *Arethusa* 22 (1989): 5–18.

———. "Nossis *Thelyglossos:* The Private Text and the Public Book." In *Women's History and Ancient History.* Edited by Sarah B. Pomeroy. Chapel Hill, N. C., 1991.

———. "Woman and Language in Archaic Greece, or, Why Is Sappho a Woman?" In *Feminist Theory and the Classics.* Edited by Nancy S. Rabinowtiz and Amy Richlin. New York and London, 1993.

Snell, Bruno. *Poetry and Society.* Bloomington, Ind., 1961.

———. *The Discovery of the Mind: The Greek Origins of European Thought.* Translated by T. G. Rosenmeyer. Cambridge, Mass., 1953.

Snyder, Jane McIntosh. *The Woman and the Lyre: Women Writers in Classical Greece and Rome.* Carbondale and Edwardsville, Ill. 1989.

———. "Public Occasion and Private Passion in the Lyrics of Sappho of Lesbos." In *Women's History and Ancient History.* Edited by Sarah B. Pomeroy. Chapel Hill, N.C., 1991.

———. "The Configuration of Desire in Sappho Fr. 22 L-P." *Helios* 21 (1994): 3–8.

Stanley, K. "The Role of Aphrodite in Sappho Fr. 1." *Greek, Roman, and Byzantine Studies* 17 (1976): 305–21.

Stehle, Eva. "Sappho's Gaze: Fantasies of a Goddess and Young Man." *Differences* 2 : 1, special issue on sexuality in Greek and Roman society (1990): 88–125.

Stigers, Eva S. "Retreat from the Male: Catullus 62 and Sappho's Erotic Flowers." *Ramus* 6 (1977): 83–102.

———. "Romantic Sensuality, Poetic Sense: A Response to Hallett on Sappho." *Signs* 4 (1979): 465–71.

———. "Sappho's Private World." In *Reflections of Women in Antiquity.* Edited by Helene P. Foley. New York, 1981.

Svenbro, Jesper. "La stratégic de l'amour. Modèle de la guerre et théorie de l'amour dans la poésie de Sappho." *Quaderni di Storia* 19 (1984): 57–79.

———. *Phrasikleia: An Anthropology of Reading in Ancient Greece.* Translated by Janet Lloyd. Ithaca, N.Y., and London, 1993.

Treu, Max. *Sappho.* Munich, 1963.

Vernant, Jean-Pierre. *Mythe et société en Grèce ancienne.* Paris, 1974.

Vickers, Nancy J. "The Body Re-membered: Petrarchan Lyrics and the Strategies of Description." In *Mimesis: From Mirror to Method, Augustine to Descartes.* Edited by J. D. Lyons and S. G. Nichols. Hanover, N.H., 1982.

Voigt, Eva-Maria. *Sappho et Alcaeus: Fragmenta.* Amsterdam, 1971.

Waern, Ingrid. "Flora Sapphica." *Eranos* 70 (1972): 1–11.

West, M. "Burning Sappho." *Maia* 22 (1970): 307–33.

Williams, Bernard. *Shame and Necessity.* Berkeley and Los Angeles, 1993.

Von Wilamowitz-Moellendorff, Ulrich. *Sappho und Simonides.* Berlin, 1913.

Winkler, John J. *The Constraints of Desire: The Anthropology of Sex and Gender in Ancient Greece.* New York and London, 1990.

———. "Sappho and the Crack of Dawn." *Journal of Homosexuality* 20:3–4 (1990): 227–33.

Wolin, Richard. *Walter Benjamin: An Aesthetic of Redemption.* New York, 1982.

Young, Robert. *White Mythologies: Writing History and the West.* London and New York, 1990.

Žižek, Slavoj. "Eastern Europe's Republics of Gilead." *New Left Review* 183 (1990): 51–56.

Zuntz, G. "On the Etymology of the Name Sappho." *Museum Helveticum* 8 (1951): 12–35.

INDEX